IMAGES
of America

AMHERST AND HADLEY THROUGH THE SEASONS

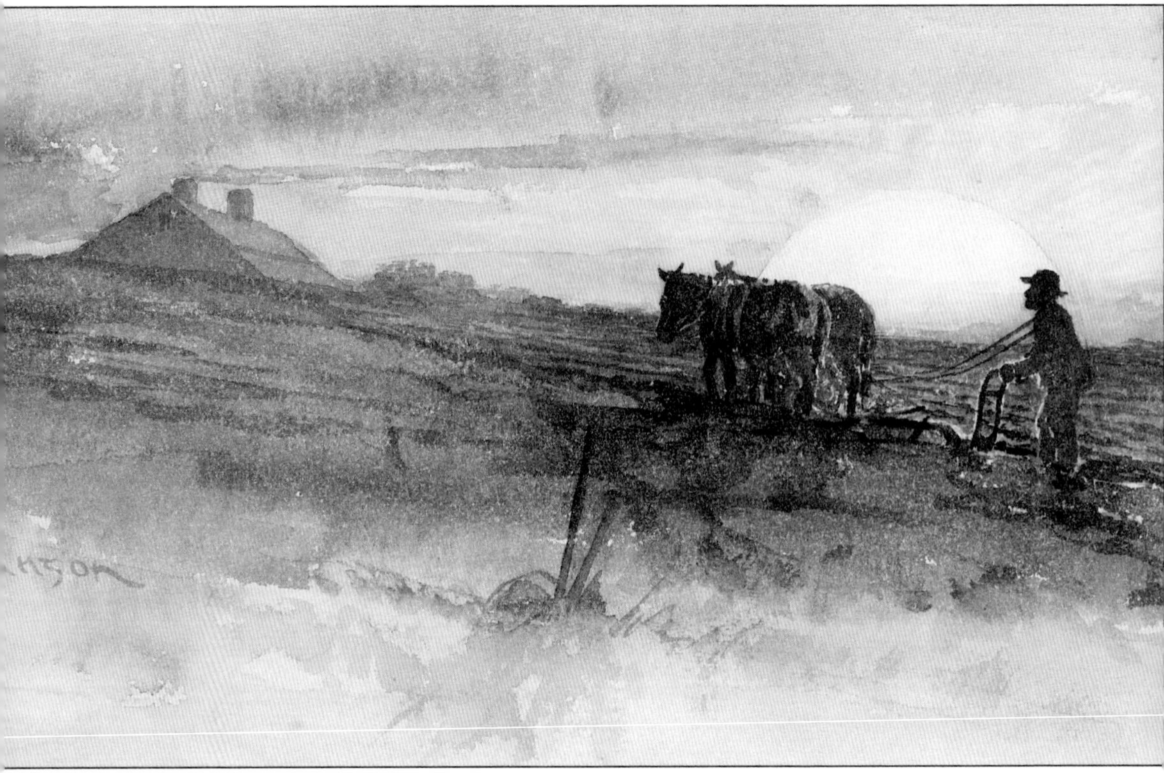

Sketch of a plowman at sunset by Clifton Johnson.

IMAGES
of America

AMHERST AND HADLEY THROUGH THE SEASONS

Daniel Lombardo

ARCADIA
PUBLISHING

ISBN 978-07385-6272-8

Published by Arcadia Publishing
Charleston, South Carolina

Printed in the United States of America

Library of Congress Catalog Card Number: 2008933036

For all general information contact Arcadia Publishing at:
Telephone 843-853-2070
Fax 843-853-0044
E-mail sales@arcadiapublishing.com
For customer service and orders:
Toll-Free 1-888-313-2665

Visit us on the Internet at www.arcadiapublishing.com

Dedicated to Robert Lombardo Jr. and Beckett McEwen.
Special thanks to Karen Banta.

Contents

Introduction

In small New England towns like Amherst and Hadley, life was dominated by the seasons—the eternal, revolving changes in climate that bring delirious beauty and the threat of swift destruction. Early on, survival itself in agricultural towns was dependent on the fickle gifts of nature. The warm spring sun of 1876 turned deadly by July. It scorched and burned the corn and tobacco crops it had encouraged in the flatland by the Connecticut River. In 1874, the streams that powered small grist- and cotton mills on the Fort and Mill Rivers suddenly flooded and washed away the work of a generation. In 1847, the snow underneath Edmund Smith's sleigh clogged the horses' hooves and pitched sleigh, horses, and rider headlong off Rattlesnake Gutter Road into the ravine.

The world knows of Emily Dickinson, whose poetry in the mid-1800s grew out of both that mysterious place within her and out of the Amherst earth that she loved. When Robert Frost lived and taught in Amherst he considered the extremes of New England seasons, and wrote, "Some say the world will end in fire, Some say in ice . . ." Indeed, this land's blistering sun and bitter winters have led many to make the leap from wonder to thoughts of biblical apocalypse.

So many writers have been inspired while living in or traveling through Amherst and Hadley that we have a natural prism through which to see this valley. The seasons and the daily labors, loves, and sorrows of the people here become vivid through the clear, inspired words of great writers.

Few know that from 1795 through 1817, Timothy Dwight, the president of Yale College, often visited this place. In his words, with "numerous churches lifting their spires in frequent succession, the neat schoolhouses everywhere occupied, and the mills busied on such a multitude of streams, it may be safely asserted that a pleasanter journey will rarely be found than that which is made in the Connecticut Valley."

Noah Webster helped shape our language and helped shape Amherst when he lived in town between 1812 and 1822. He worked on his famous dictionary and was a founder of both Amherst Academy and Amherst College. The great transcendentalist Ralph Waldo Emerson sometimes dined with the Dickinsons. Emerson visited his aunt, Deborah Haskins Shepard, in Amherst, and he lectured in the valley many times, noting his impressions in his journal. Poet and journalist Eugene Field, author of "Little Boy Blue," moved to Amherst as a boy in 1856, after his mother's death.

In that same year, the great Amherst photographer John Lovell began recording classic street scenes, clear and natural portraits, lively images of holiday celebrations, and the tragedies of fire and storm.

The most famous of all Amherst writers was Emily Dickinson, and her work was unlike the artistic efforts of others in or out of the area. Among the many people who knew her were Helen Hunt Jackson and MacGregor Jenkins. Jackson became a celebrated poet in her time and urged Dickinson to publish. Jenkins, on the other hand, was one of the neighborhood children who played under Dickinson's window. His recollections give a unique portrait of the poet and her town through the eyes of a child.

Harlan Fiske Stone, the great chief justice of the Supreme Court, studied at the Massachusetts Agricultural College in Amherst. His fond memories of the seasons during his Amherst days were hardly affected by his having been expelled in 1890 and having later taken part in a rebellion at Amherst College: "We swam in and skated and boated on the Freshman River. We roamed the surrounding hillsides in search of the first wild flowers of spring and of chestnuts and hickory nuts in the fall. We sought out the trout streams which nestle in the Pelham Hills and in the woods on the south side of Norwottuck. . . . We knew and understood the people of the countryside and, knowing them, the pious devotion, with which in an earlier day the farmers of the Pelham Hills and of the Connecticut River Valley had brought gifts for the founding of the College, was to us no mystery."

The writer who wrote most directly and most prolifically about the landscape and seasons of Amherst and Hadley was Ray Stannard Baker. A pioneering investigative journalist and Pulitzer Prize-winning biographer of Woodrow Wilson, Baker moved to Amherst in 1910. Under the pseudonym David Grayson, he wrote wildly popular books in which he described life in the country, just as that life was being forever changed by the developments of the early 20th century. From his small farm on Sunset Avenue he tended bees, raised onions, and contemplated the view over Hadley and Mount Warner, out toward the Connecticut River.

The valley's finest photographer came along, like Baker, just in time to capture the kind of natural, agrarian poetry the land was about to lose. Clifton Johnson was born along the Connecticut River in Hadley in 1865. His beautifully composed, often romantic images of farm and village life and his extraordinary images of farmers, working people, and children grace many pages of this book. With over one hundred books to his credit and thousands of images taken throughout this country and abroad, Johnson is slowly being rediscovered.

Robert Francis can, from a certain perspective, be seen as Amherst's 20th-century Emily Dickinson. He lived a solitary, though not reclusive, life and wrote much that came from his intimate awareness of the hills, fields, and people around his three-room house. He transformed what he observed around him into words as universally potent as the changing seasons.

This Connecticut River Valley has attracted and continues to attract writers into whose work the land seeps. Sylvia Plath attended Smith College and taught there in the 1950s. Her poems describing the "truncated hillocks" we call mountains and the oxbow that has become our spiritual emblem may have given some solace to her agonized life. The Poet Laureate Richard Wilbur, still living and writing in the hills beyond the Connecticut River, is undoubtedly one of this century's best. We are fortunate to have his voice in the autumn of the 20th century, to continue the work of others in renewing our love of both this valley's harshness and its beauty, its fire and its ice.

One

Wintertime

"They sigh and dream, maybe, and snore
While snow piles on the bedroom floor."

—Robert Francis

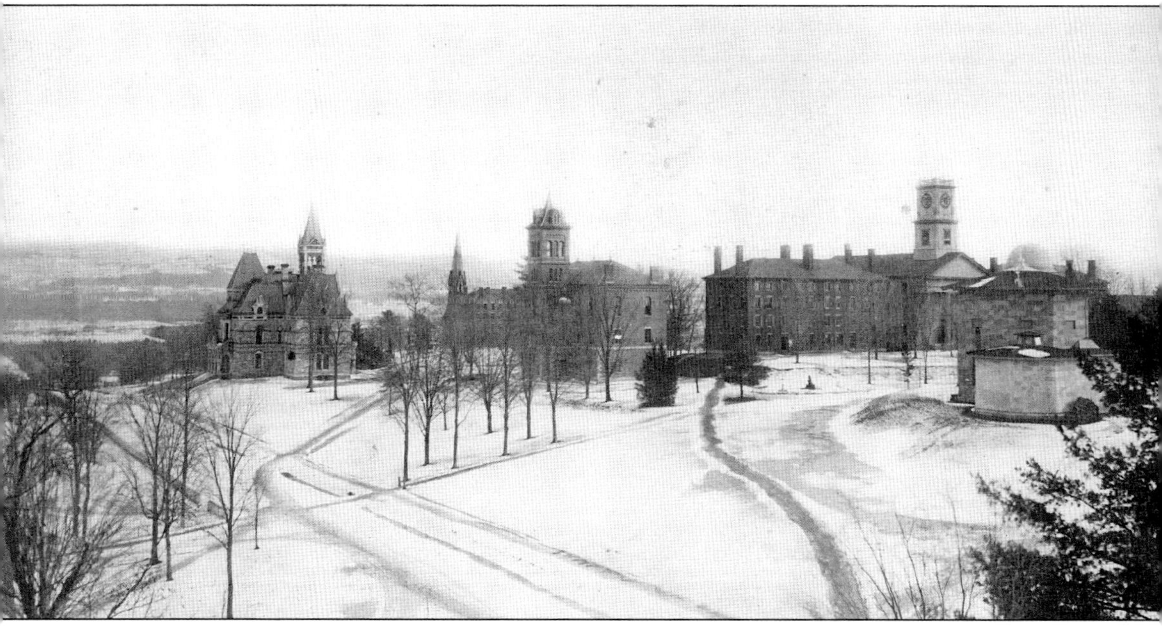

"Amherst clustered around the college where serious men, with sober faces, talked in solemn voices to younger men. The college gave a peculiar tone and flavor to the life of the village. The long, cold winter, with perpetual snow, was a season of labor and rigorous living, tempered by hospitality and genuine, if restrained enjoyment. There was much social life of a simple and delightful sort . . ." (MacGregor Jenkins, *Emily Dickinson, Friend and Neighbor*. Boston: Little, Brown, 1939, p. 6.)

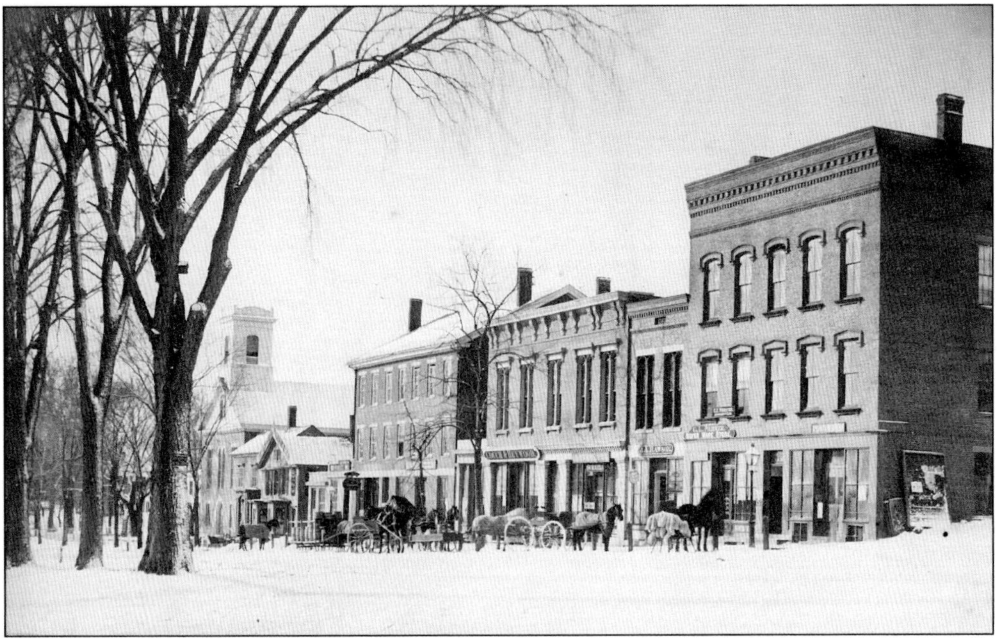

CELEBRATING THE HOLIDAY. At Christmastime each shop around the Amherst Common stocked holiday presents and decorated windows. In 1878, Mirick Spear's shop on Main Street advertised, "Do You Want to Buy Christmas Presents? Then go to M.N. Spear's and Look at Them. This store is packed with fresh goods for the Holiday trade. Children can find here Games, Pictures, Story Books, Dolls, Sleds, Rocking Horses, Trumpets, Drums, Wagons, Carts, Skates, Bracket Saws, and hundreds of toys of every conceivable kind and description."

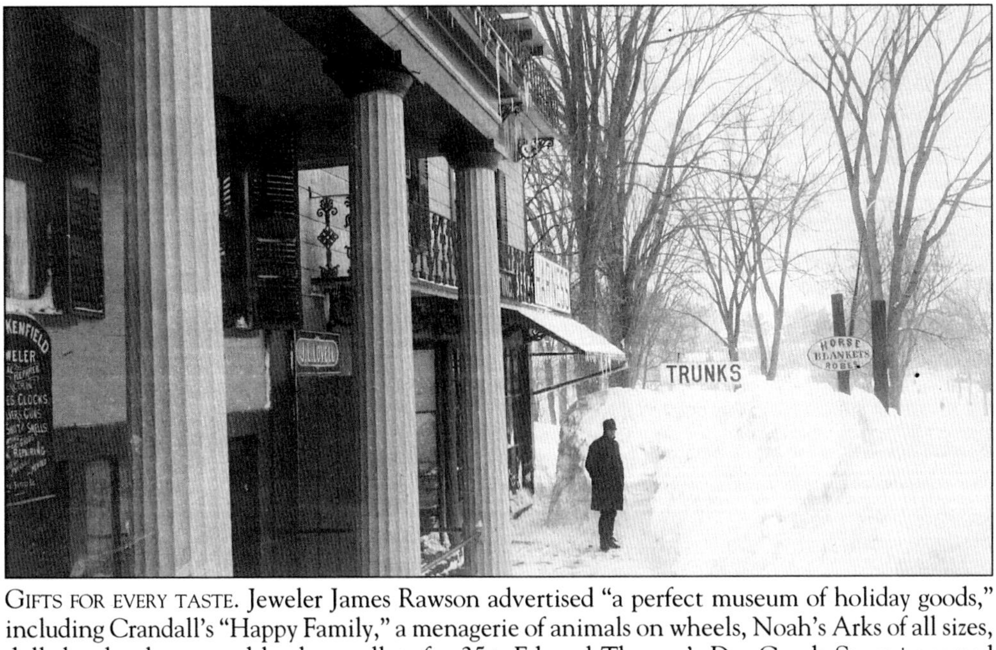

GIFTS FOR EVERY TASTE. Jeweler James Rawson advertised "a perfect museum of holiday goods," including Crandall's "Happy Family," a menagerie of animals on wheels, Noah's Arks of all sizes, dolls by the dozen, and leather wallets for 35¢. Edward Thomas's Dry Goods Store imported Japanese collar and cuff boxes and many other Asian gifts, available only since Commodore Matthew Perry opened Japan to trade in the 1850s.

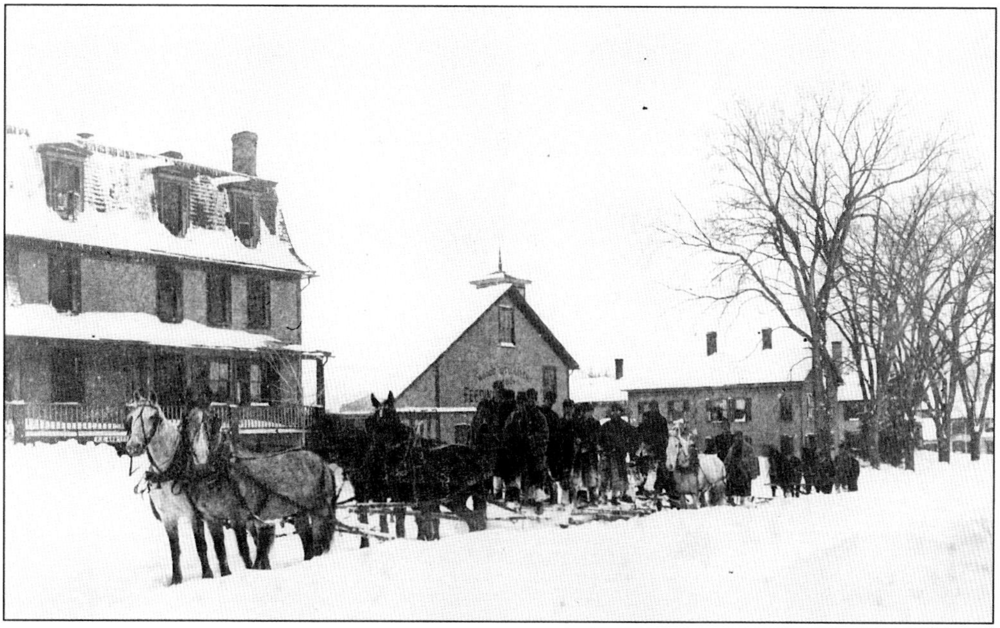

AFTER THE FIRST GREAT SNOWSTORM OF 1898. *The Amherst Record* reported that "Saturday the sleighs were out in force and Sunday the local liverymen did a business that gladdened their hearts . . . For the past two or three days zero weather had prevailed, making all the conditions for a real old-fashioned winter."

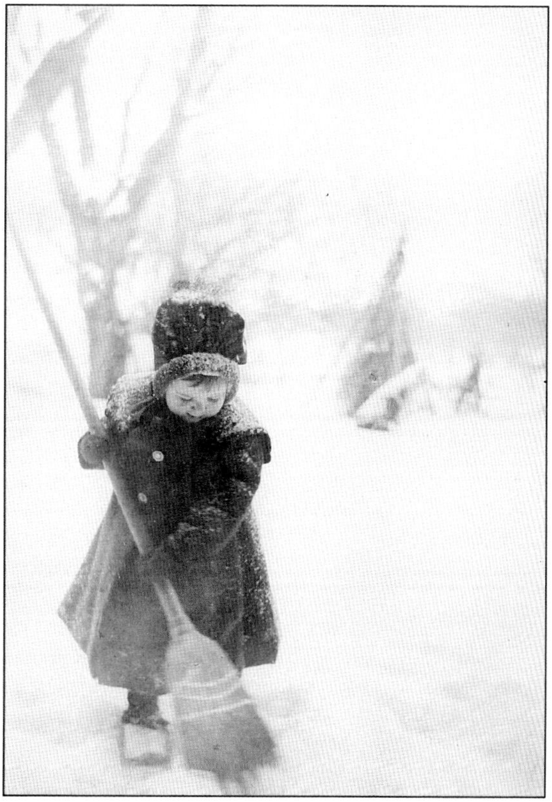

A CLIFTON JOHNSON PHOTOGRAPH OF HIS DAUGHTER MARGARET. "Atmospherically it was the most beautiful Christmas on record. The hens came to the door with Santa Claus, the pussies washed themselves in the open air without chilling their tongues, and Santa Claus—sweet old gentleman—was even gallanter than usual. Visitors from the chimney were a new dismay, but all of them brought their hands so full and behaved so sweetly only a churl could have turned them away. And the ones at the barn were so happy! Maggie gave the hens a check for potatoes, each of the cats had a gilt-edged bone, and the horse had a new blanket from Boston." (Emily Dickinson, from MacGregor Jenkins, *Emily Dickinson, Friend and Neighbor*, p. 63.)

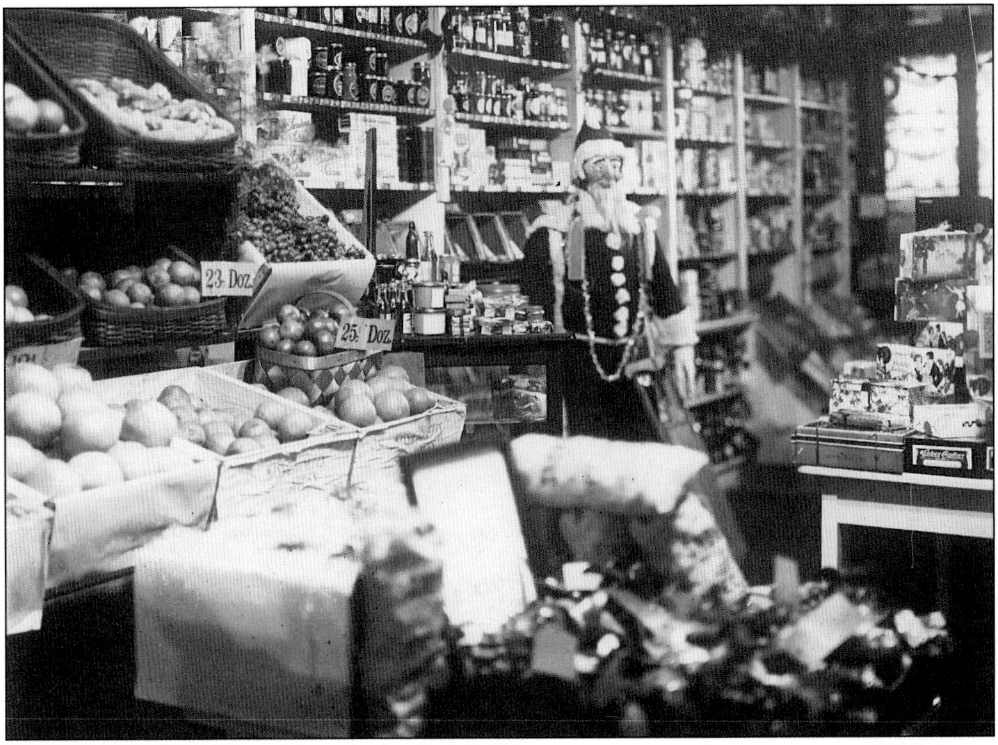

MASON DICKINSON'S GRANGE STORE, NORTH PLEASANT STREET, AMHERST. Saint Nicholas is surrounded by fresh fruits, canned goods, nuts, dried fruit, and candy for the holidays.

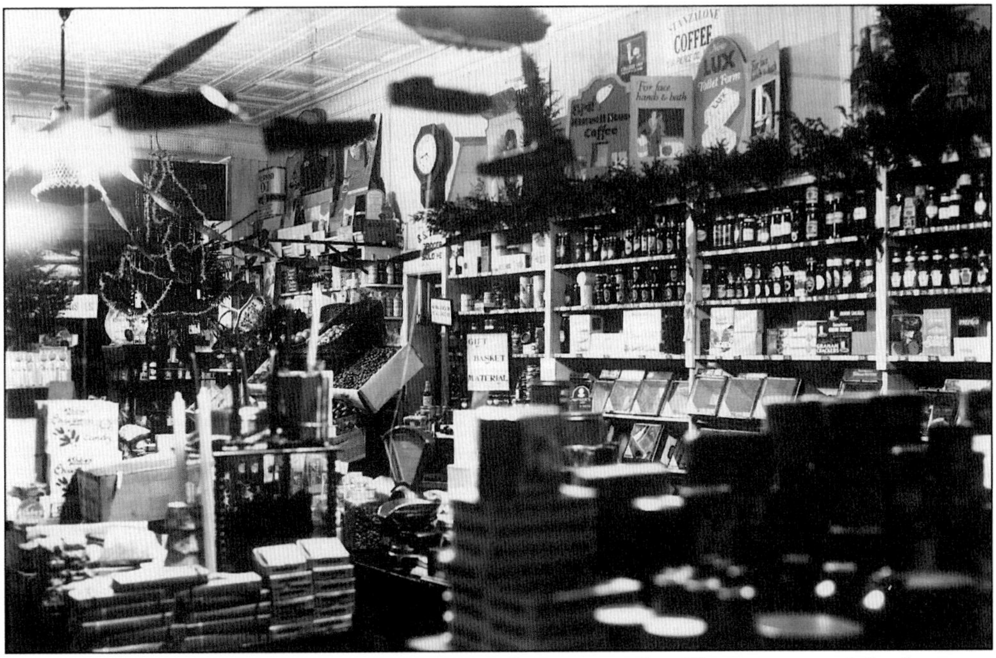

CHRISTMAS DECORATIONS AT THE GRANGE STORE. Greenery and a Christmas tree fight for space among stacks of graham crackers (named for nearby Northampton's Sylvester Graham), candles, gift baskets, and Stanzalone coffee.

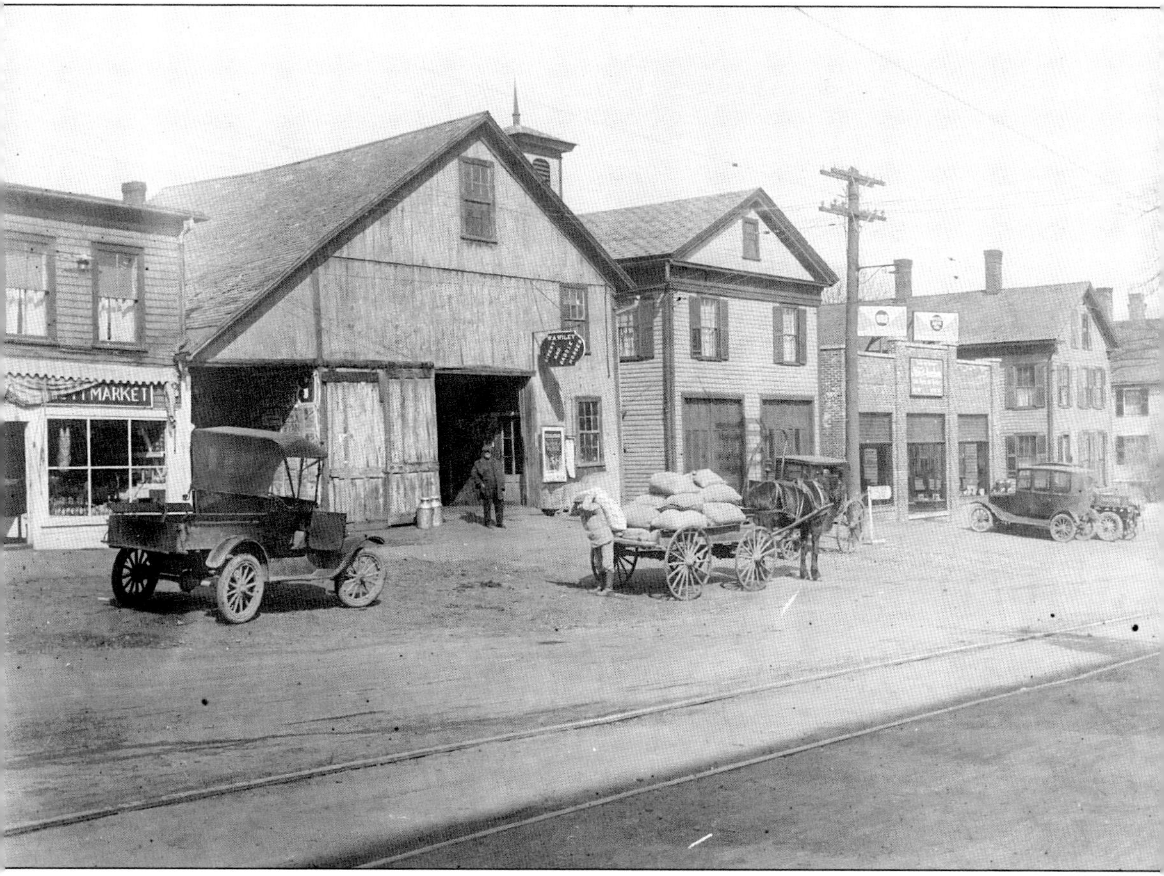

THE AMHERST JAIL BEHIND THE BLACKSMITH SHOP AND FIREHOUSE ON NORTH PLEASANT STREET. Christmastime, as Charles Dickens had written, had its dark side. So many cases were heard before the Hampshire County Grand Jury that extra benches had to be set up for prisoners. In 1878, cases included the following: Mrs. Thayer indicted for a second case of adultery ("the mother of seven children and is yet only thirty years old"), Charles Beaman for adultery, Erlon Benjamin for burglary and polygamy, John Stein for stealing Horace Lamb's horse, John Shay for assault on an officer, six men from Williamsburg for creating a riot, and Margaret Noonan for concealing the death of a child. All pleaded not guilty.

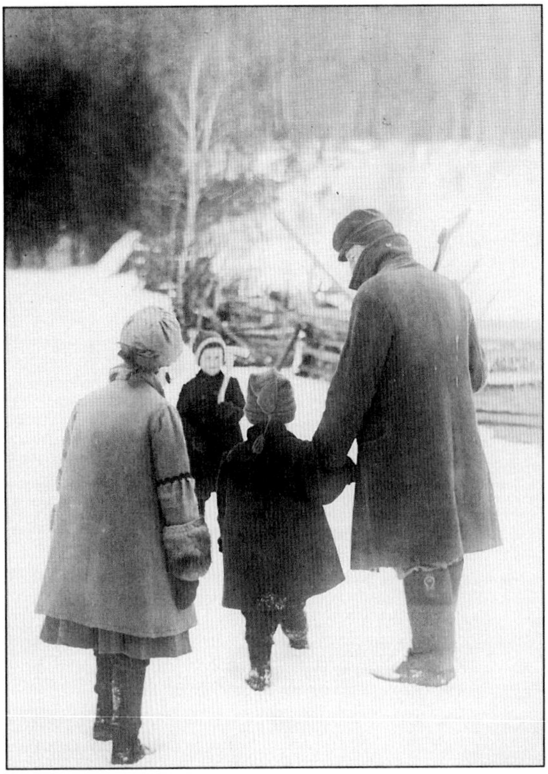

CHOOSING A TREE. Hadley writer and photographer Clifton Johnson documented the annual trek to the woods to cut down a Christmas tree. Here, his children Margaret, Arthur, and Roger are accompanied by their grandfather, Chester Johnson.

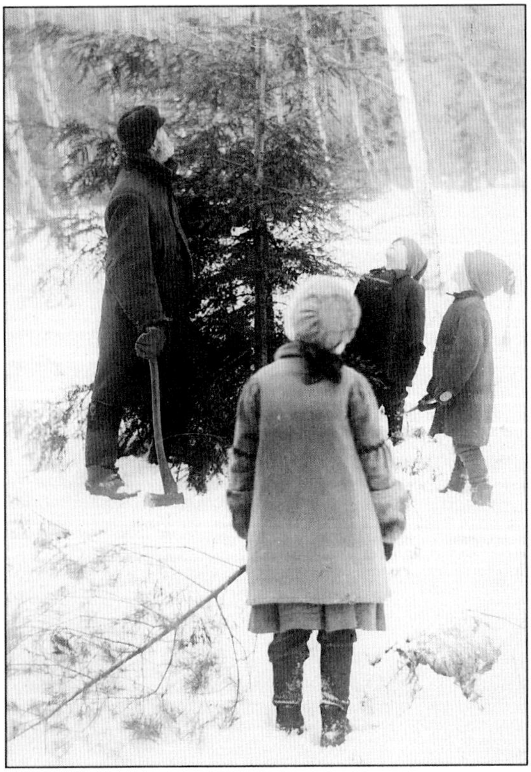

THE IDEAL SPECIMEN. "To Shutesbury hill for Christmas greens. Silent wintry woods, full of snow. The last pink sky of an early sunset with the exquisite tracery of bare trees against it." (David Grayson, *The Countryman's Year*, December 23.)

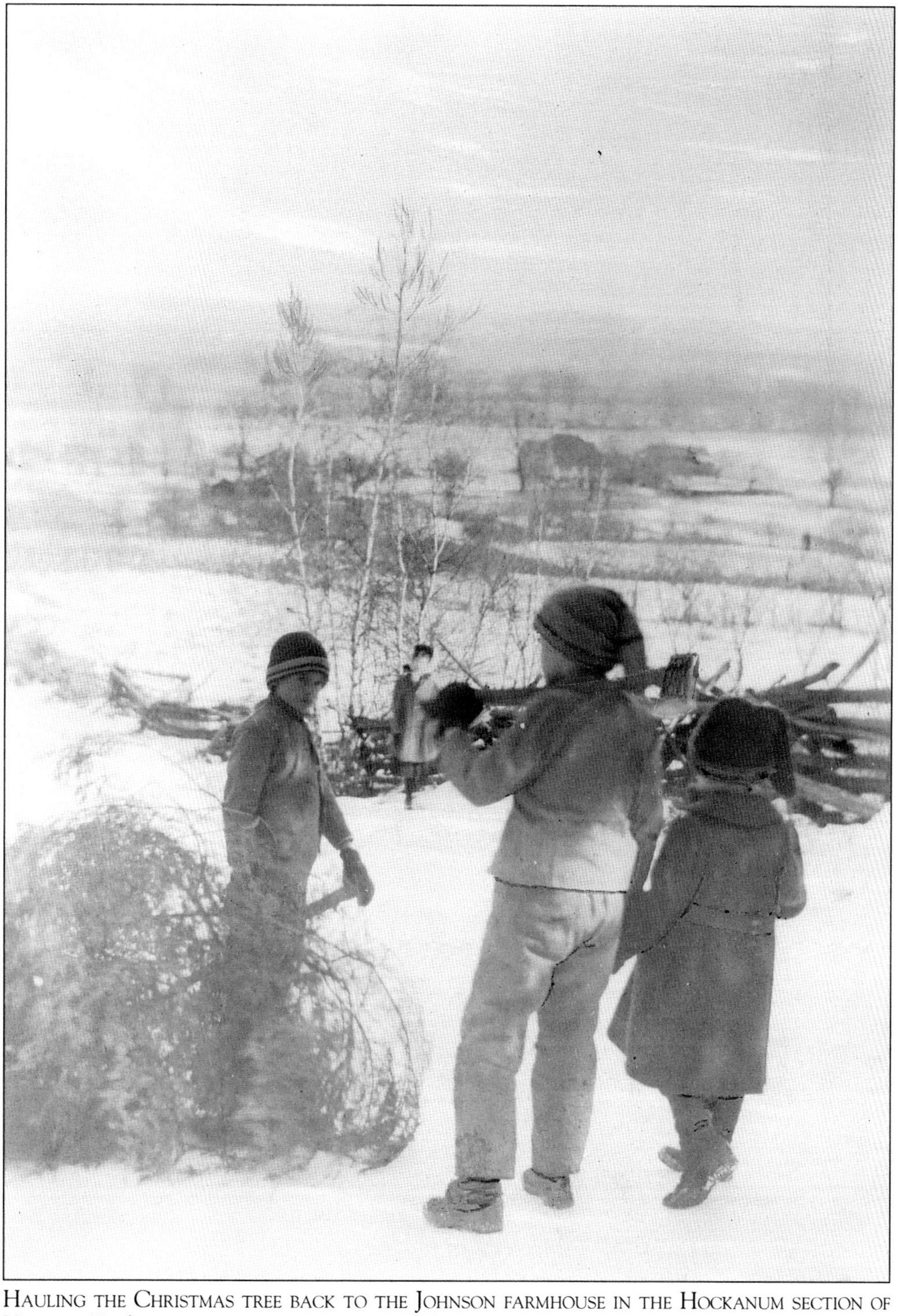

HAULING THE CHRISTMAS TREE BACK TO THE JOHNSON FARMHOUSE IN THE HOCKANUM SECTION OF HADLEY. "Lights coming on in evening windows, cattle bawling, dark figures in snow-filled roads, going home. The spell of New England winter days." (David Grayson, *The Countryman's Year*, December 23.)

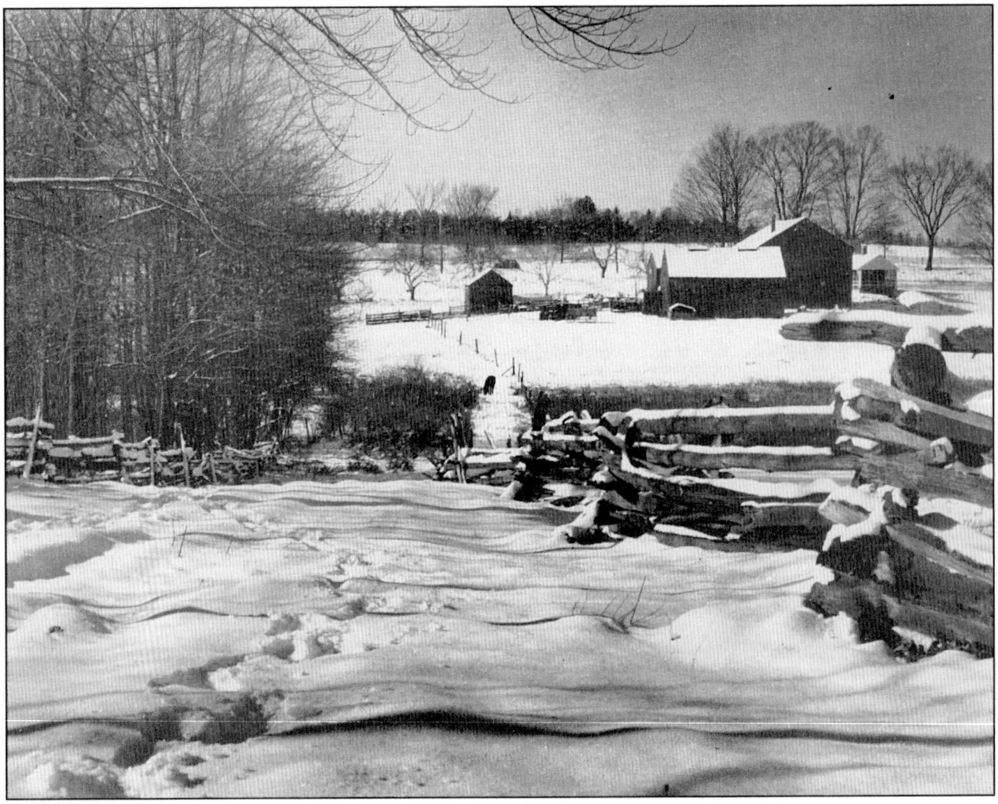

AN OLD AMHERST FARM IN WINTER, EAST PLEASANT STREET.

Good Night Near Christmas

And now good night. Good night to this old house
Whose breathing fires are banked for their night's rest.
Good night to lighted windows in the west.
Good night to neighbors and to neighbors' cows

Whose morning milk will be beside my door.
Good night to one star shining in. Good night
To earth, poor earth with its uncertain light,
Our little wandering planet still at war.

Good night to one unstarved and gnawing mouse
Between the inner and the outer wall.
He has a paper nest in which to crawl.
Good night to men who have no bed, no house.

—Robert Francis, *Collected Poems*, p. 135.
(Amherst: University of Massachusetts Press, 1976.)

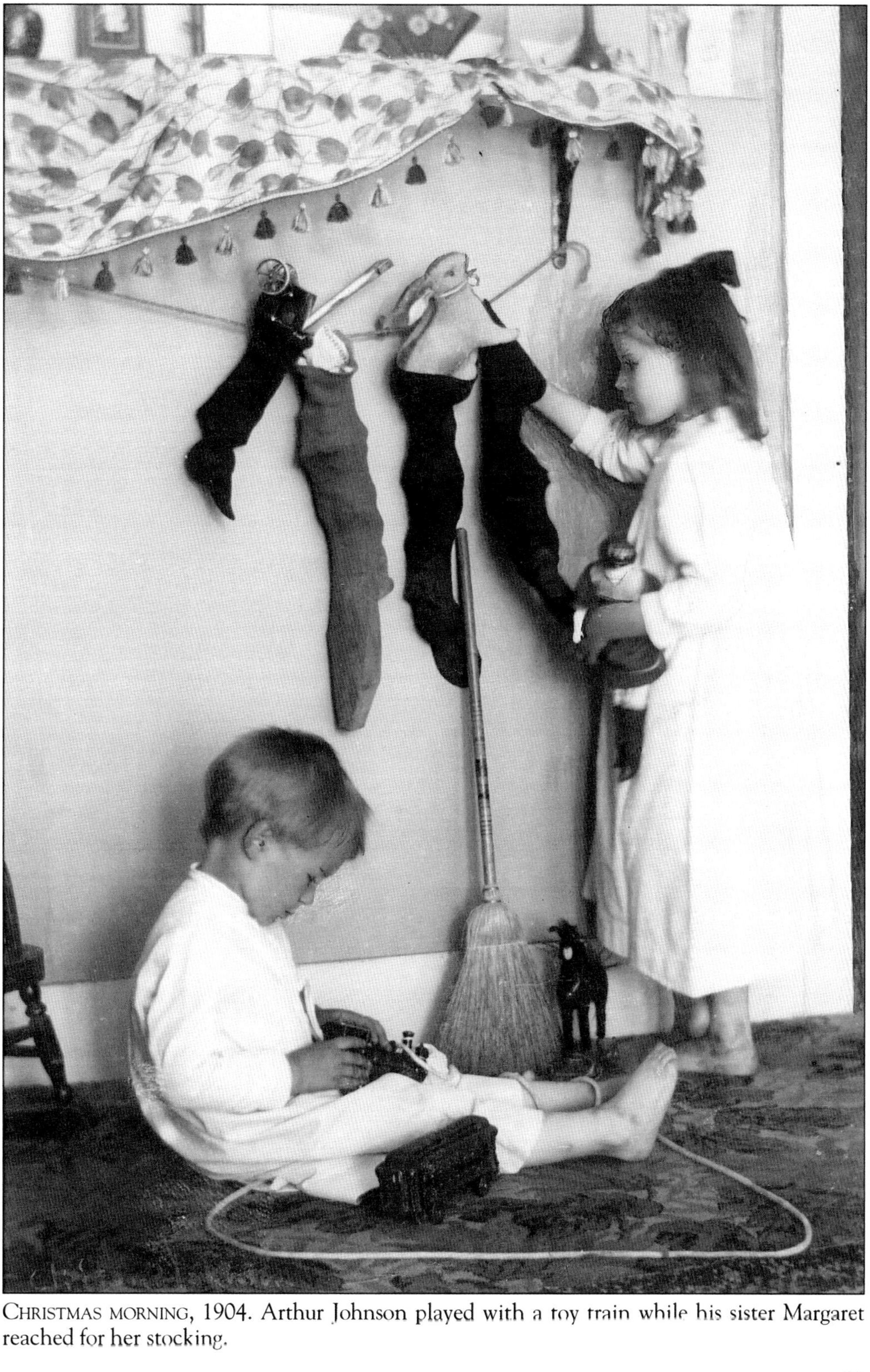

CHRISTMAS MORNING, 1904. Arthur Johnson played with a toy train while his sister Margaret reached for her stocking.

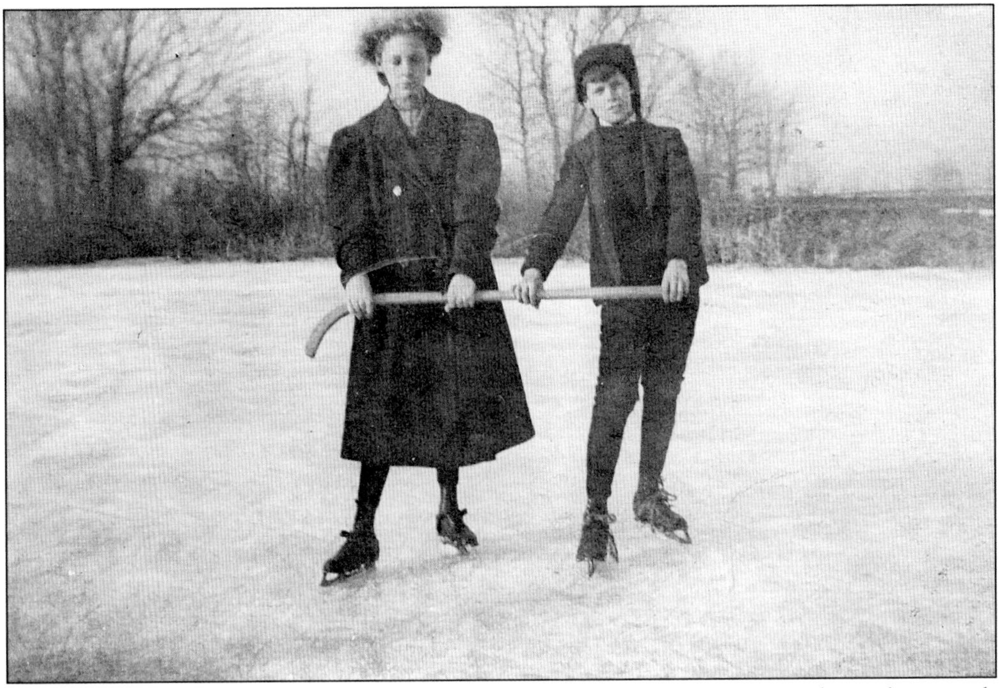

CHRISTMAS DAY. "Fierce cold, yet dry and clear, the snowy earth radiant with sunshine, such a day as only the north can know. The newspapers say that all records for low temperature for this time of year have been broken, but our gaiety has in no wise been dimmed. We have skated—all hands—on the pond . . ."

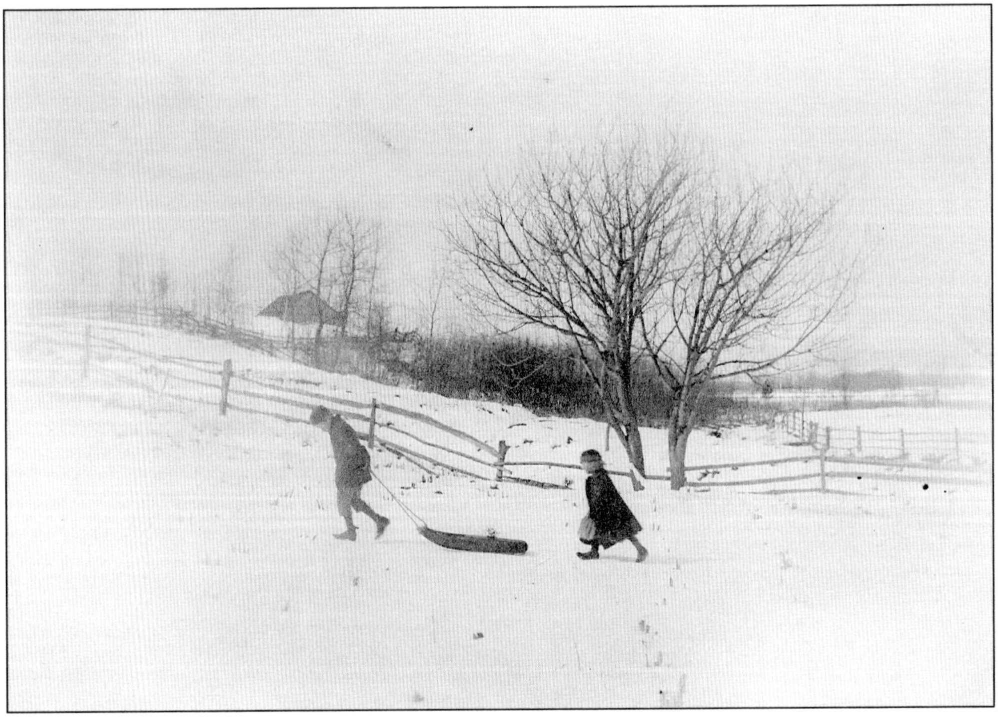

". . . we have coasted on the hill . . ."

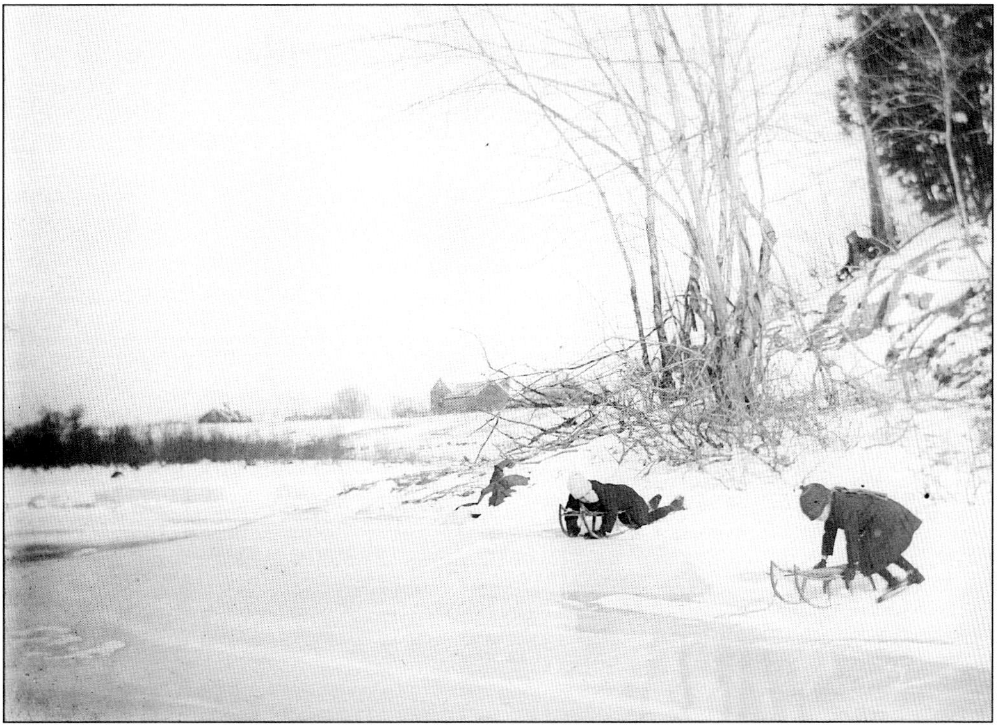

Above: CHILDREN SLEDDING AT RUSSELL'S COVE IN HADLEY, BY CLIFTON JOHNSON.
Below: ". . . we have tramped the wintry roads . . ." (Photograph of Mount Nonotuck by Clifton Johnson.)

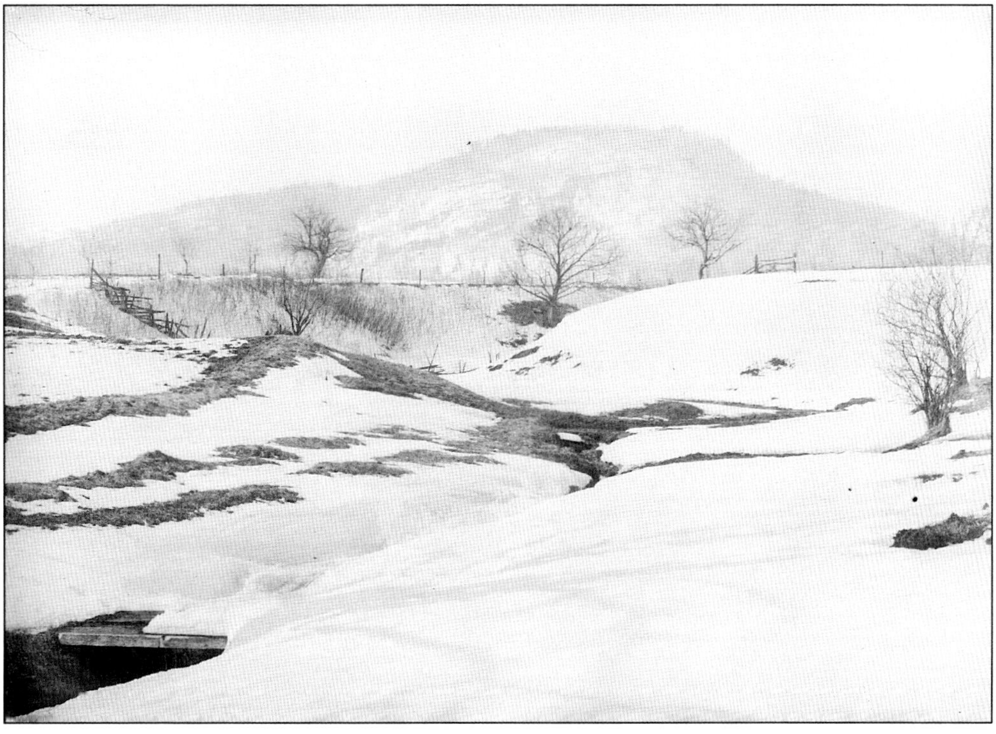

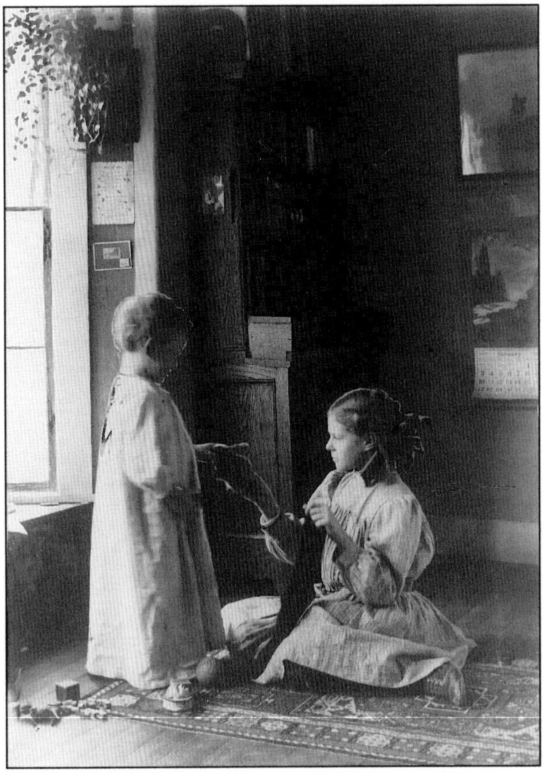

". . . and come in glowing, to shake ourselves out of coats and mufflers and seek the roaring open fires. At noon what a turkey, and everything that goes with it—what pumpkin pies! . . ." Margaret Johnson hands a toy rabbit to brother Irving on Christmas, 1909.

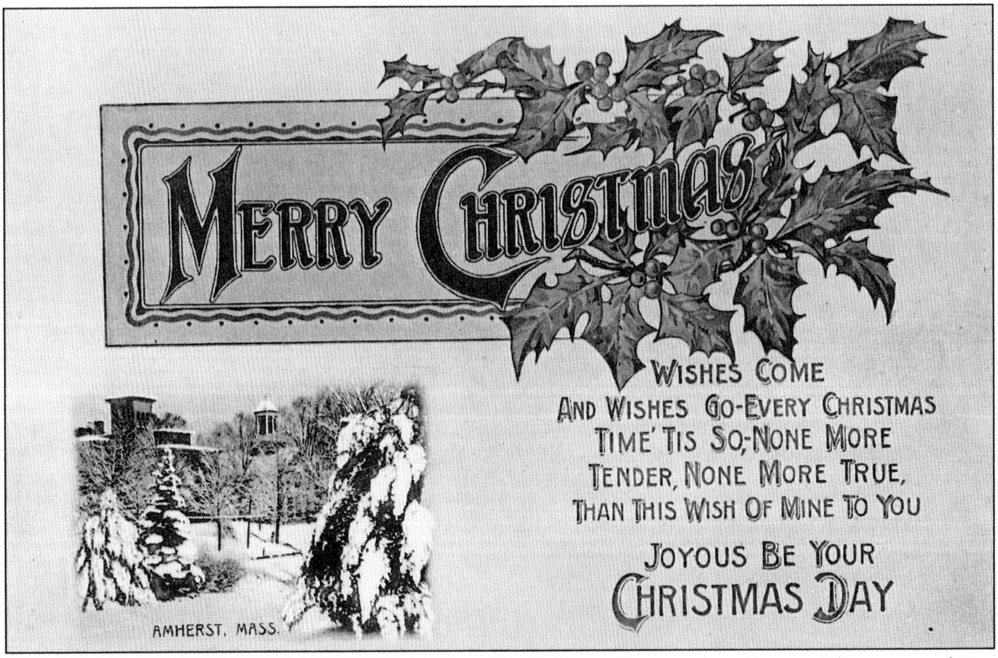

". . .The long table quite full, a tree that touched the ceiling, cries of astonishment and joy from all the little boys and girls, and many surprises and much laughter—and music in the house—and dancing. It has been a good Christmas Day." (David Grayson, *The Countryman's Year*, December 25.)

THE SNOWMAN. Clifton Johnson photographed his children Margaret, Arthur, and Roger putting the finishing touches on a snowman at their Hadley farmhouse about 1908.

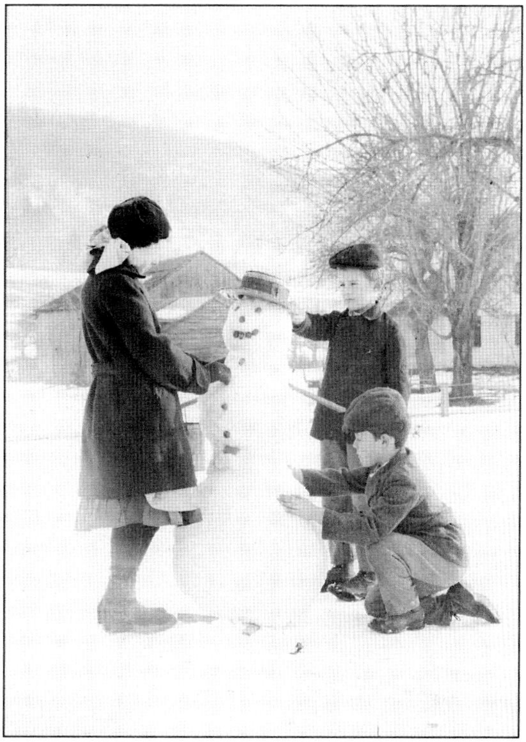

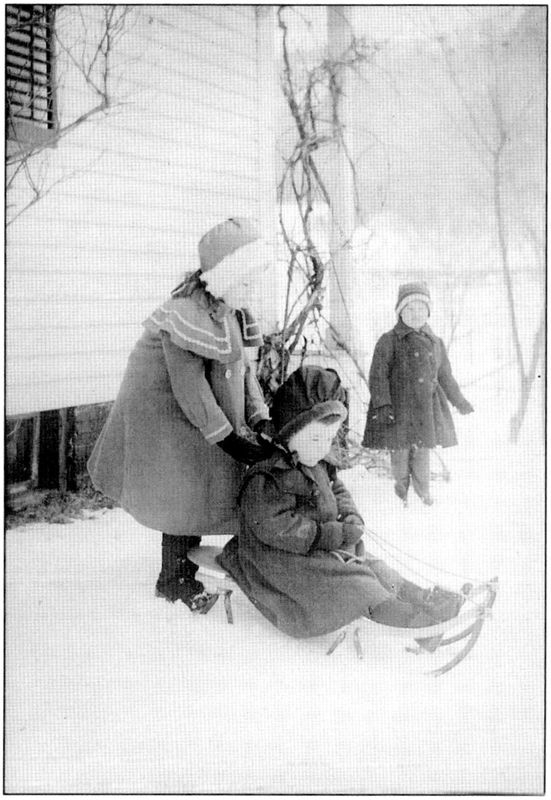

SLEDDING, C. 1904. Margaret Johnson pushed Roger on a sled as Arthur watched.

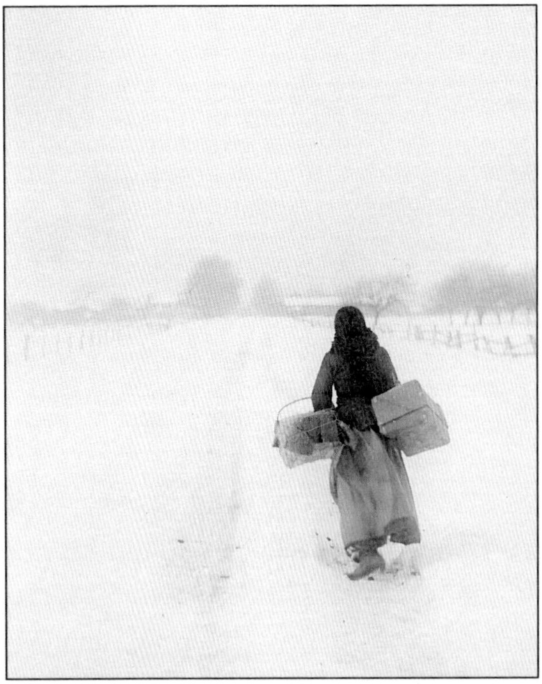

ROUGH GOING. Clifton Johnson captured a lonely peddler woman on film as she tramped the snowy roads of Hadley at the turn of the century.

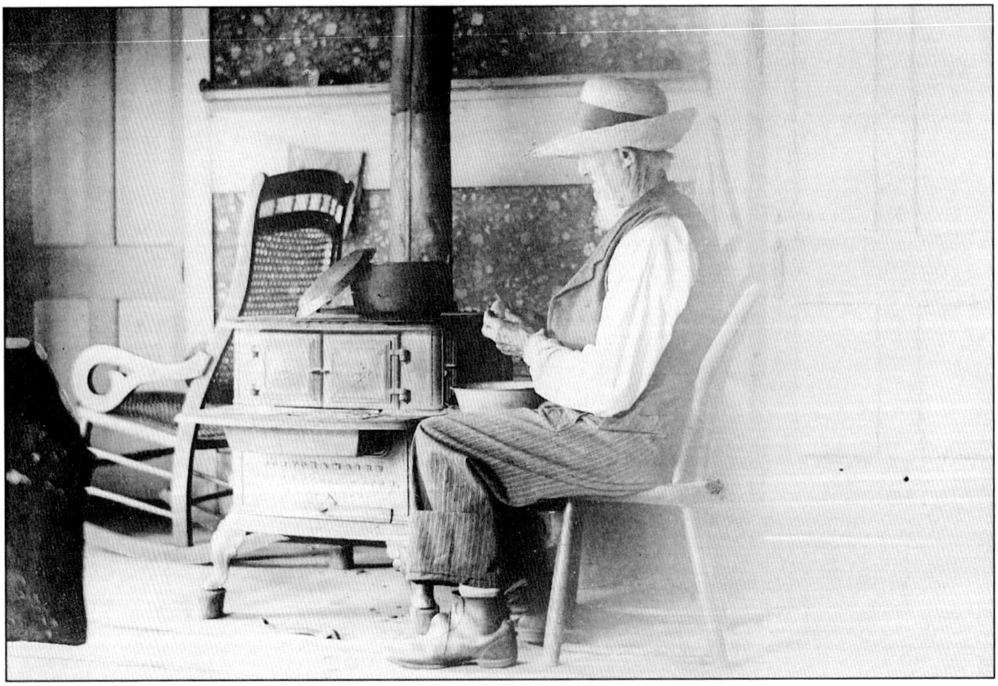

"GRANDPA" LOREN PEASE OF HADLEY BY THE WOOD STOVE IN WINTER. "Winter, too, brought plenty of work . . . There was the stock to feed and water and keep comfortable; the threshing to do; trees must be felled in the woods and sledded to the home yard, there to be worked up into fireplace length; tools needed mending; there was the flax to attend to, and, if new fencing was to be done in the spring, rails must be split." (Clifton Johnson, *The New England Country*. Boston: Lee and Shepard Publishers, 1896, p. 17.)

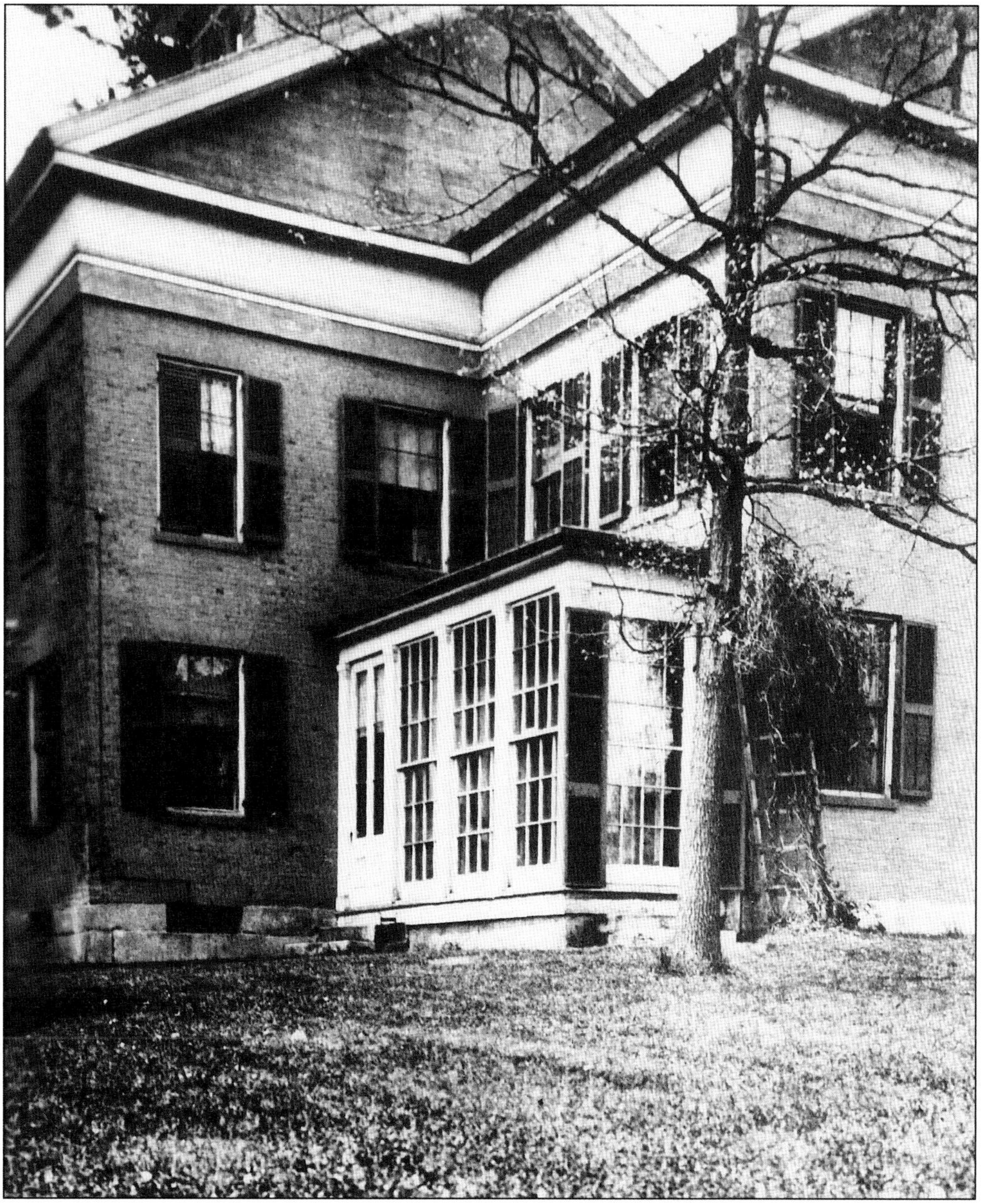

EMILY DICKINSON'S CONSERVATORY. "I think the only prolonged interview I ever had with [Emily Dickinson] alone was on a bleak winter day when an errand of some sort took me to 'The Mansion.' I was just leaving when Miss Emily called me back. She seemed to be in an unusual state of excitement . . . She took me to her conservatory where she labored all winter to keep a succession of flowers in bloom. No one equaled her in her skill with flowers and . . . her conservatory was a dream of loveliness. But she had more than a flower to show me that day. 'Come quickly,' she said, 'if you want to see something beautiful.' I followed her and she pointed out a wonderful moth which had broken its chrysalis and was fluttering about among her flowers. I wish I could now recall what she said, but small boy as I was, I knew the manner of a prophetess when I saw it, and recognized the voice when I heard it." (MacGregor Jenkins, *Emily Dickinson, Friend and Neighbor*, pp. 121–122.)

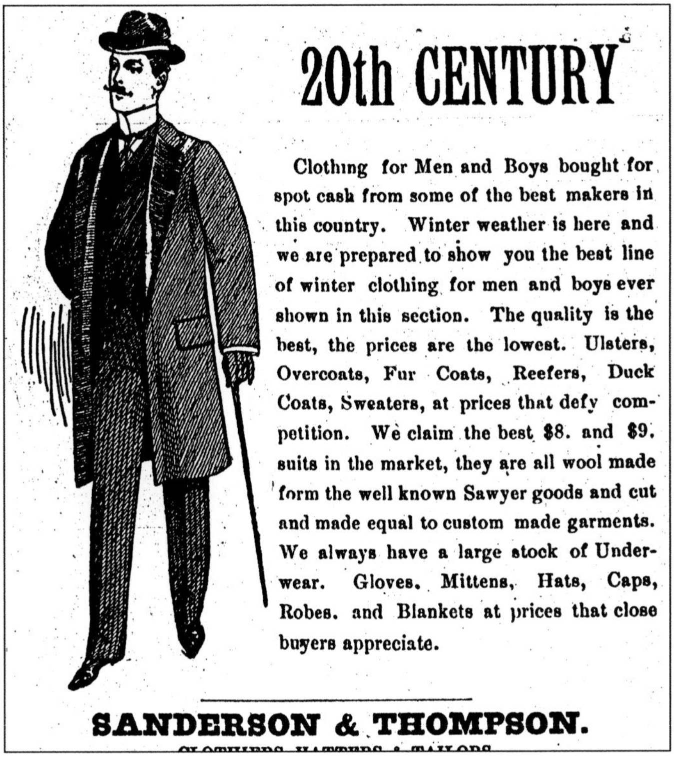

"On Monday, at midnight, Father Time turned over another leaf in his big ledger and wrote at the top of a clean white page the figures '1895.' It seems hardly possible that a full year has elapsed since we shook hands in greeting with 1894 and invited him to make himself at home, but Time and the Old Farmers' Almanac never lie." (*The Amherst Record*, January 1895.)

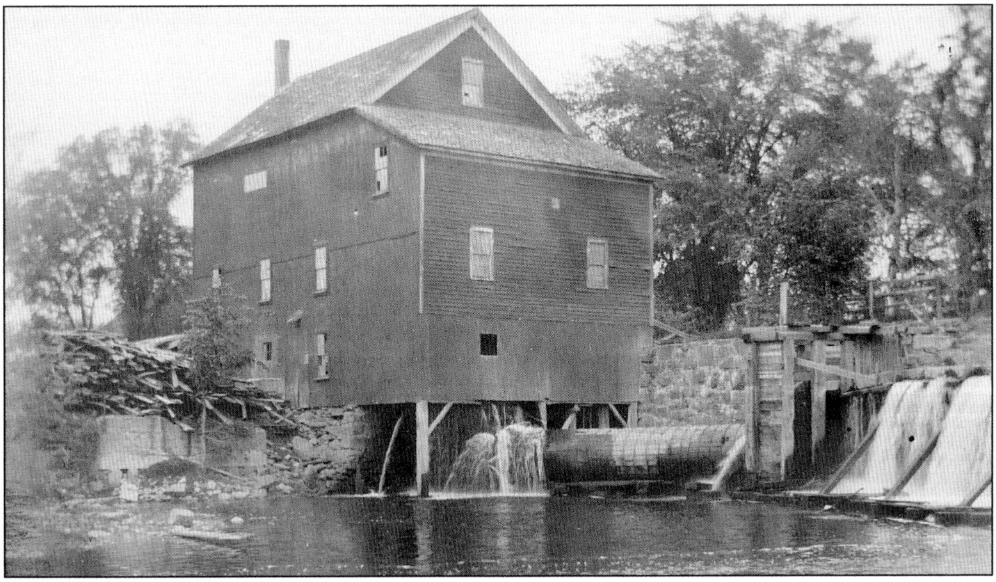

A Mill Valley gristmill, South Amherst. "In the afternoon I tramped to Mill Valley to see the ice cutters at work . . . I stopped at the mill, sniffing at the doorway, looking in with pleasure at the great fat bags of grain, the ancient noisy machinery, the rafters gray with the undisturbed dust of half a century. I walked on up the road, meeting many wood sleds, full-loaded, on their way to town, the brass bells hung from the horses' collars jangling in the still air. A jolly driver waved his mittened hand at me as he passed." (David Grayson, *The Countryman's Year*, February 22.)

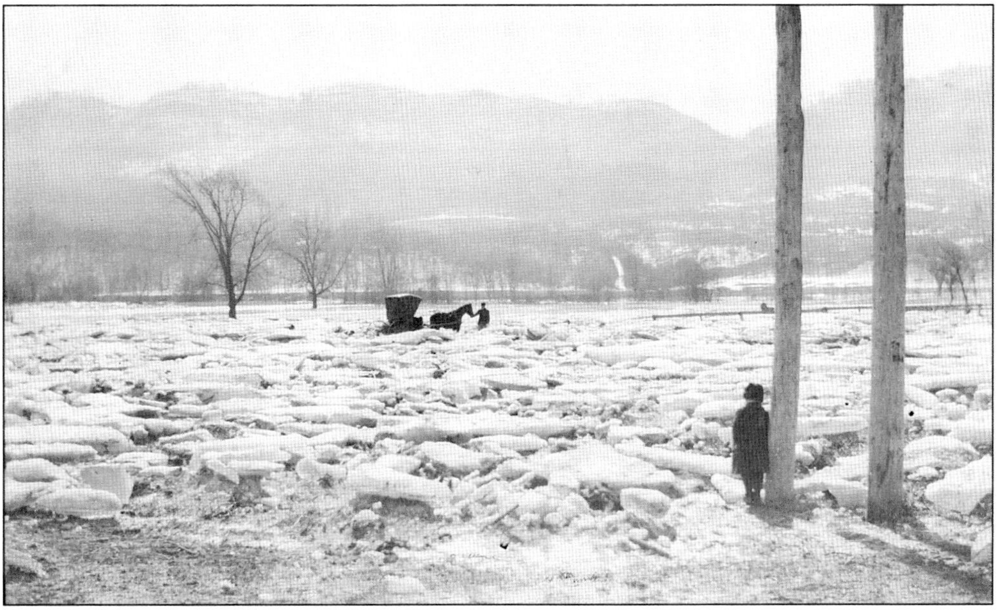

THE FORT MEADOW IN HADLEY AFTER AN ICE FLOOD.

February Snow

Far and near and high and low
The world is nothing now but snow.

It sweeps and swoops down slanting-wise
In flakes of February size.

White is where black used to be.
Every tree is a snowtree.

Up in the steeple the hands of the clock
Reached almost III before they stuck.

This is a world without a bell.
Sleepers in their beds sleep well.

They sigh and dream, maybe, and snore
While snow piles on the bedroom floor.

Everything drifts or lies undone.
There is no time. There is no sun.

—Robert Francis, *Collected Poems*, p. 16.
(Amherst: University of Massachusetts Press, 1976.)

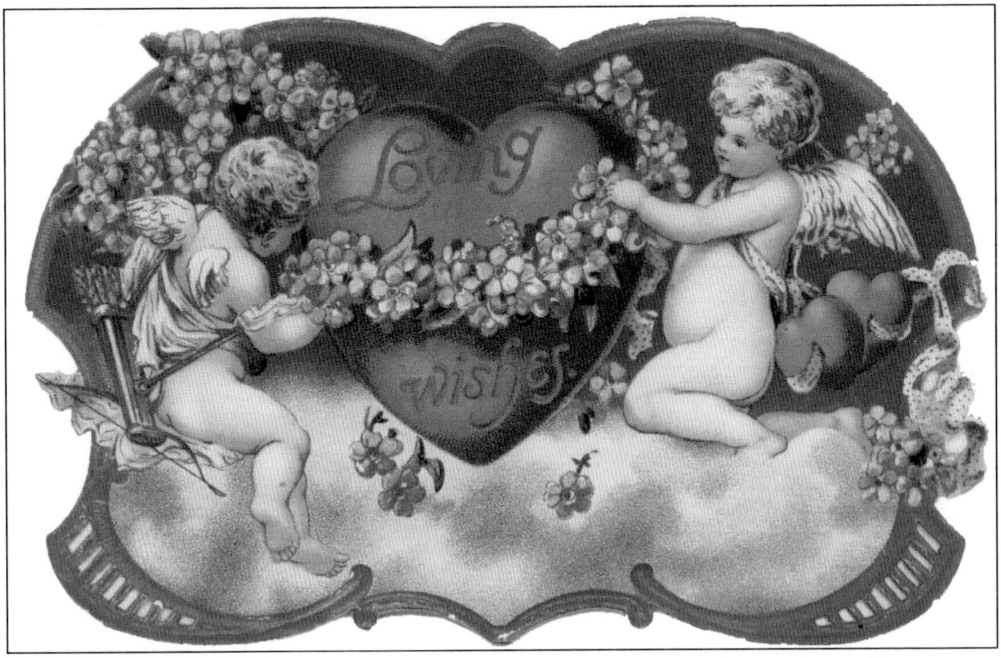

NINETEENTH-CENTURY COURTSHIP. Young women were warned to be vigilant and avoid being swept away: "Since women are prone to think much of love, to read books of sickly sentimentality and the poetry of amatory bards; since girls will put it into each other's heads, that they are in love, it is desirable that they should understand the first symptoms of the disorder, and take early and vigorous measures to stop its dangerous course." (Elizabeth Tobey, *The Young Lady's Friend*. Boston: American Stationers Company, 1837.)

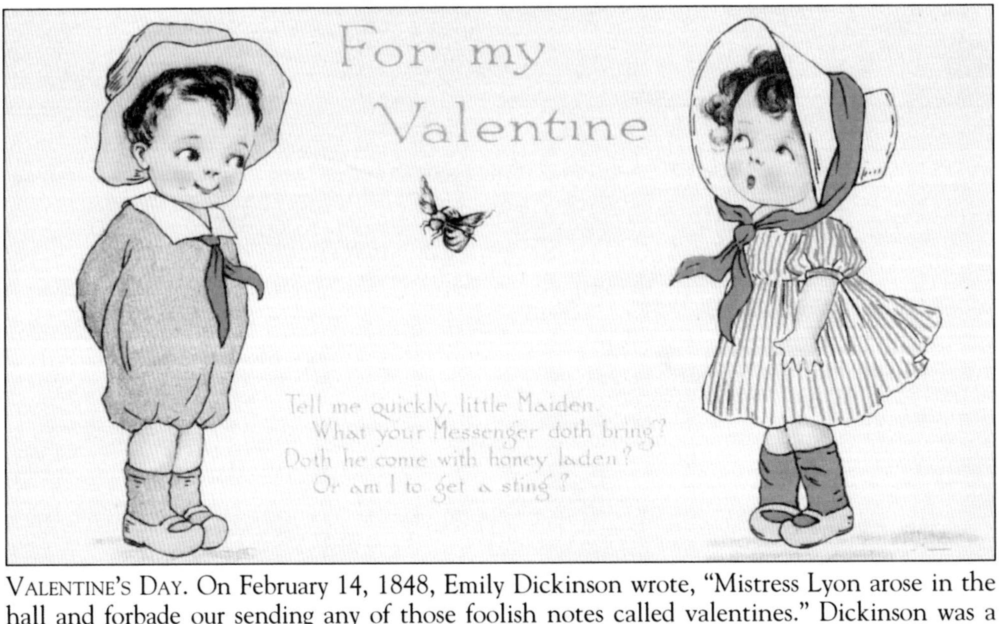

VALENTINE'S DAY. On February 14, 1848, Emily Dickinson wrote, "Mistress Lyon arose in the hall and forbade our sending any of those foolish notes called valentines." Dickinson was a student at Mount Holyoke Seminary at the time. Ironically, another student, Esther Howland, created such innovative valentines she became a wealthy woman and is considered the mother of American valentine cards.

LAVINIA DICKINSON IN THE 1860S. Many bent the rules of courtship, as did Emily Dickinson's sister Lavinia when courted by Joseph Lyman. He wrote of his visits to Lavinia in the 1840s: "I read her Virgil lessons to her & walked with her to the Amherst Academy gate carrying her books . . . I was happy once in Vinnies arms—very happy. She sat in my lap and pulled the hairpins from her long soft chestnut hair and tied the long silken mass around my neck and kissed me again & again."

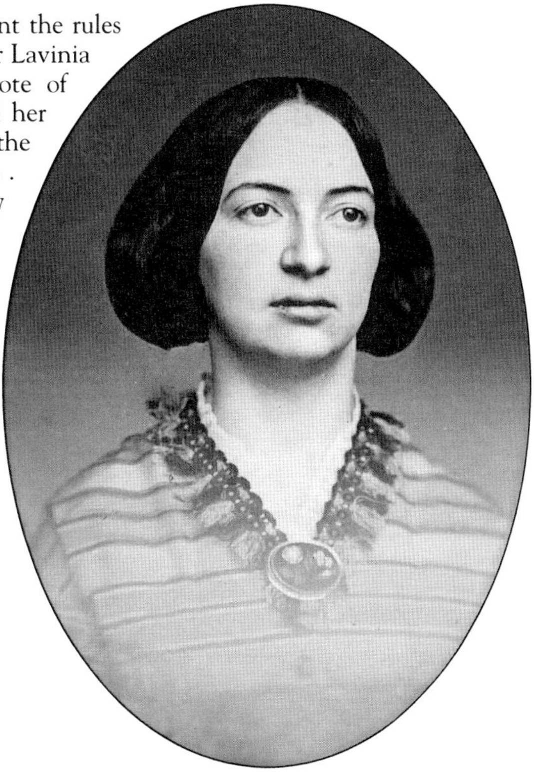

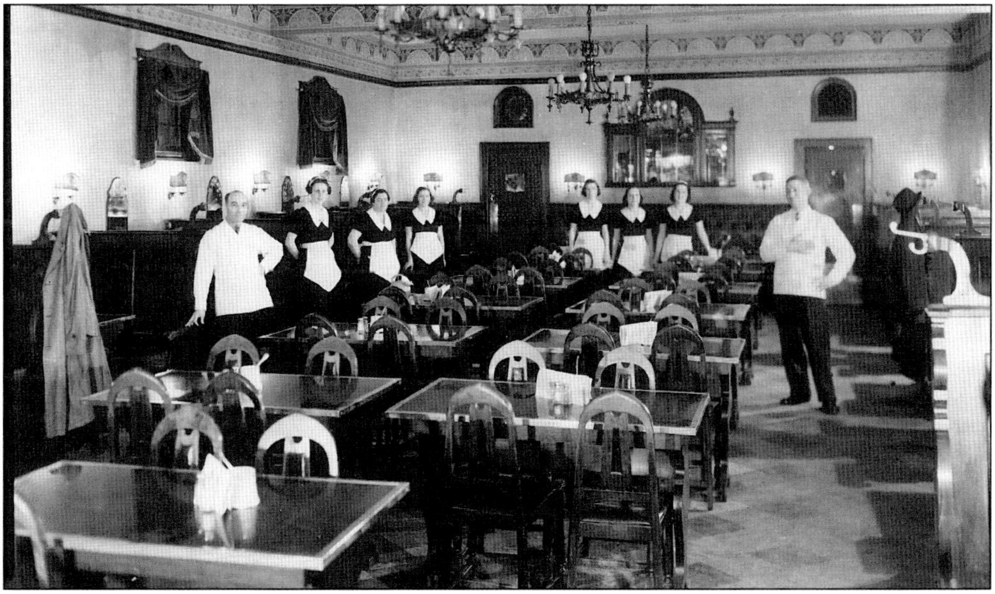

A SPARK OF FIRE IN THE MIDST OF WINTER. February doldrums were enlivened by the class rivalries of Amherst College. In 1927, freshmen built a bonfire on the Common and burned their hated pea-green caps. They rushed the new Amherst Theatre and the College Candy Kitchen on Main Street (above), turned cars around, sent them in the opposite direction, and disconnected the trolley lines. The Amherst newspaper's reaction? "From now on the landscape should be more pleasing, with the disappearance of the suicide-green of the Amherst freshmen caps."

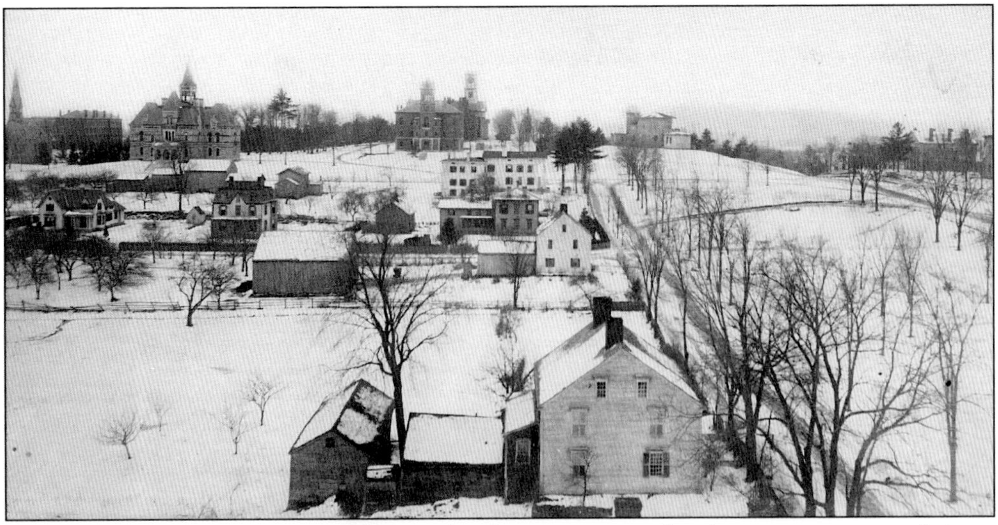

IN THE DAYS BEFORE ANTIBIOTICS. "The grip has long since ceased to be a jesting matter. It is no imaginary complaint . . . but a genuine malady, unpleasant and painful to its victim, and apt to be attended with complications that lead to serious and in some cases fatal, results . . . a great many people in Amherst are sick with the grip . . . The disease is confined to no section of the town nor in any class of people; it attacks young and old, rich and poor, sickly or healthy with genuine impartiality." (*The Amherst Record*, December 1891.)

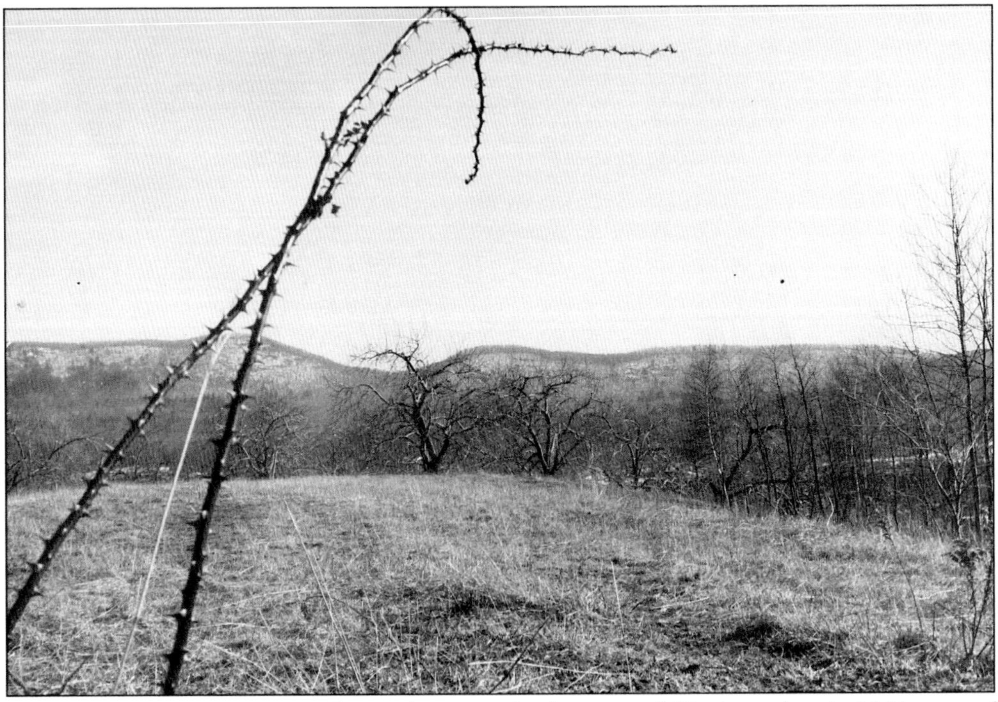

BARE APPLE TREES AND BRIARS IN SOUTH AMHERST. In the space of 12 winter days in 1864, most of a South Amherst family was wiped out. On February 10, Charles M. Smith died at the age of 12; the following day his 13-year-old brother Chester died; 6 days later their father, Chileab, died at 57; and 4 days later 7-year-old George died. All were stricken by the then-mysterious disease of diphtheria. Only the mother—Susan Pettengill Smith—and one daughter survived.

WILLIAM BURNETT, AMHERST HAT FACTORY HEIR. In 1904, the Connecticut River froze solid for months, with ice 3 feet thick in some places. Freezing and flooding in the basement of the Amherst House hotel caused the sidewalks on South Pleasant Street to collapse. Gaping cavities opened up before startled shoppers. A fortunate few could escape winter's brutalities by sailing away. Burnett sailed for the warmer climate of Cairo on a luxury liner in 1904.

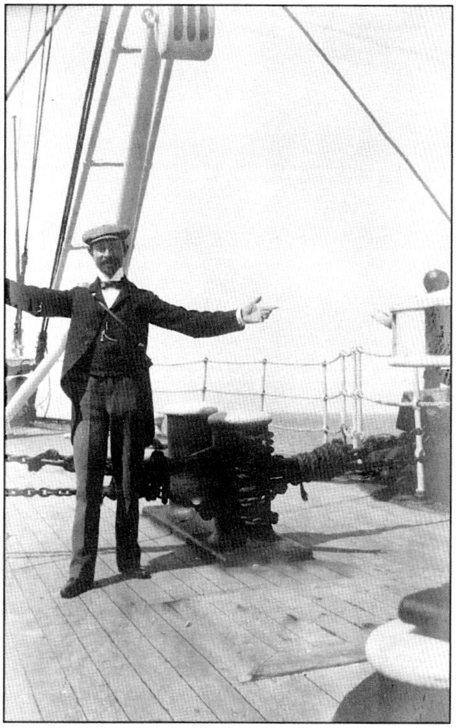

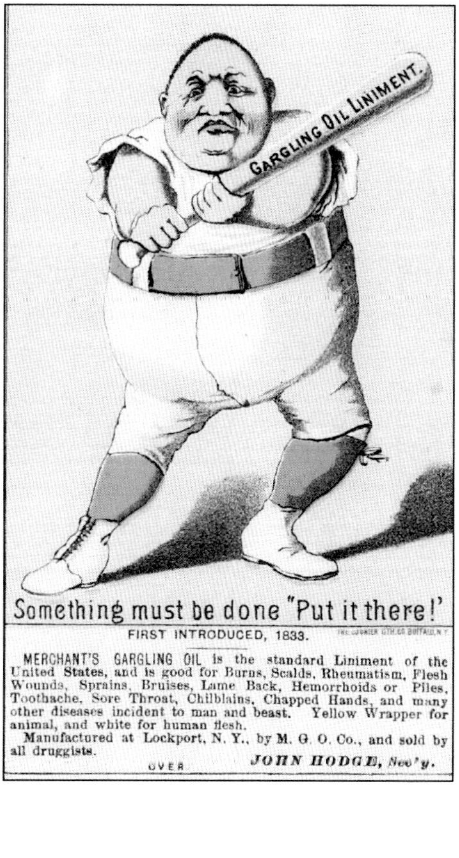

QUESTIONABLE REMEDIES. "Run Down, Tired, Nine-tenths of the Amherst People are in this Condition. Our Local Druggists, Henry Adams & Co., Say 'Vinol is What Every Man, Woman and Child Needs at This Season of the Year.' Many people right in this vicinity are all run down, no strength, hardly able to drag about . . . Our Vinol is the one great tonic reconstructor which they need. It will create strength, tone up the digestive organs, cure all stomach troubles, create a healthy appetite, make rich, red blood and strengthen every organ in the body."

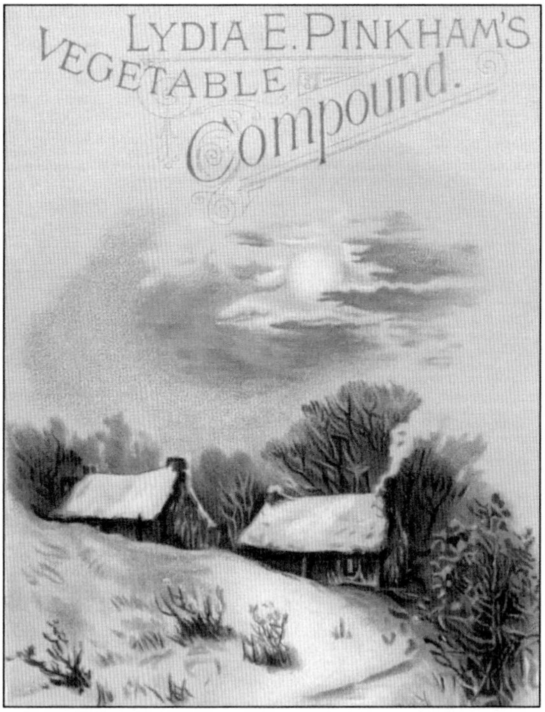

HENRY ADAMS'S ADVERTISEMENT "GOOD ADVICE TO NERVOUS WOMEN." "Has anyone ever told you what it means to feel restless?—flighty?—unsettled?—unable to concentrate yourself on your work?—unable to find pleasure or satisfaction in anything? One after another the organs become deranged . . . Sleeplessness, nervousness, melancholy and despair follow . . . WE GUARANTEE THAT MUCO-TONE WILL CURE YOU."

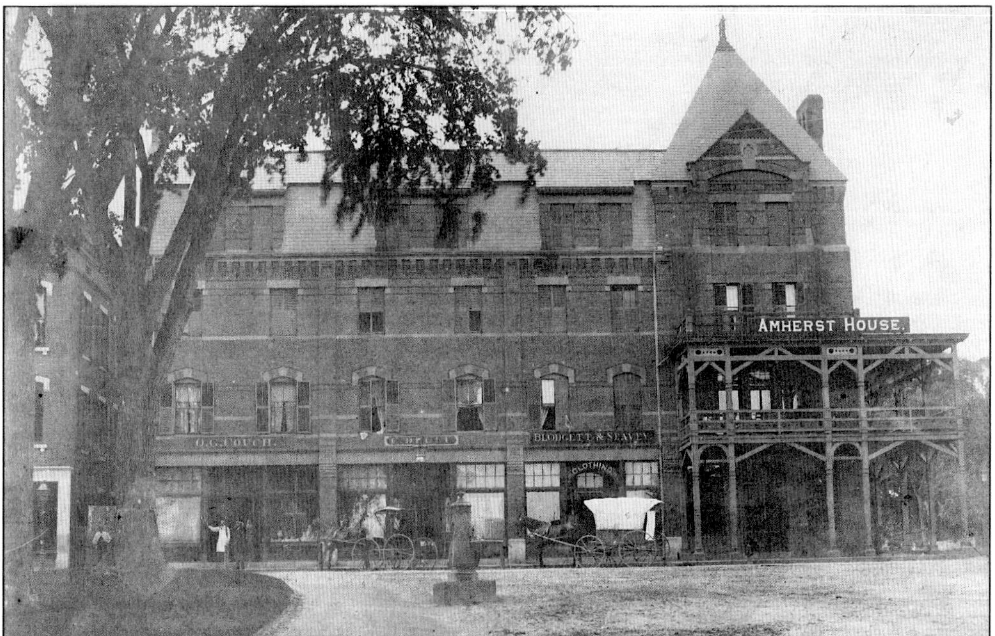

DEUEL'S DRUGSTORE (LEFT CENTER), SOUTH PLEASANT STREET, AMHERST, 1888. Pharmacist Charles Deuel touted something called Hyomei: "Hyomei is nature's own method for curing catarrh, colds, coughs and diseases of the respiratory organs . . . Breathed through the neat pocket inhaler that comes with every outfit, the air passed into the throat and lungs, is identical with that on the mountains, where it is laced with healing and health-giving balsams. It searches out and kills disease germs in the most remote and minute cells."

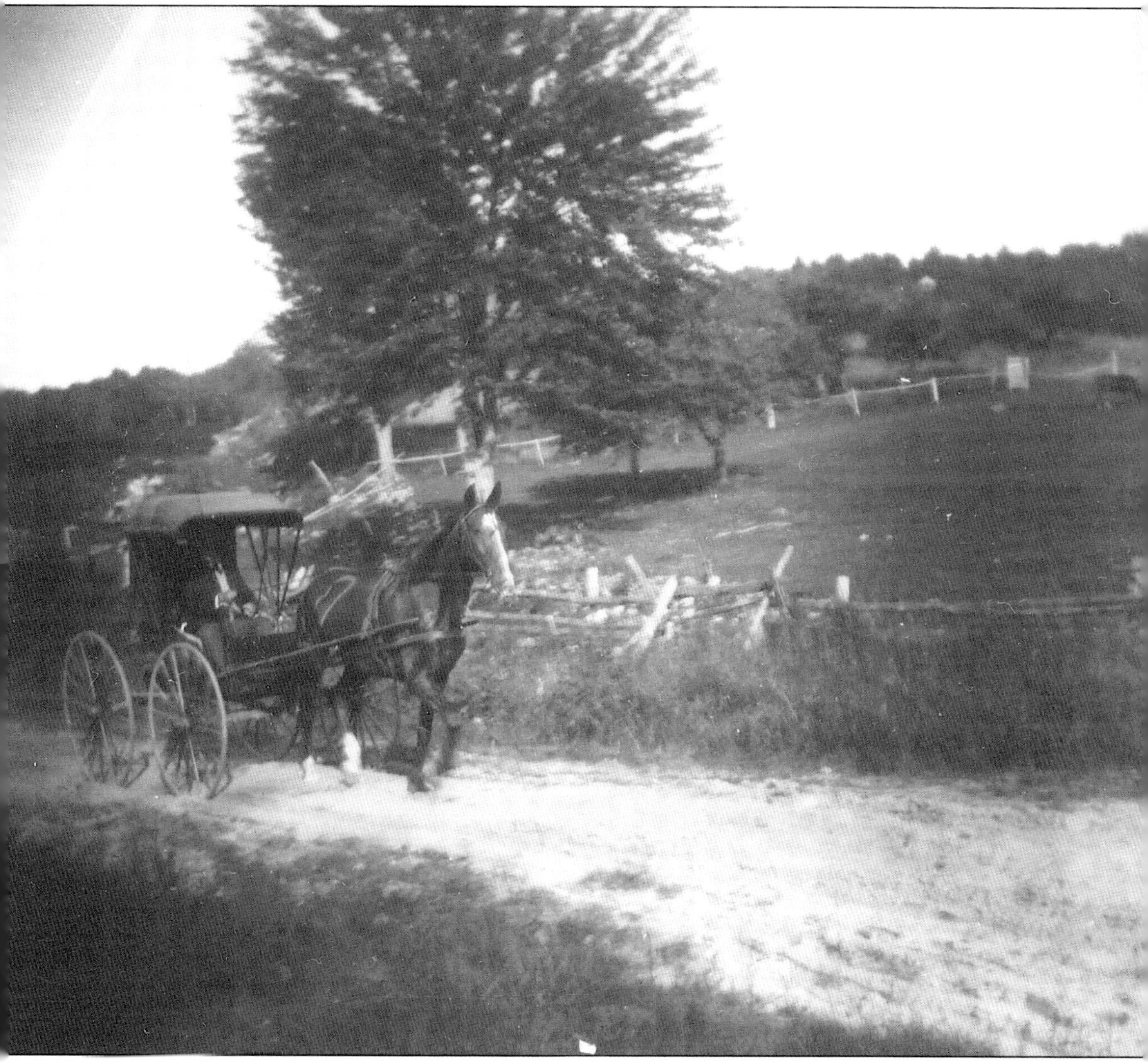

CHARLES O. PARMENTER ON THE ROAD FROM PELHAM TO AMHERST. Parmenter satirized quack remedies in an 1875 article in *The Amherst Record*. To cure the common cold, he suggested the "arctic sweat," produced by filling a flour barrel with cold water and having the patient sit on a cake of ice "dressed in his nudity" while sticking his legs in the barrel. Barrel, ice, and sufferer are covered with blankets. "Just as soon as the patient is found to be reeking with sweat, turn him through a wringer and rub dry." The "rum sweat" was produced by setting fire to half a barrel of rum. The patient is covered with blankets and suspended over the flaming rum while "a total abstinence man" simultaneously gives him rum to drink "until the rum is gone or until he is fit to ring out."

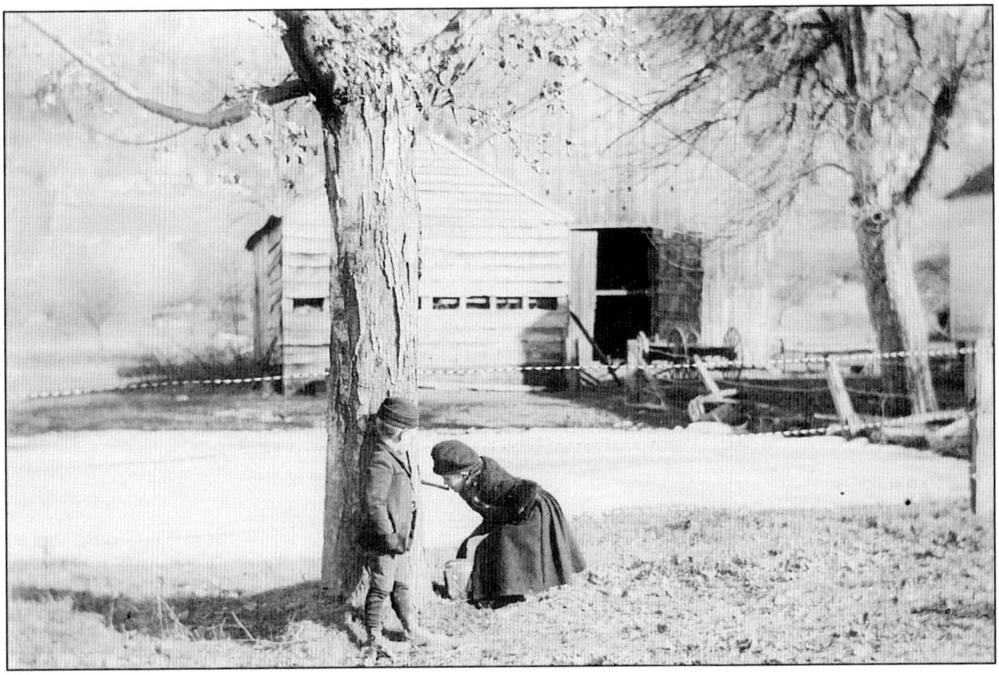

Oscar and Hettie Johnson, seen in a Clifton Johnson photograph tasting maple sap in Hadley. Weeks before the first day of spring, sap invisibly rises in the sugar maple trees. Centuries ago, Native Americans slashed the bark of maples and boiled the sap into syrup. By the 18th century, New Englanders were doing the same.

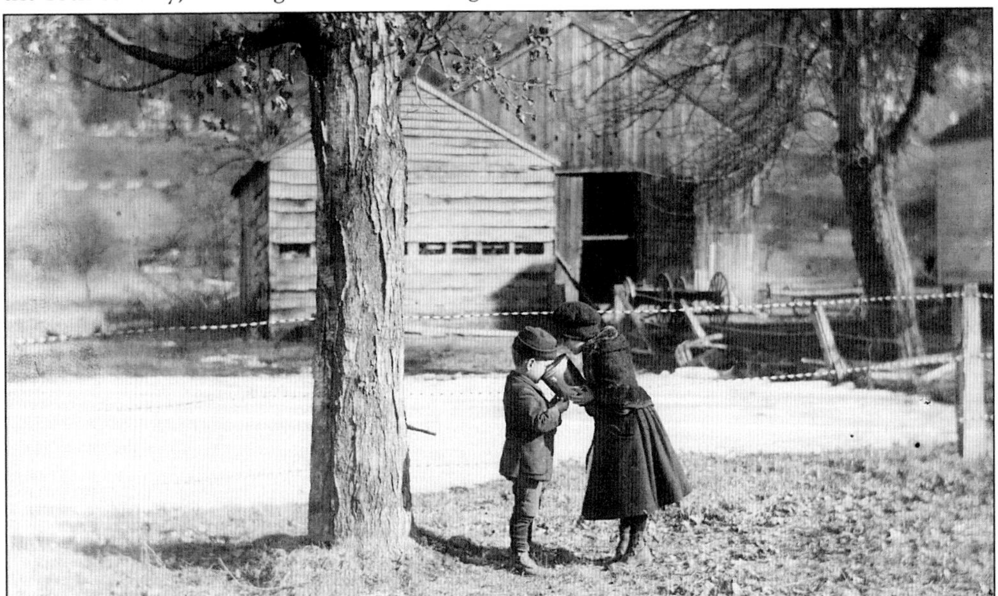

The sugaring season. In 1876, an Amherst writer known only as "Smith" commented on the prevalence of sap: "Sap in its raw state is only a juice, and is generally found in trees, some trees containing more and others less, though trees do not by any means monopolize all of this fluid. A great many heads contain this juice in abundance, such heads being known by the technical name of 'sap-heads,' and are distressingly common."

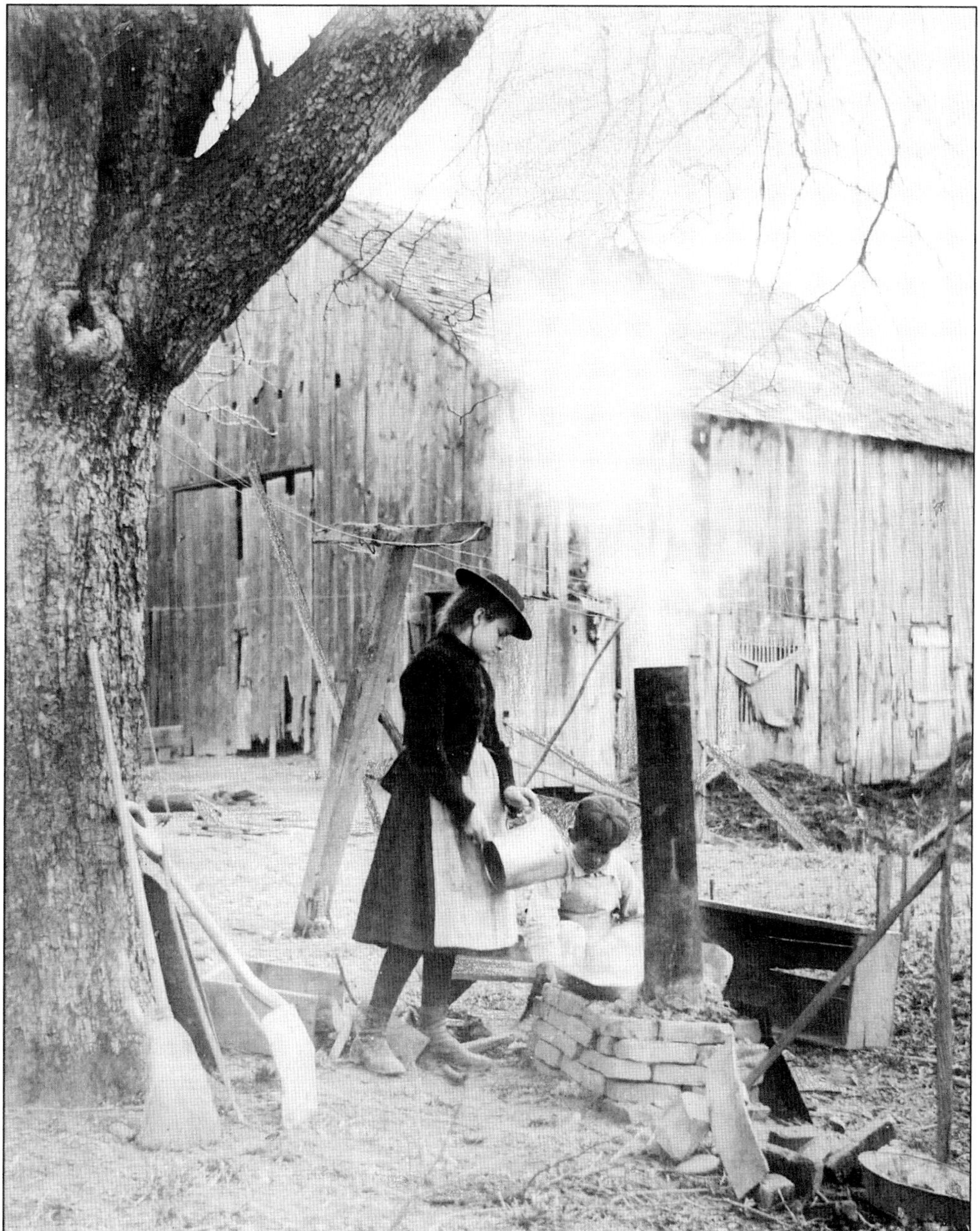

HETTIE AND OSCAR BOILING SAP ON A STOVE THEY MADE THEMSELVES. Smith continued: "The sap must be cooked before it is fit for anything. This is accomplished by the process of 'bilin',' or to use a more scientific term, by evaporation, and is one of the fine arts; this process reduces the quantity of sap but improves the quality. This fact leads us to suggest the propriety of applying this 'bilin' down' test to political candidates; many of them if evaporated a while would have little or nothing left to vote for, as no grain or fibre appears until all aqueous secretions have been given off. A fair trial would show that there is an astounding quantity of sap or water on the brain sent into our offices of trust, in which the wigglers of dishonesty and corruption soon breed."

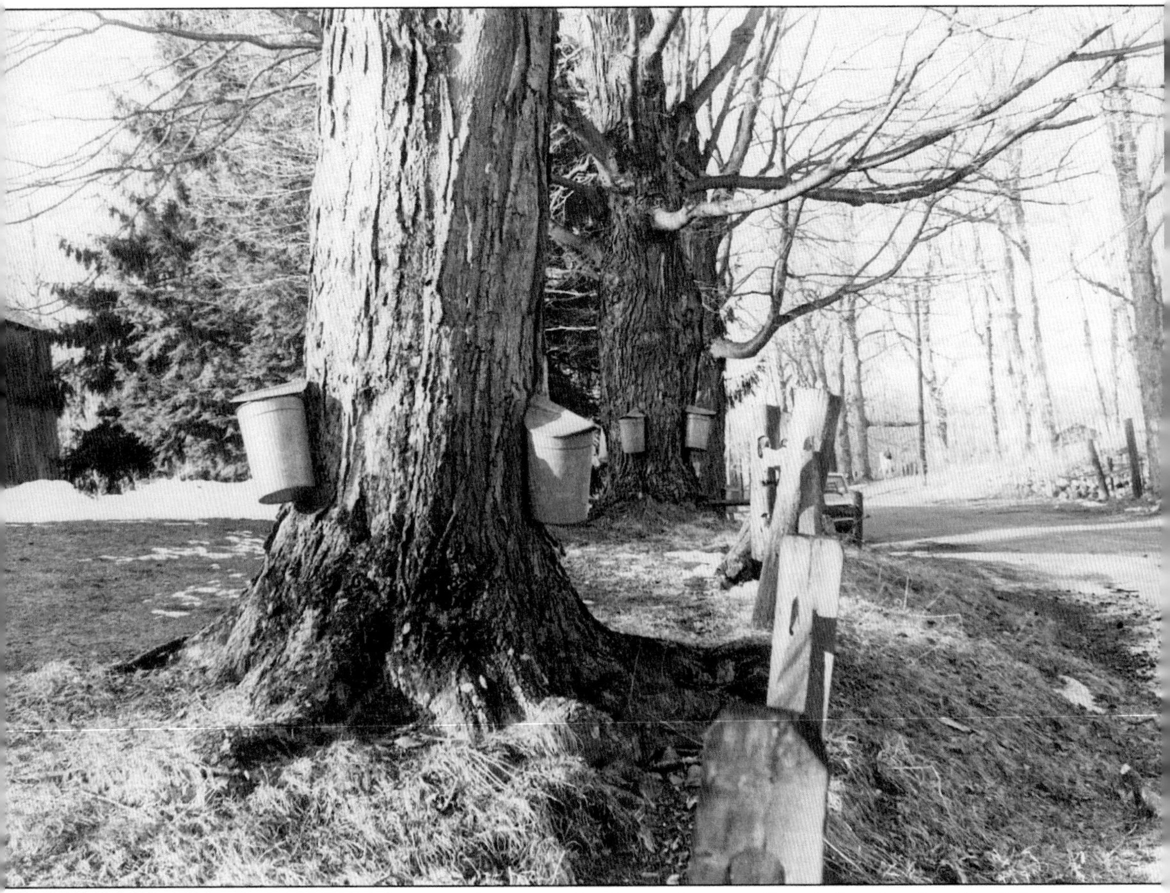

"Our friends having invited us to visit their sugarbush, we drove to Sunderland and walked three miles up Mount Toby . . . Hubbard's bush is in a rocky field on the flank of the mountain—an ancient wooden shack standing among magnificent old maple trees. When we came first in sight of it, it looked as though it were on fire, for the steam from the boiling sap was pouring out through every crack. It was indeed a stirring place—men and boys hallooing in the woods as they chopped fuel for the fire, or drove the sledges down the mountainside with barrels of sap, or ran in and out of the sugarhouse. As we came nearer we caught the ambrosial odor of the steaming syrup, and a moment later we were welcomed by Hubbard and his boys." (David Grayson, *The Countryman's Year*, March 25.)

Two

Springtime

"A sanguine madness attacks the countryman in spring."

—David Grayson

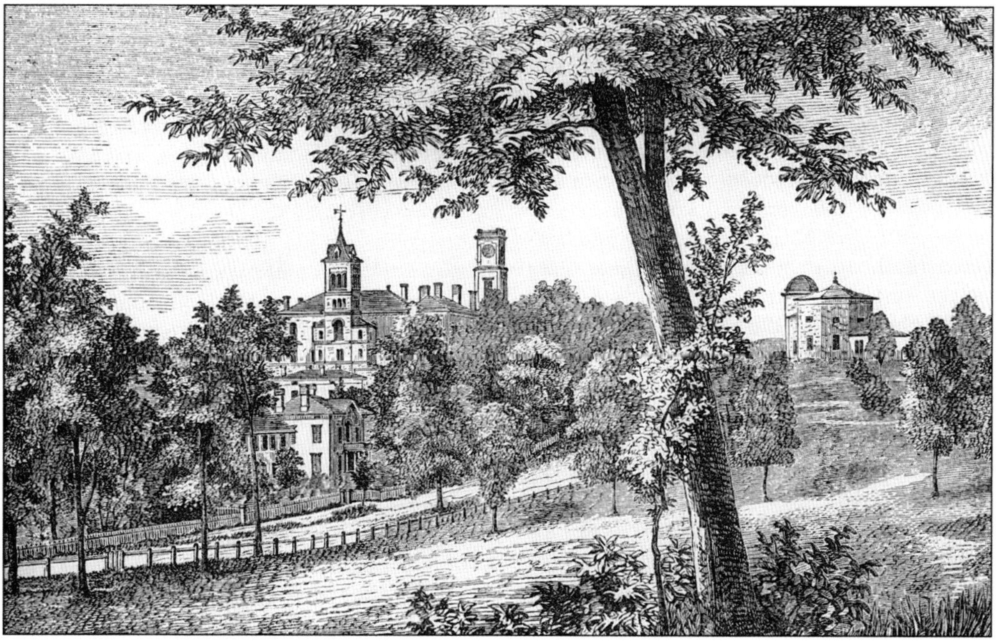

ENGRAVING OF AMHERST COLLEGE FROM *POTTER'S AMERICAN MONTHLY*, DECEMBER 1877, P. 401. "There never was a lovelier place than Amherst in the spring. As a boy I felt the intoxication of it. We had skated all winter on the shallow, frozen places in the Dickinson meadows, but now they were fair and green. Each year it was a mystery that those bleak acres of snow and ice and tufts of dead, brown grass should suddenly, almost overnight, become a paradise of green and gold and white." (MacGregor Jenkins, *Emily Dickinson, Friend and Neighbor*, p. 119.)

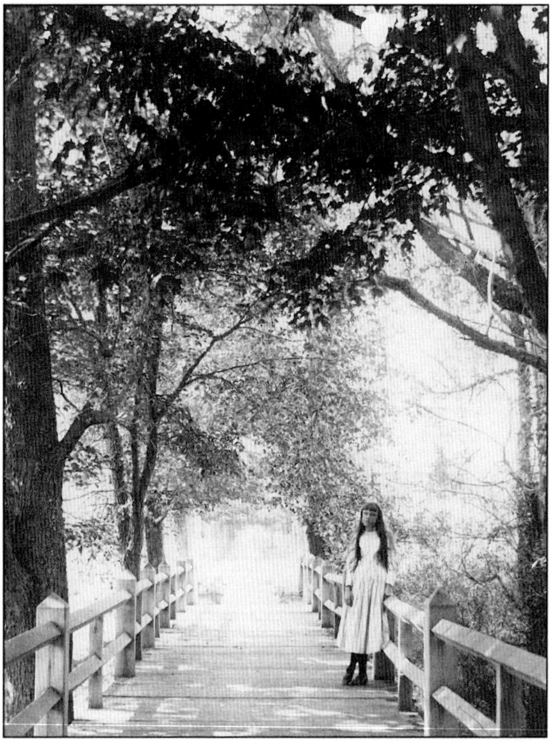

A girl on the bridge between the Dakin and Snell Houses, off of South Pleasant Street, Amherst. "Youth is, of course, the season for romance. Its buoyant spirit must soar, till weighed down by earthly care. It is in you that the feelings are warm, and the fancy fresh." (*The Young Lady's Own Book*. Philadelphia: Published by John Locken, 1841, p. 295.)

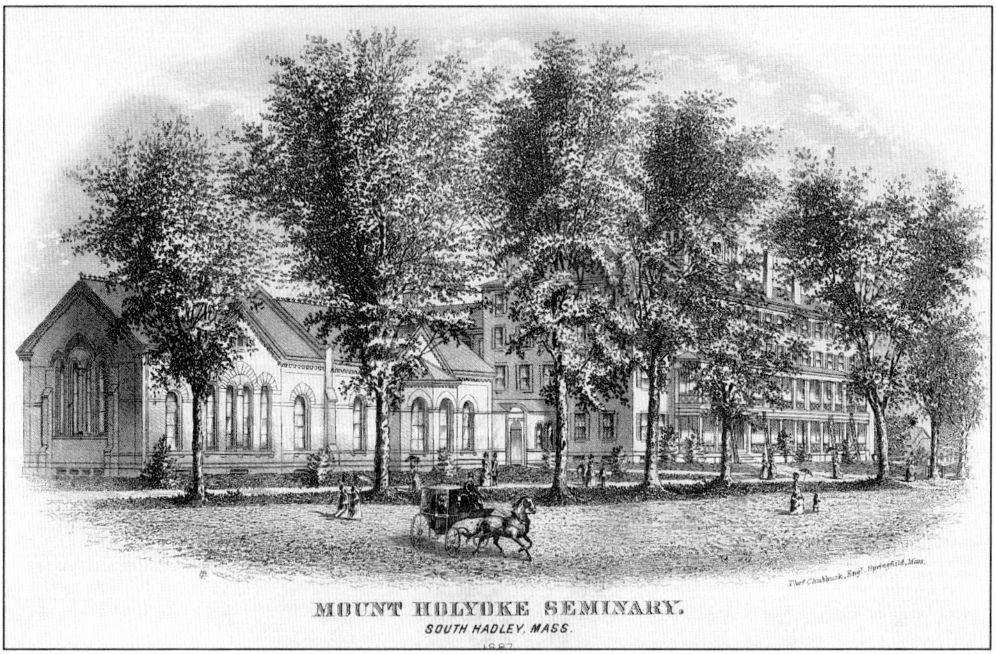

Mount Holyoke Seminary, South Hadley, 1887. Spring in a college town was a time for youth and romance. In May of 1866, the men of Amherst College realized that on just the other side of the Holyoke Range in South Hadley, were the women of Mount Holyoke Seminary. The mountains made courtship a challenge, which the young men met by reaching back to the ancient practice of the serenade.

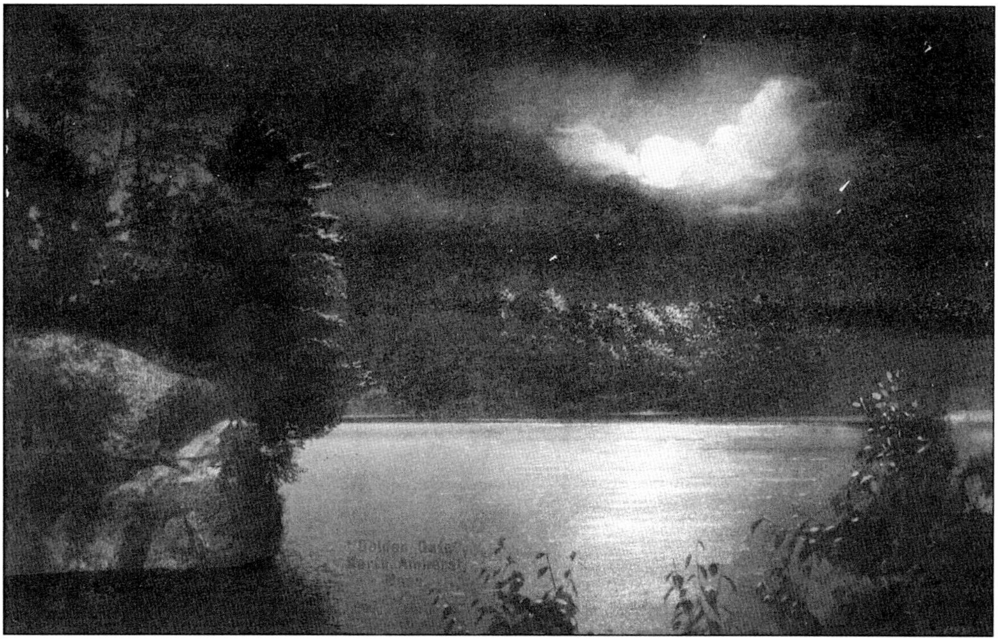

RECOLLECTIONS OF THE SERENADE. At the end of April 1866, a party of Amherst College seniors picked up their instruments and crossed the notch to South Hadley and serenaded the young women of Mount Holyoke Seminary. In response, one wrote:

'Tis the gallant Amherst students,
Amherst students, so they said,
They have come to old South Hadley,
To give us a serenade.
Round the south wing and the north wing,
Passed the serenaders then,
While Mt. Holyoke's daughters listened
Eagerly to catch the strain.

One of the serenading Amherst students penned his own poem about the occasion:

The vision passed. Yet, Hadley!
When again your maidens go to dreaming,
If, fancy free, their brains are teeming,
With visions of Old Amherst, gleaming
In moonlight—perhaps their dreaming
May prove again much more than seeming,
And they again be frightened sadly,
To see Old Amherst come to Hadley.

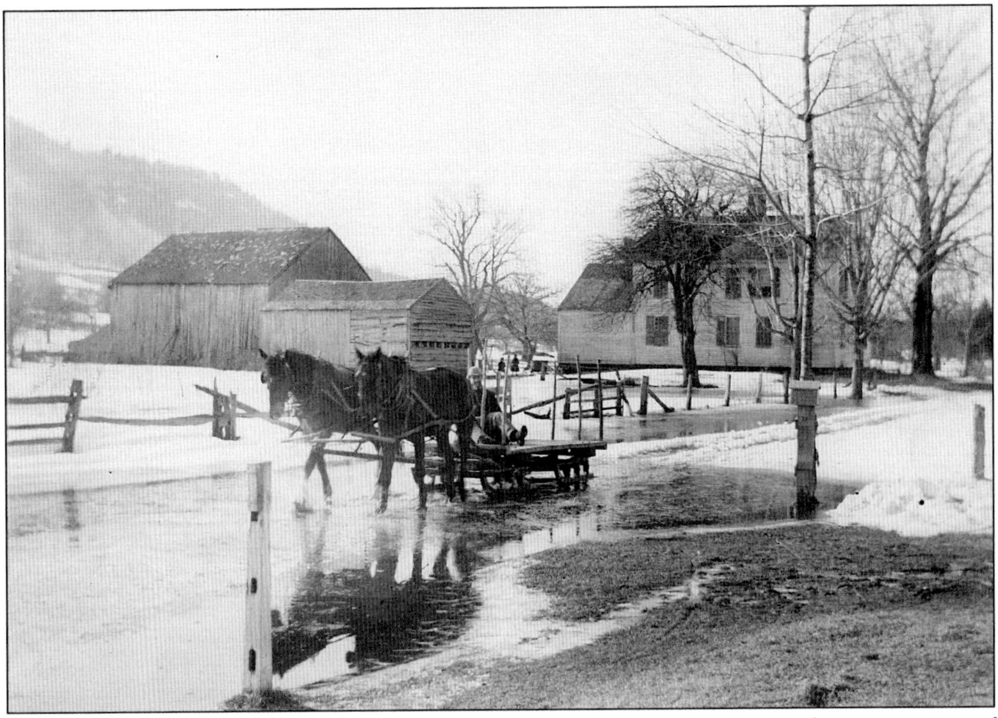

THE SPRING THAW. The road in front of Clifton Johnson's house in the Hockanum section of Hadley flooded every spring.

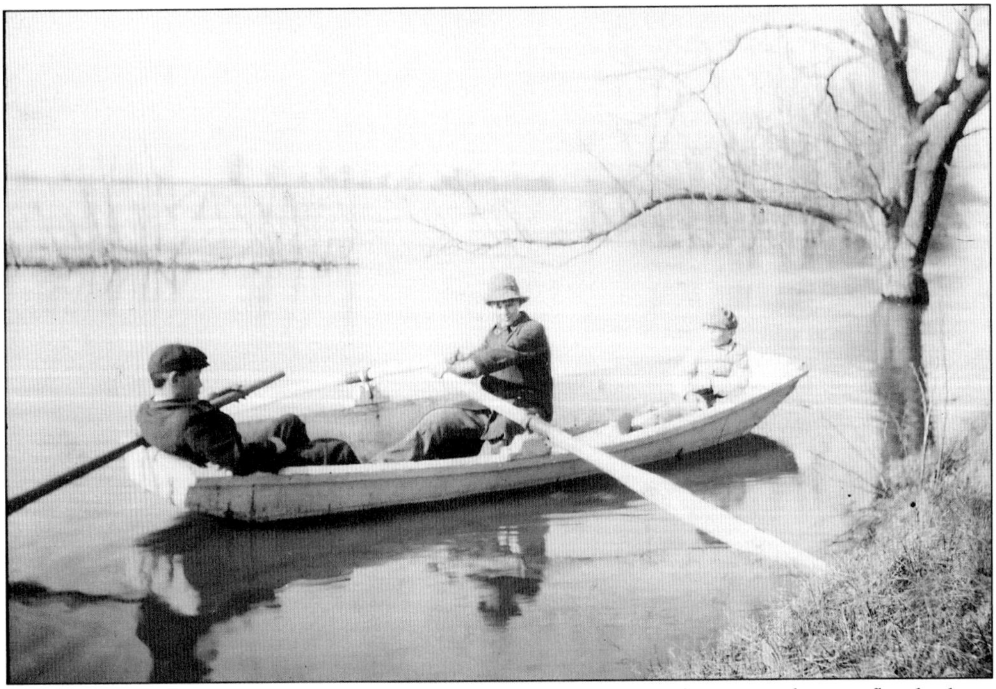

AQUEOUS EXPLORATION. Roger, Arthur, and Irving Johnson took advantage of spring floods along the Connecticut River to explore farm fields by boat in 1906.

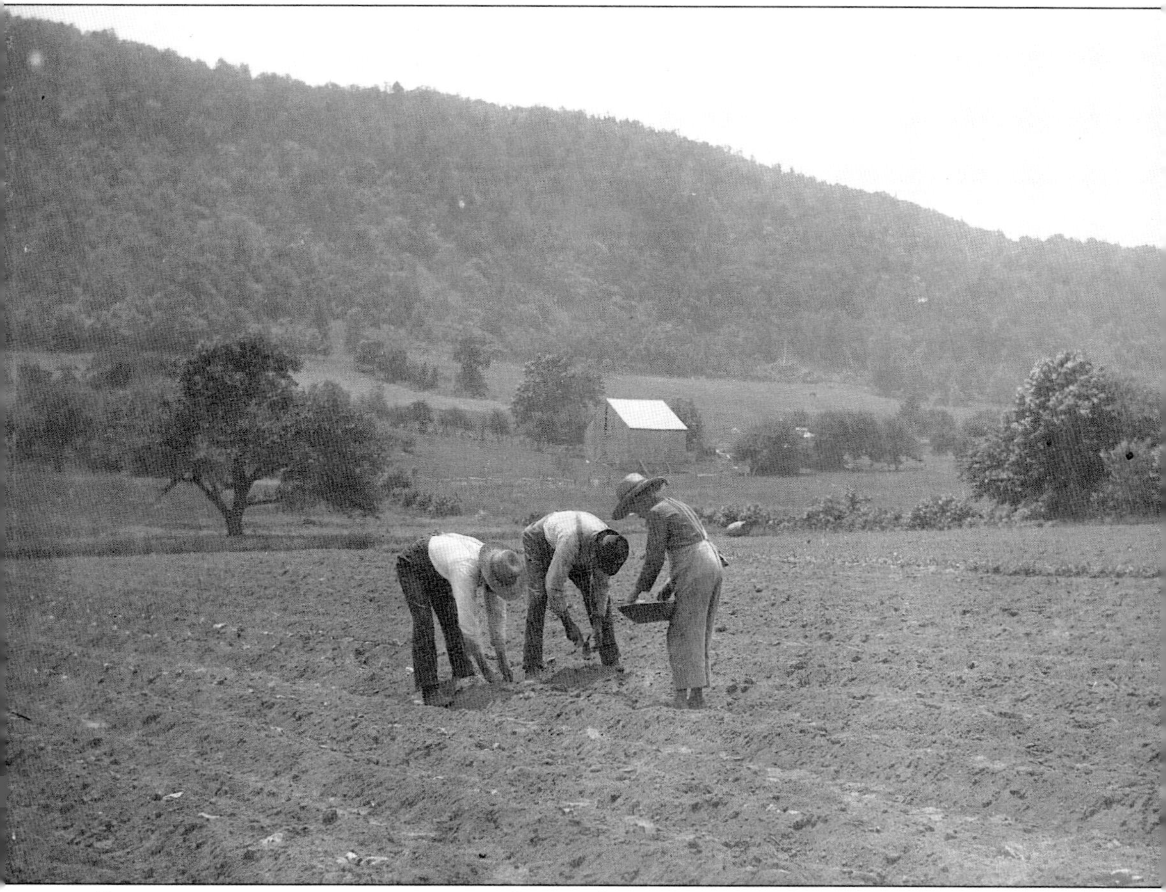

SPRING PLANTING AS PHOTOGRAPHED BY CLIFTON JOHNSON IN THE HADLEY FIELDS. "When I go to Boston or New York I begin to worry about the state of the nation—and civilization generally. So much unrest, such unreason, such violence, such utter folly! But when I come home to my own hills and get down to work among these everyday, normal people, I am reassured. So many millions there are leading their steady quiet lives, absorbed in the common processes of existence: working, eating, sleeping, hoping, struggling, failing, loving. All their thinking seems somehow to have its roots in the soil." (David Grayson, *The Countryman's Year*, April 4.)

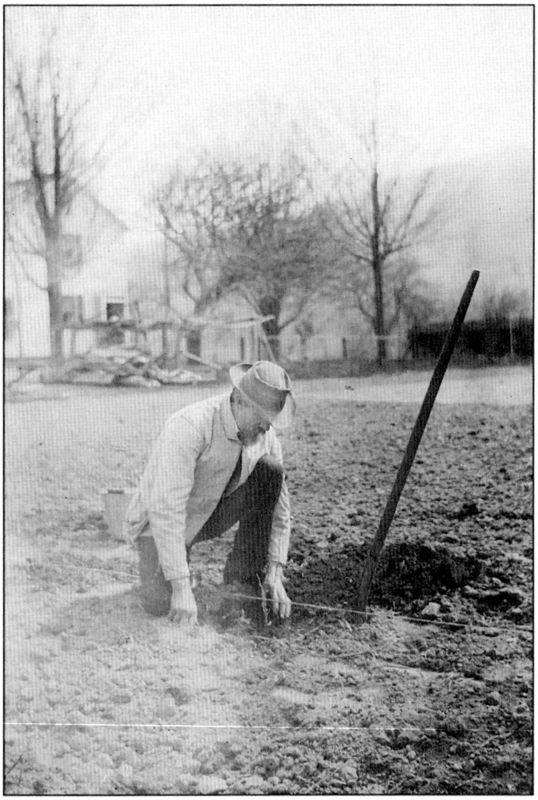

A HADLEY FARMER SETTING OUT CURRANT BUSHES IN THE FARMHOUSE GARDEN AT THE TURN OF THE CENTURY. "I never come home to my hillside without a renewed sense of the assured soundness and continuity of life." (David Grayson, *The Countryman's Year*, April 4.)

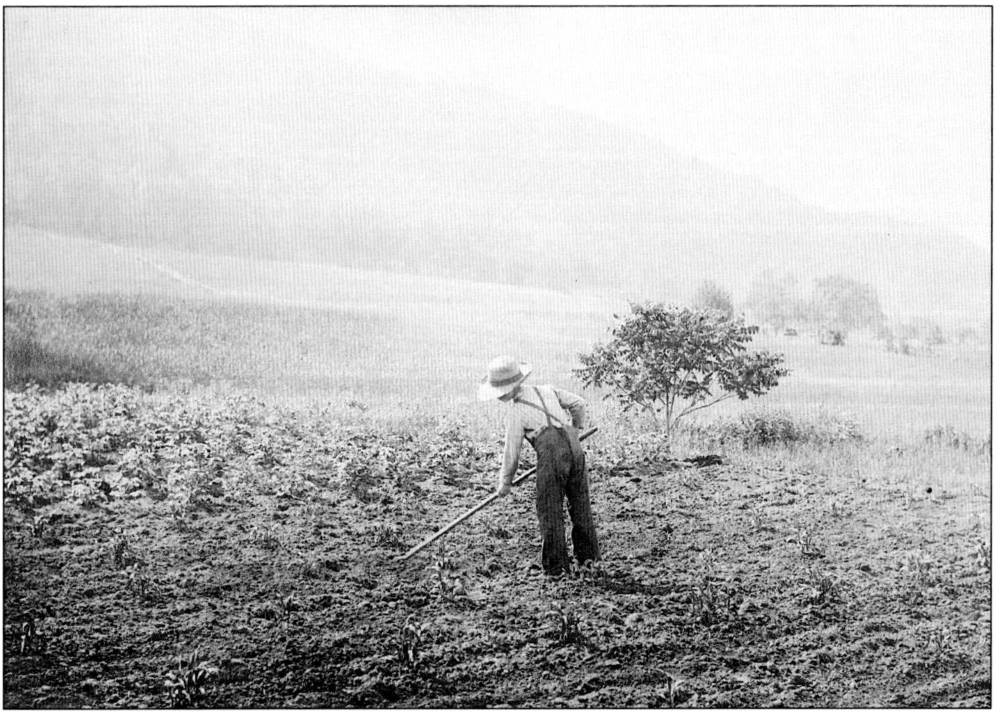

HOEING CORN IN HADLEY.

ED JOHNSON AND A STATE-SUPPORTED BOY HOEING ONIONS IN HADLEY, 1895. "I stopped today to talk with S——, Polish onion grower, at the edge of his field. He is ignorant and wise. Certain subjects one can talk about with people anywhere upon terms of equality—that is, upon death and birth and love and work, which, after all, are the principal subjects of all conversations upon this planet." (David Grayson, *The Countryman's Year*, May 6.)

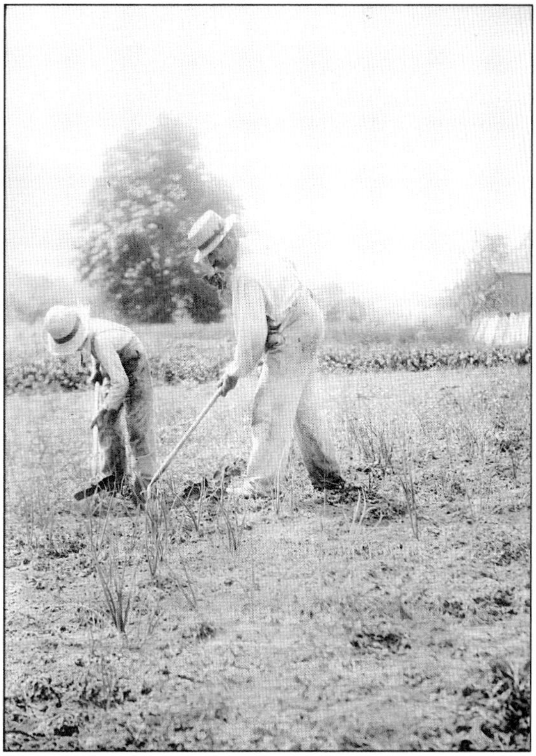

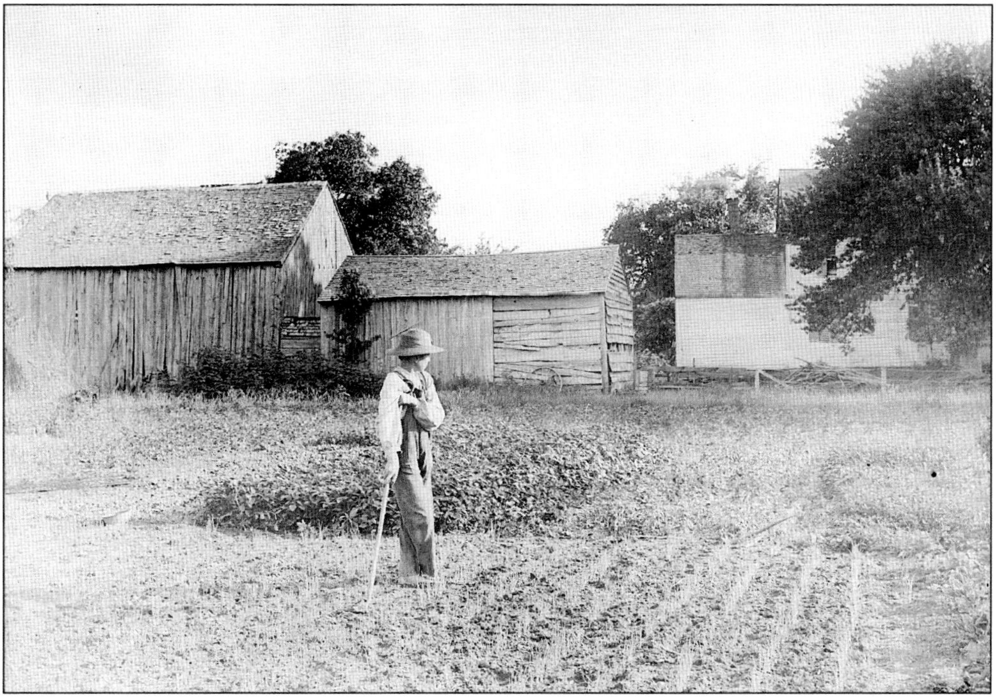

THE ONION PATCH AT ED JOHNSON'S HADLEY FARM, 1895. "S—— said to me that 'a man can pay his way out of almost any trouble but death.' I have had this day a strange sense of unexplained well-being." (David Grayson, *The Countryman's Year*, May 6.)

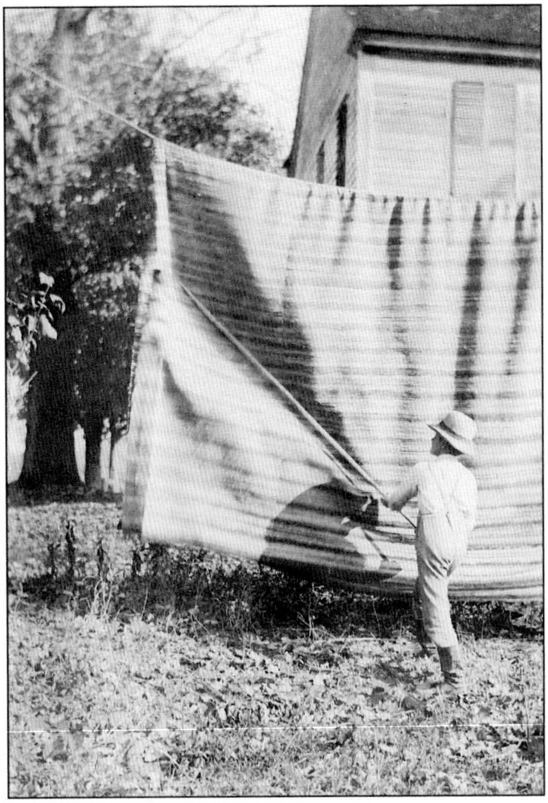

OSCAR JOHNSON BEATING THE DUST OUT OF A RAG CARPET AS PART OF THE ANNUAL SPRINGTIME CHORES ON A HADLEY FARM.

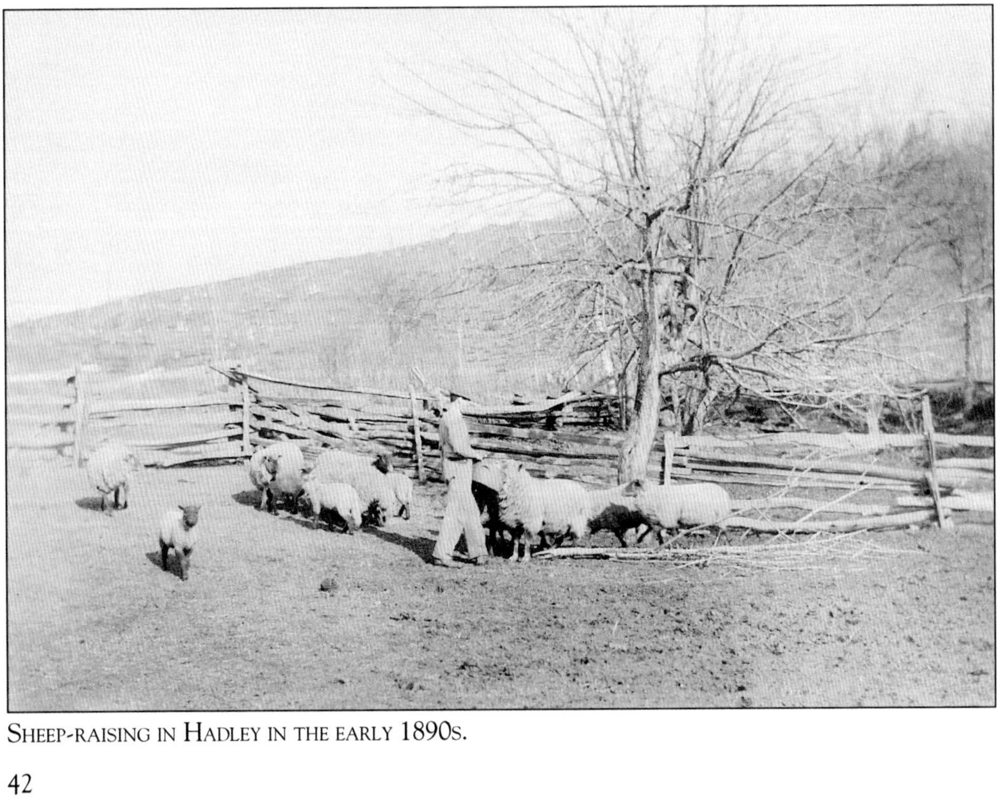

SHEEP-RAISING IN HADLEY IN THE EARLY 1890S.

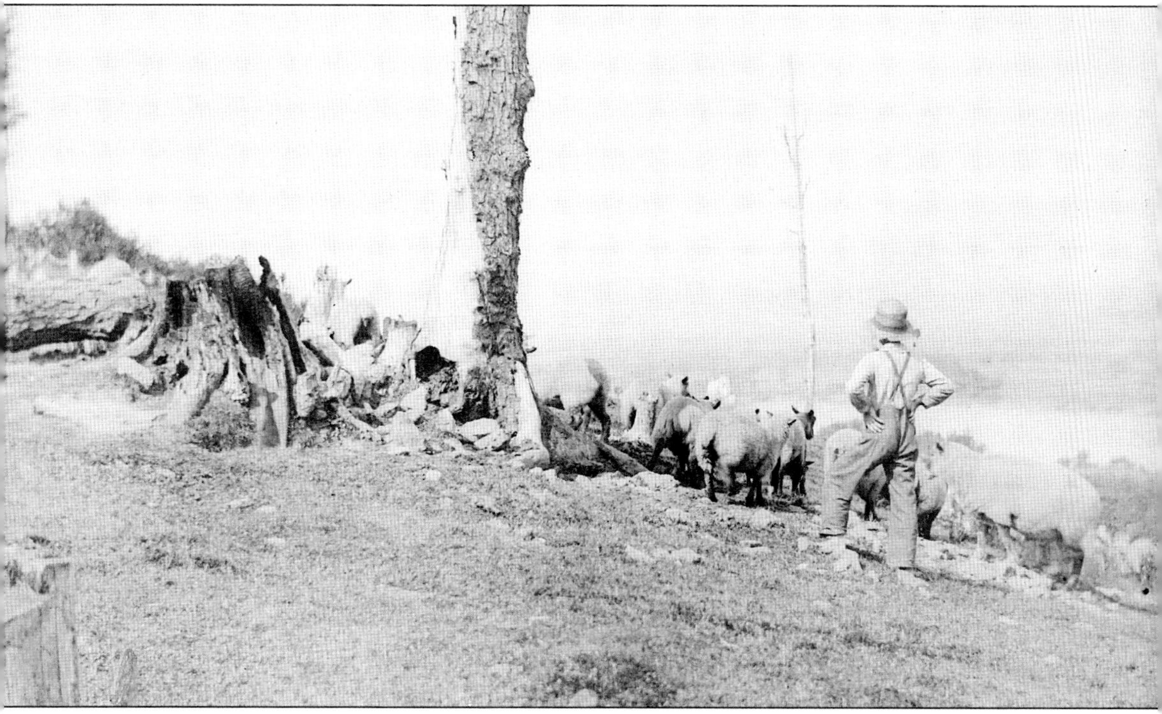

A FARM BOY WATCHING OVER SHEEP IN AN UPLAND PASTURE, OVERLOOKING THE CONNECTICUT RIVER AND THE HAZY MOUNTAINS.

March

Beneath the sheltering walls the thin snow clings,—
Dead winter's skeleton, left bleaching, white,
Disjointed, crumbling, on unfriendly fields.
The inky pools surrender tardily
At noon, to patient herds, a frosty drink
From jagged rims of ice; a subtle red
Of life is kindling every twig and stalk
Of lowly meadow growths; the willows wrap
Their stems in furry white, the pines grow gray
A little in the biting wind; midday
Brings tiny burrowed creatures, peeping out
Alert for sun.
Ah March! we know thou art
Kind-hearted, spite of ugly looks and threats,
And out of sight, art nursing April's violets!

—Amherst poet Helen Hunt Jackson's *Verses by H.H.*, p. 149.
(Boston: Roberts Brothers, 1888.)

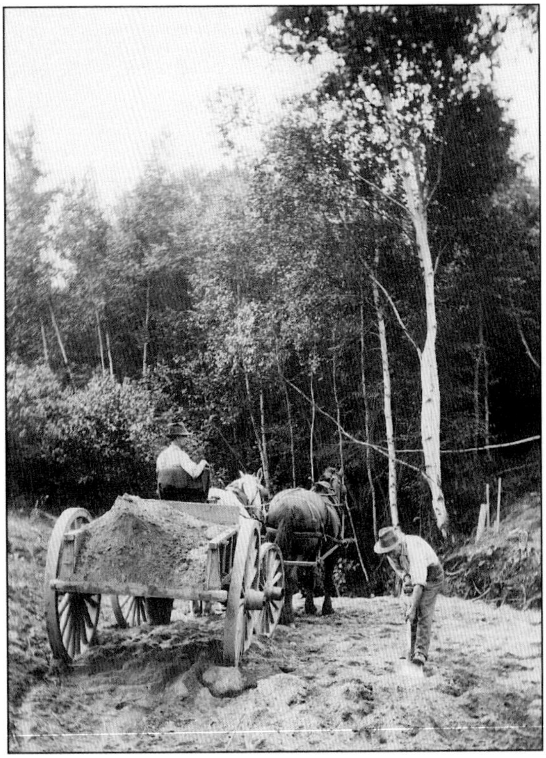

MEN REBUILDING THE COUNTRY ROADS AFTER A TOUGH WINTER.

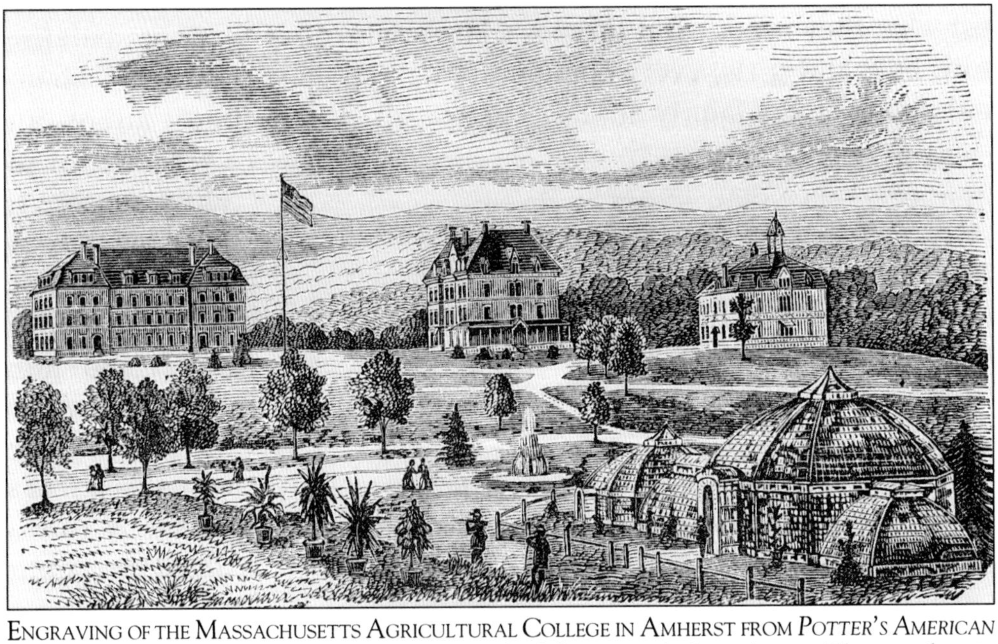

ENGRAVING OF THE MASSACHUSETTS AGRICULTURAL COLLEGE IN AMHERST FROM *POTTER'S AMERICAN MONTHLY*, 1887, P. 415. "Every one in the town had flowers and planted trees. This was due, in part, to the influence of the Agricultural College, from the greenhouses of which many flowers were supplied for the parties, without charge. For the grander and more elegant affairs immense quantities of beautiful flowers could be secured for a trifling sum." (MacGregor Jenkins, *Emily Dickinson, Friend and Neighbor*, p. 9.)

UNCLE WIGGILY. Howard Garis, the creator of Uncle Wiggily, moved to Amherst in 1952. In 1949, he had written a story called "Uncle Wiggily Comes to Amherst." Wiggily set off for Amherst in his "funny auto with bologna sausages for tires," and stayed with his rabbit friend Bill Springer, who lived in a hole under the Lord Jeffery Inn. It was ideal for rabbits interested in leftover carrots, lettuce, and cabbage. The only drawback was a nearby wolf, but Wiggily thought he could outwit him. But his friend told him, "This is an Amherst wolf, Wiggy. He's been to college."

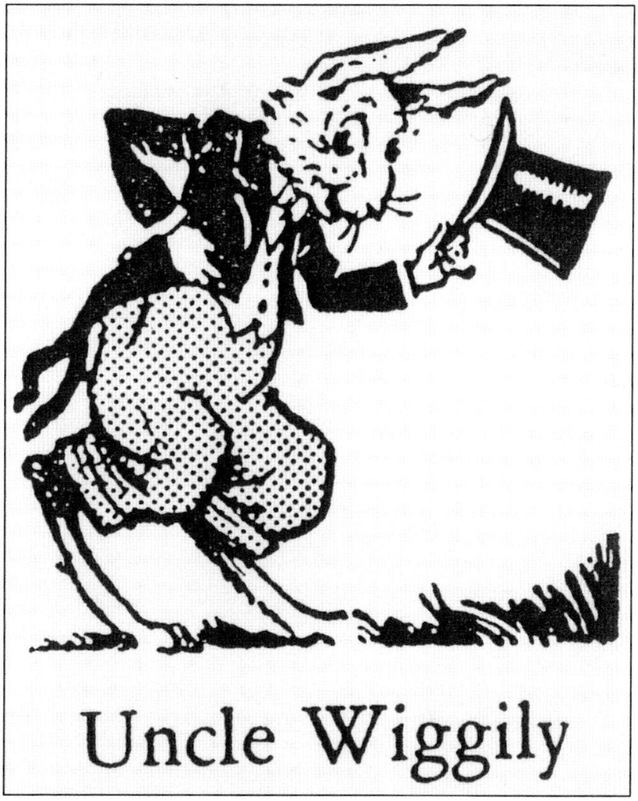

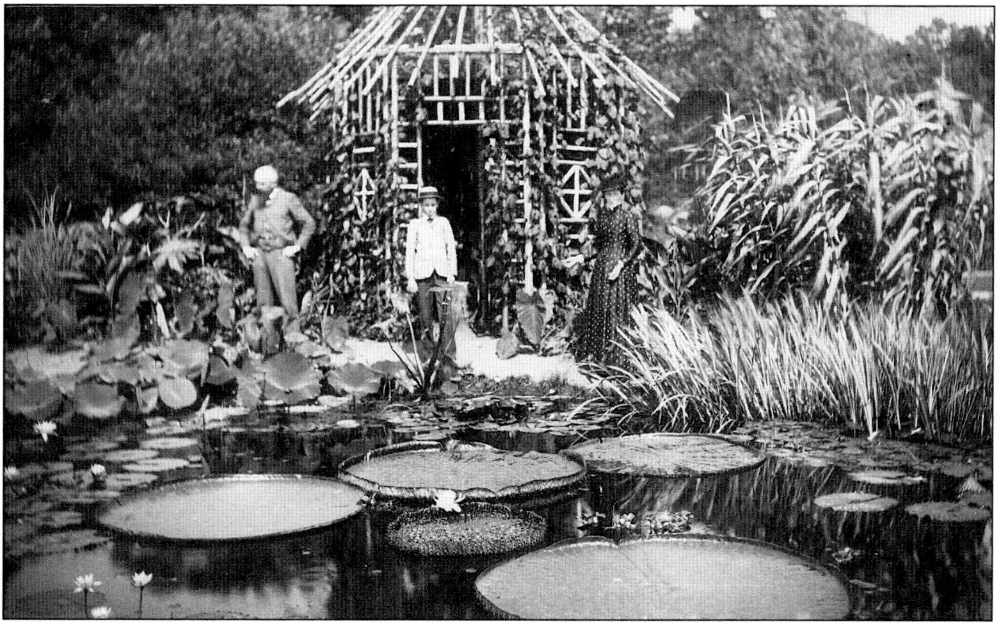

LAFAYETTE W. GOODELL, SEED SUPPLIER. Goodell supplied the valley, the country, and beyond with seeds from Pansy Park in Belchertown. He began with $25 in 1868, and by the 1890s he was sending catalogs to 200,000 customers. In addition to exotic water lilies and lotuses, he grew cherries, quinces, apricots, plums, pears, grapes, peaches, gooseberries, and currants.

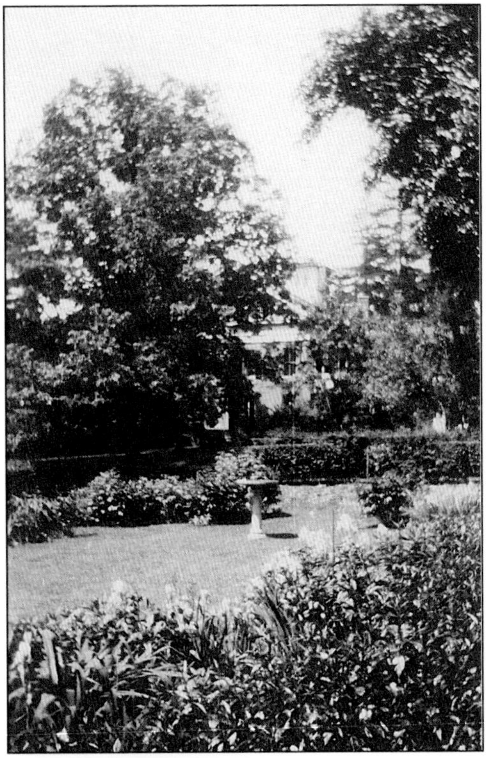

THE GARDEN AT THE EMILY DICKINSON HOMESTEAD. "Spring was to [Emily Dickinson] the summit of the year. There were now near her hand a hundred symbols of it. Her garden and her world behind the hedge was full of them. She gathered them that she might express through them the affection she felt for her friends and her desire to share with them her ecstasy." (MacGregor Jenkins, *Emily Dickinson, Friend and Neighbor*, p. 120.)

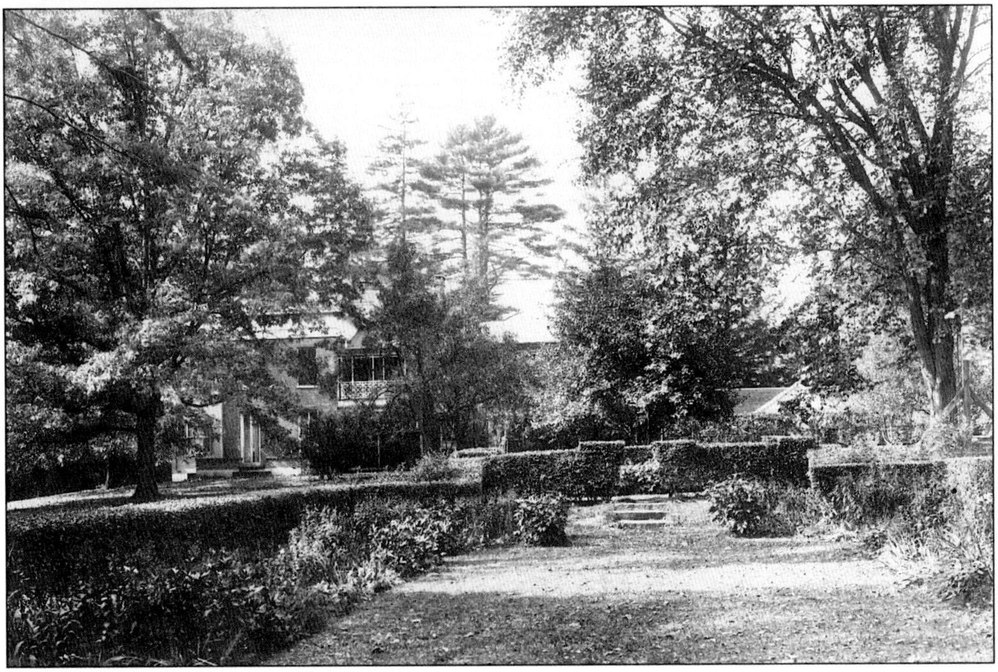

"[Emily Dickinson's] garden was to her the source of constant joy, and on it she lavished the most affectionate care and attention. I have often seen her there. She sometimes stood on an old red army blanket when the ground was damp, and frequently kneeled on it to reach her flowers." (MacGregor Jenkins, *Emily Dickinson, Friend and Neighbor*, p. 89.)

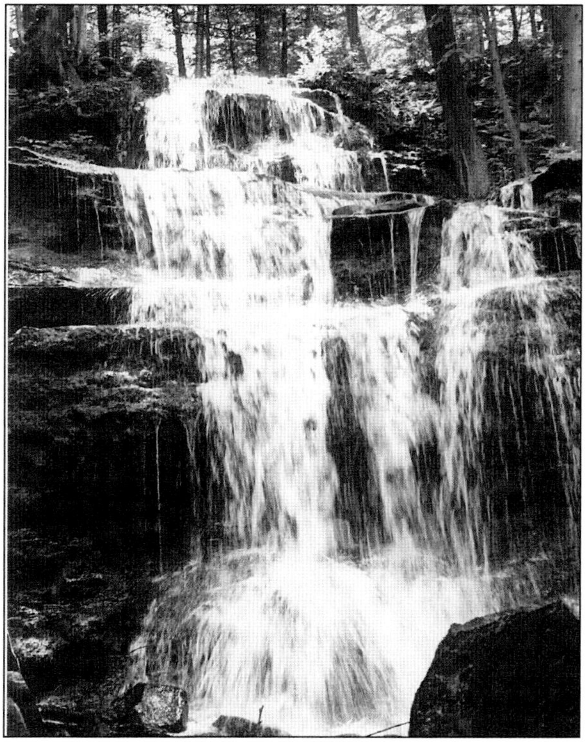

FERNS AND A WATERFALL IN THE HILLS OF HAMPSHIRE COUNTY.

Fern-Beds in Hampshire County

Although from them
Steep stands of beech and sugar-maple stem,
Varied with birch, or ash, or basswood trees
Which spring will throng with bees,
While intervening thickets grow complex
With flower, seed, and variance of sex,
And the whole wood conspires, by change of kind,
To break the purchase of the gathering mind,
The ferns are as they were.
Let but a trifling stir
Of air traverse their pool or touchy beds
And some will dip their heads,
Some switch a moment like a scribbling quill
And then be still,
Sporadic as in guarded bays
The rockweed slaps a bit, or sways.
Then let the wind grow bluff, and though
The sea lies far to eastward, far below,
These fluent spines, with whipped pale underside,
Will climb through timber as a smoking tide
Through pier-stakes, beat their sprays about the base
Of every boulder, scale its creviced face
And, wave on wave, like some green infantry,
Storm all the slope as high as eye can see.
Whatever at the heart
Of creatures makes them branch and burst apart,
Or at the core of star or tree may burn
At last to turn
And make an end of time,
These airy plants, tenacious of their prime,
Dwell in the swept recurrence of
An ancient conquest, shaken by first love
As when they answered to the boomed command
That the sea's green rise up and take the land.

—Richard Wilbur, from *Walking to Sleep: New Poems and Translations*, p. 11.

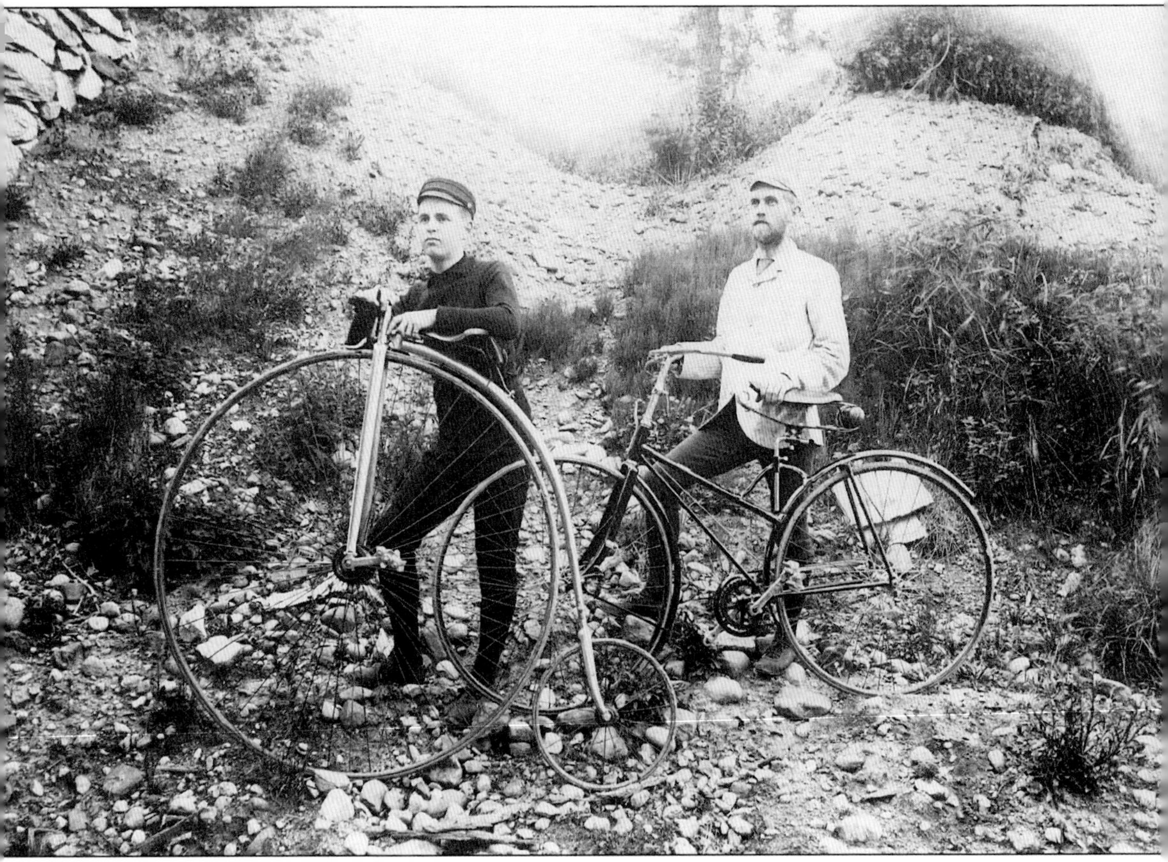

FIRST NATIONAL BANK CLERKS SHERWIN AND LYMAN ESCAPING AMHERST FOR A BIKE RIDE. "Freedom—that was the word. That was what everyone wanted. To a boy freedom was a bicycle; and if he could ride without feet on the pedals or hands on the handlebar, that was so much freedom more. Freedom was going barefoot in green grass in May: freedom from shoes. Freedom was walking out a road into the country, choosing your own direction, your own gait, your own time of going, and not having to think about coming back." (Robert Francis, *We Fly Away*. New York: The Swallow Press and William Morrow & Co., 1948, p. 136.)

ED PRAY AND RICHARD SCHOONMAKER ON BUTTER HILL, IN A PHOTOGRAPH BY ROBERT FRANCIS.

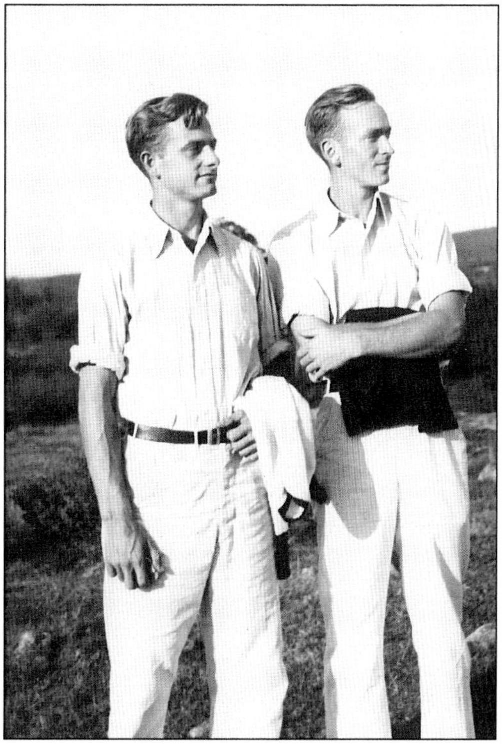

From "Butter Hill"

We didn't say the sky had cleared for us
Although it looked that way that afternoon.
What really happened was we caught the sky
In the act of clearing and went along with it.
We went along with it to Butter Hill.

Three of us . . .
Up through the lower and the upper pasture
We followed less a path than a ritual
Of certain leaves to smell and twigs to taste—
Twigs of spicebush, sassafras, black birch,
Leaves of cedar, juniper, sweet fern,
And the sweet briar equally at home
In English poetry and New England pastures,
And where the slope was steepest pennyroyal
Which stepped on stops one with its pungence.

—Robert Francis, *Butter Hill*, p. 1.
(Springfield, Mass.: Paul W. Carman's Ardsley Press, 1984.)

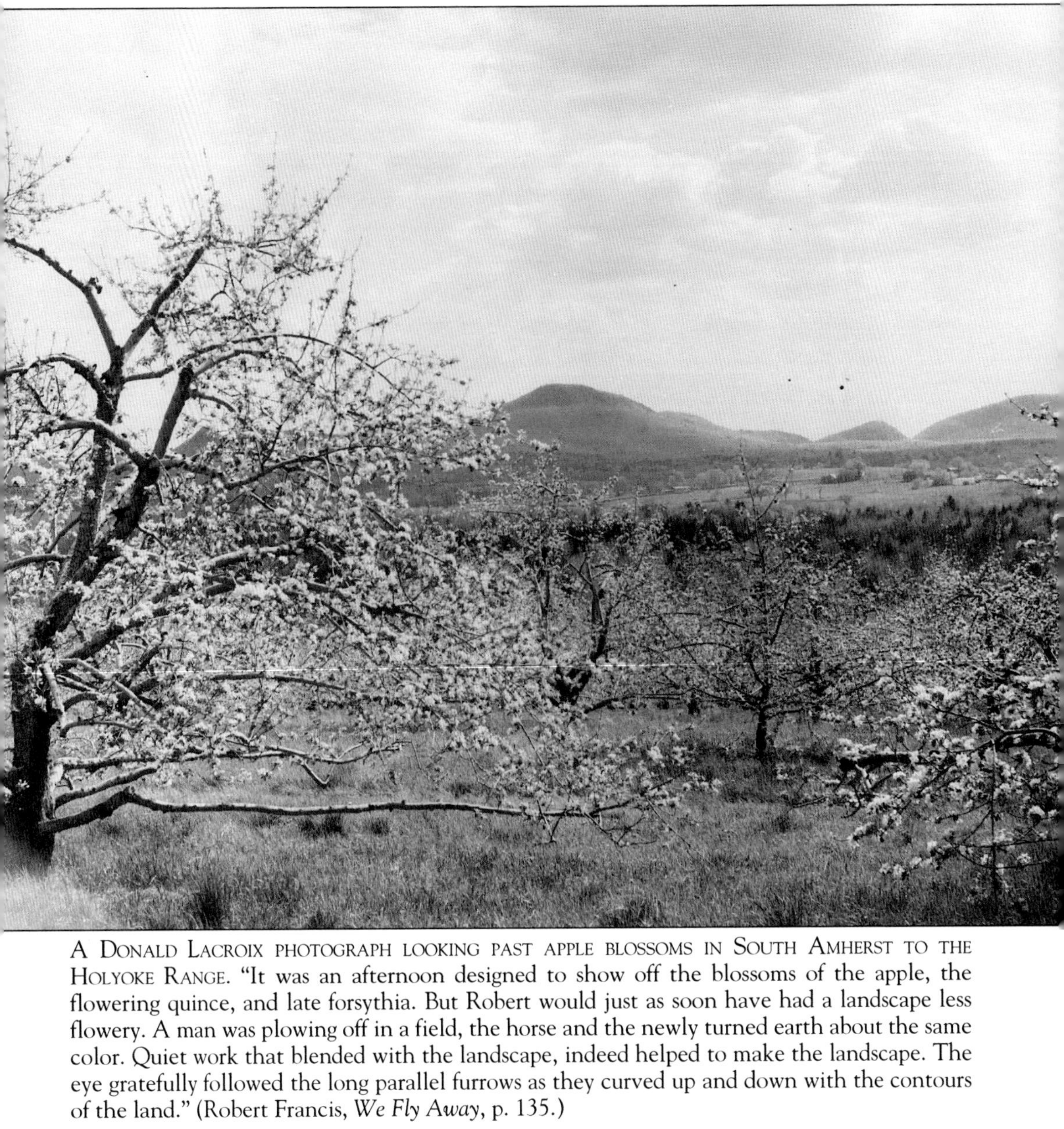

A Donald Lacroix photograph looking past apple blossoms in South Amherst to the Holyoke Range. "It was an afternoon designed to show off the blossoms of the apple, the flowering quince, and late forsythia. But Robert would just as soon have had a landscape less flowery. A man was plowing off in a field, the horse and the newly turned earth about the same color. Quiet work that blended with the landscape, indeed helped to make the landscape. The eye gratefully followed the long parallel furrows as they curved up and down with the contours of the land." (Robert Francis, *We Fly Away*, p. 135.)

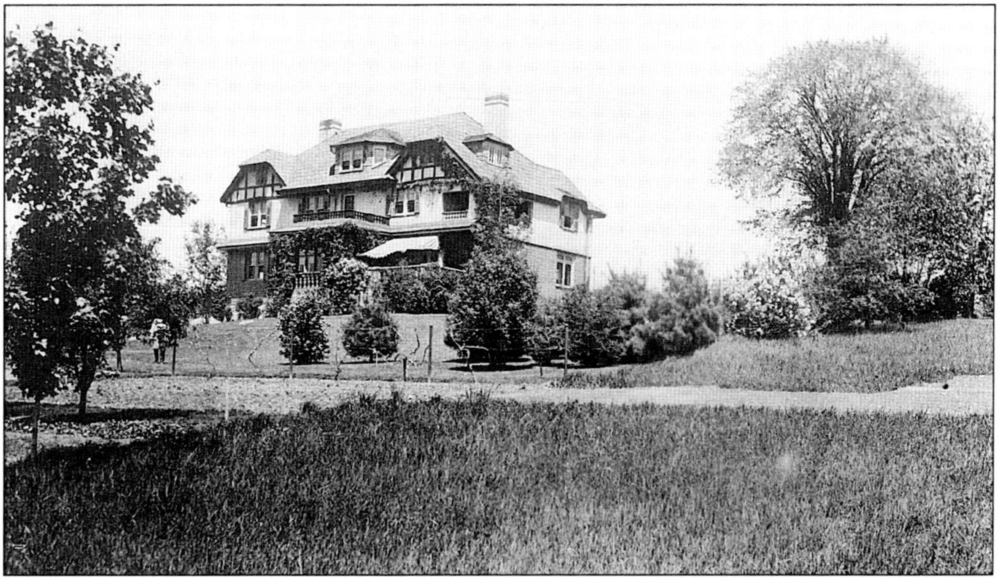

Ray Stannard Baker's house and the elm tree he wrote about under his pseudonym, David Grayson. "I fell hopelessly in love with [Amherst] and everything in it: and the next spring [1910] we moved there . . . We bought the back end of the Old Smith farm, a field of about ten acres . . . At that time no road led into it or past it. Save for one magnificent elm near the top of the hill and a fine maple in the lower pasture, it was bare of any planting." (Ray Stannard Baker, *American Chronicle*. New York: Charles Scribner's Sons, 1945, p. 289.)

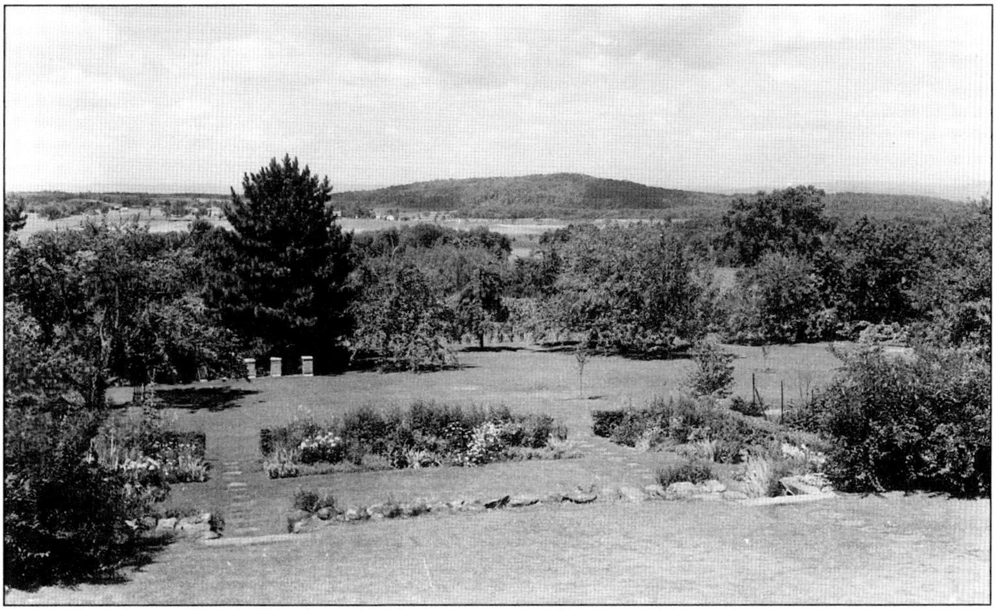

The view from the back of the Ray Stannard Baker house on Sunset Avenue. "We have lived in this home ever since. Every tree, every shrub, every berry bush around the house and in the garden we planted with our own hands. We have lived with them through many summers and winters; we have cared for them; pruned and cultivated and fed them. We know them personally and intimately: all their little individual excellencies and beauties; all their waywardnesses—and we love them." (Ray Stannard Baker, *American Chronicle*, p. 290.)

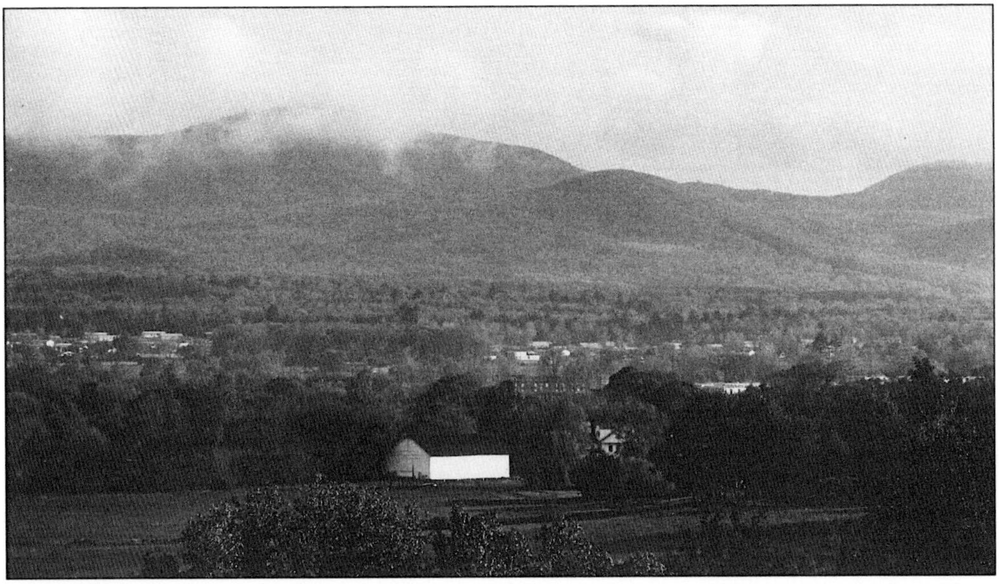

SPRINGTIME MIST OVER THE HOLYOKE RANGE. "This contrary New England spring! Hard frost last night: glorious clear summer sunshine this morning. . . . Setting out a number of new peach trees to replace weakened old ones. Trying to raise peaches in this northern climate is a perfect example of the way in which hope springs eternal in the human breast: or else it is the kind of sanguine madness that attacks the countryman in spring." (David Grayson, *The Countryman's Year*, April 26.)

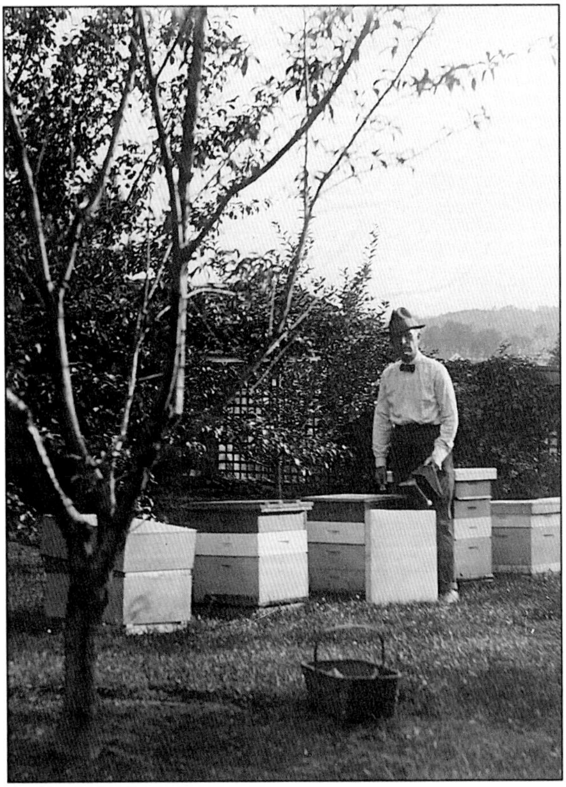

DAVID GRAYSON (RAY STANNARD BAKER) WITH HIS BEEHIVES. "This morning I had the most delightful of interruptions. Steve came to the door to tell me that the bees were swarming. I rushed to the doorway, and there, in the sunny air above the hives, I saw a great cloud of bees filling all the garden with the music of their basso. The first of the year! Already they were gathering above one of the Baldwin apple trees, and there I knew they were preparing to light." (David Grayson, *The Countryman's Year*, May 12.)

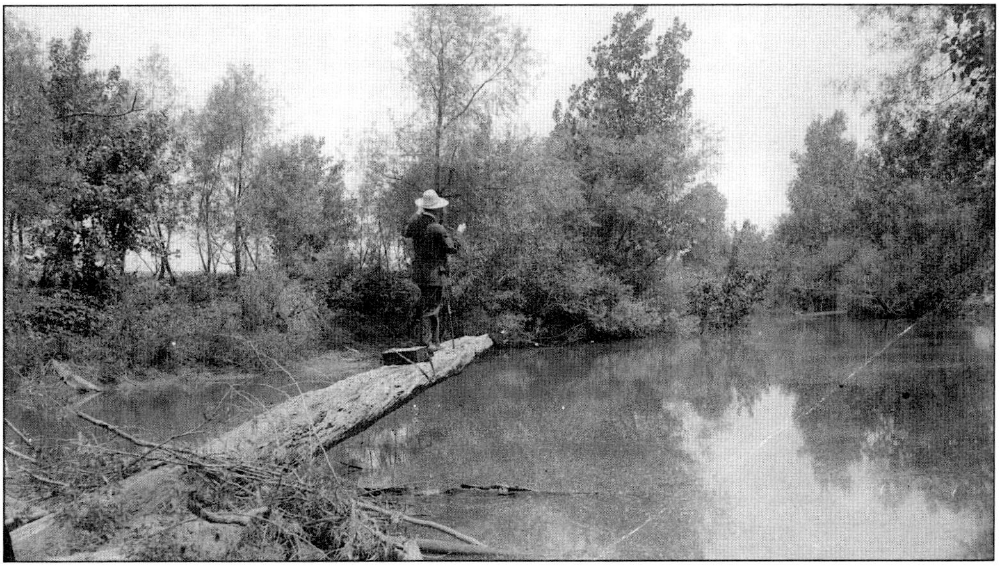

FORT RIVER. Photographer Edgar Scott perched on a log to get a photograph. It was here in May 1895 that Albert Wales and T.W. Kelley caught a 36-pound snapping turtle. They had to wrestle the monster into the boat by its tail. The turtle "showed a very pugnacious disposition and it was necessary to cut his tail off close behind his ears in order to quiet him down." It was dressed and cooked into steaks, fricassee, and turtle salad by Amos Ward, a worker at the Hills Hat Factory.

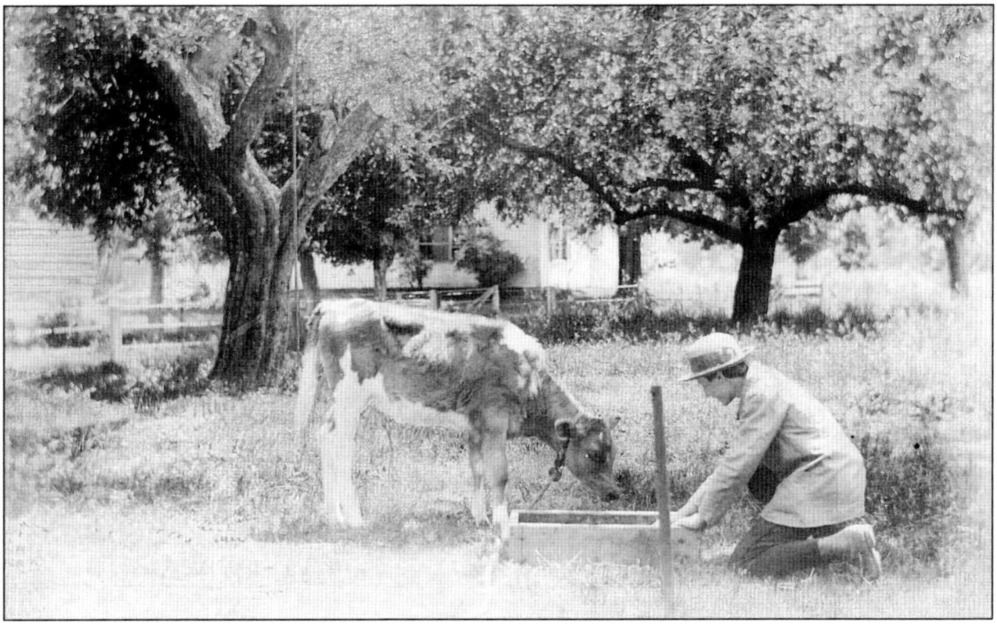

A ONE-HEADED COW IN EDWARD JOHNSON'S HADLEY ORCHARD. In 1895, blacksmith Charlie Holcomb traveled across town to see a "two-headed cow" before realizing the date was the first of April. From this, *The Amherst Record* concluded, "There are thousands of April fools in the world and hundreds of thousands of others whose folly remains with them the year round. There is the man who takes off his winter flannels as soon as he hears the first bluebird sing, and then demands successively the services of the doctor, the clergyman and the undertaker."

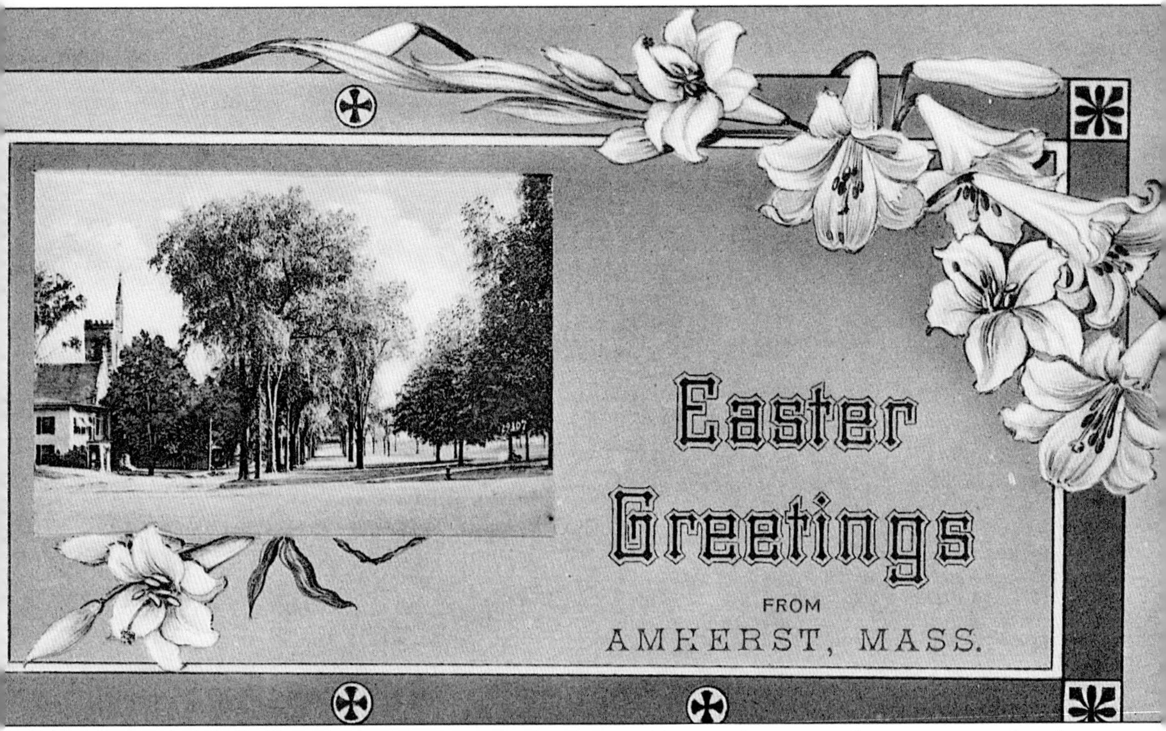

"EASTER, TO MISS EMILY, WAS A DAY FULL OF MEANING. Despite her somewhat unconventional theology, its spiritual quality touched her deeply, and it was a festival of the season of the year that stirred her to the very core of her being. It meant the miracle of spring, promise of new life, the reawakening of the world to beauty and fruitfulness. She thrilled and responded to it as she did to no other aspect of nature." (MacGregor Jenkins, *Emily Dickinson, Friend and Neighbor*, p. 118.)

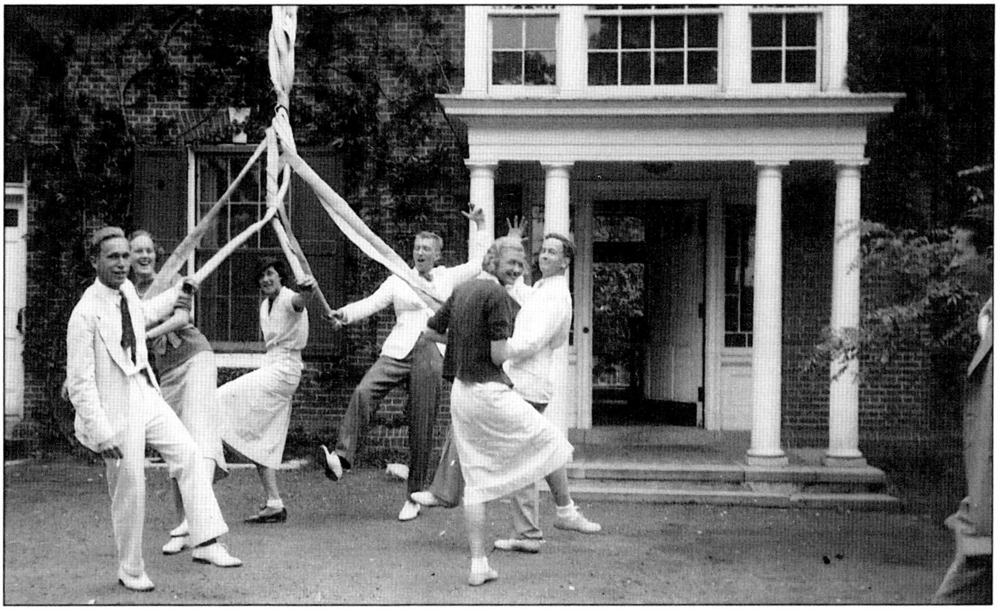

DANCING AROUND THE MAYPOLE, AMHERST COLLEGE. In the early part of the 20th century, May Festivals were still common in the valley. In 1906, Katherine Morse was crowned May Queen at Amherst Town Hall. Sixteen girls danced around the Maypole on the Common, and their performance was followed by ice cream and lemonade, a comedy, and dancing into the night. Today, Morris dancers have revived May Festivals on local town commons.

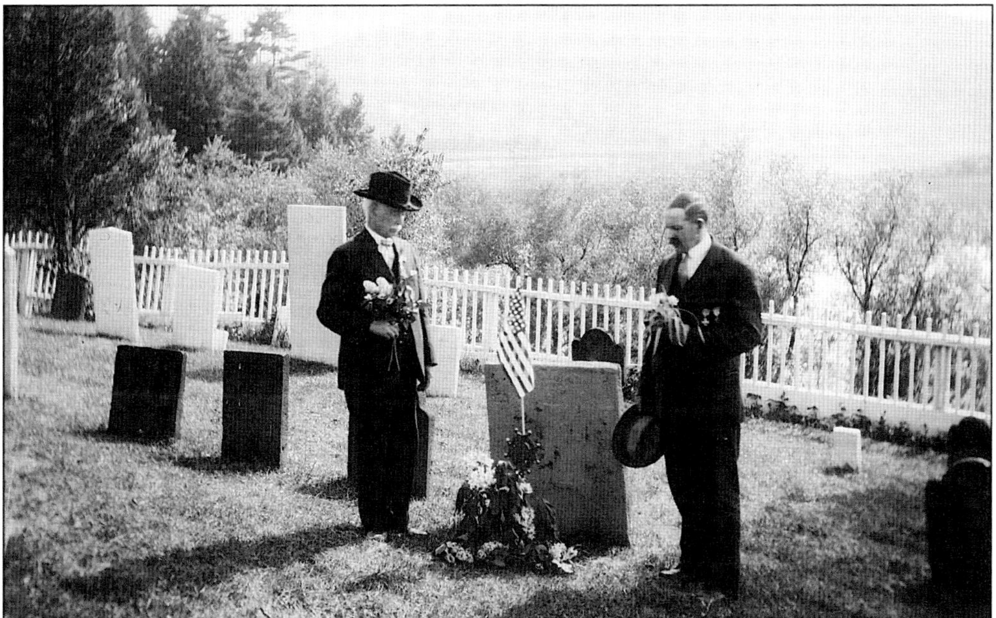

CIVIL WAR VETERANS PHOTOGRAPHED BY CLIFTON JOHNSON ON MEMORIAL DAY AT THE HOCKANUM CEMETERY IN HADLEY. A typical Memorial Day (then called Decoration Day) in 1877 Amherst included a procession to West Cemetery led by the Amherst Brass Band. It was said that the graves of those who died "at the bidding of the death angel" and joined "the grand army of the dead" were decorated on that day

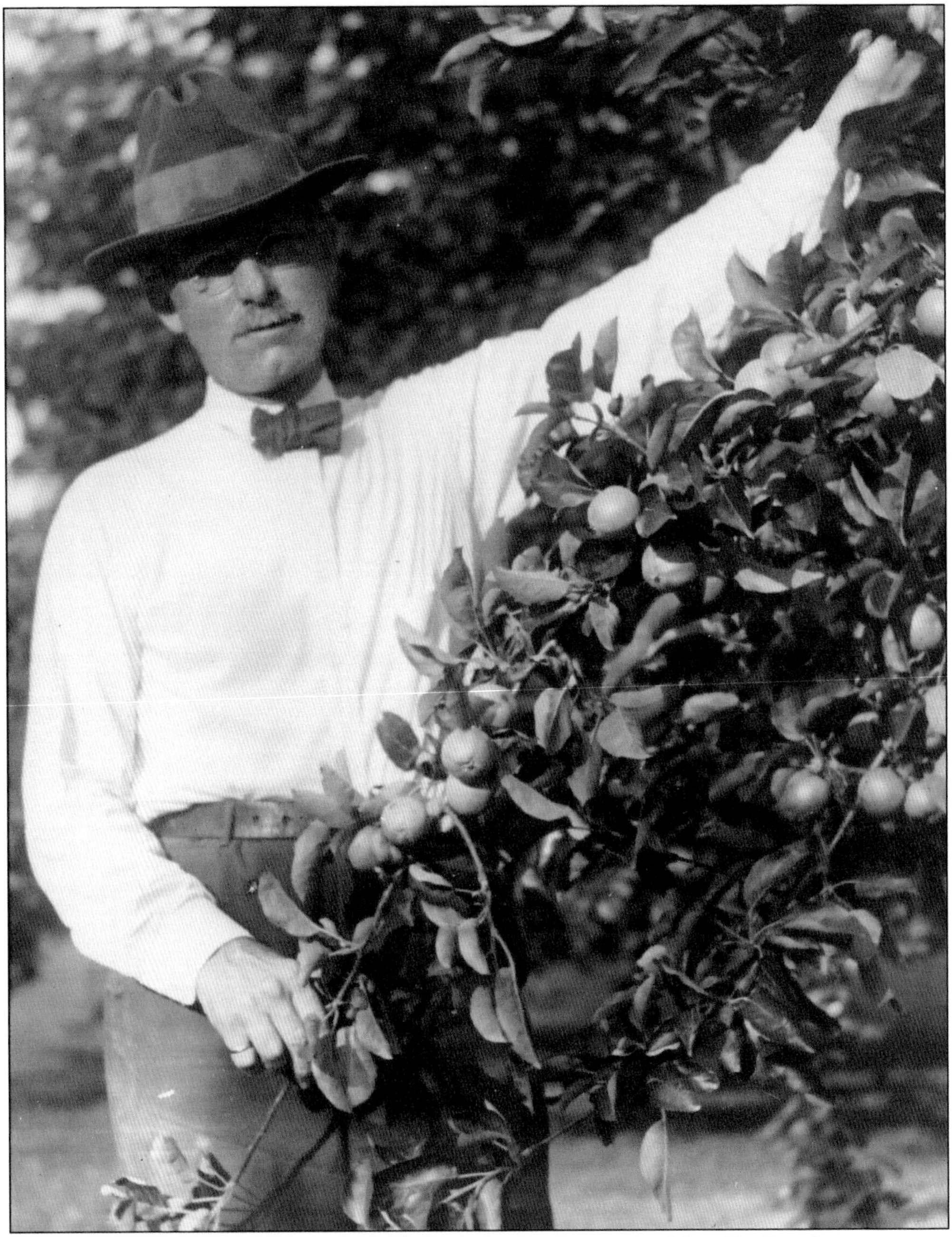

RAY STANNARD BAKER (DAVID GRAYSON) WITH HIS QUINCE BUSHES. "A still, close, hazy intimate day—one I love. Never have I known the fruit trees so heavily set, not only apples but peaches, pears, plums and quinces . . . There are also good crops of strawberries, raspberries and blackberries in sight, not yet ripe, of course. A promise of a good year." (David Grayson, *The Countryman's Year*, June 5.)

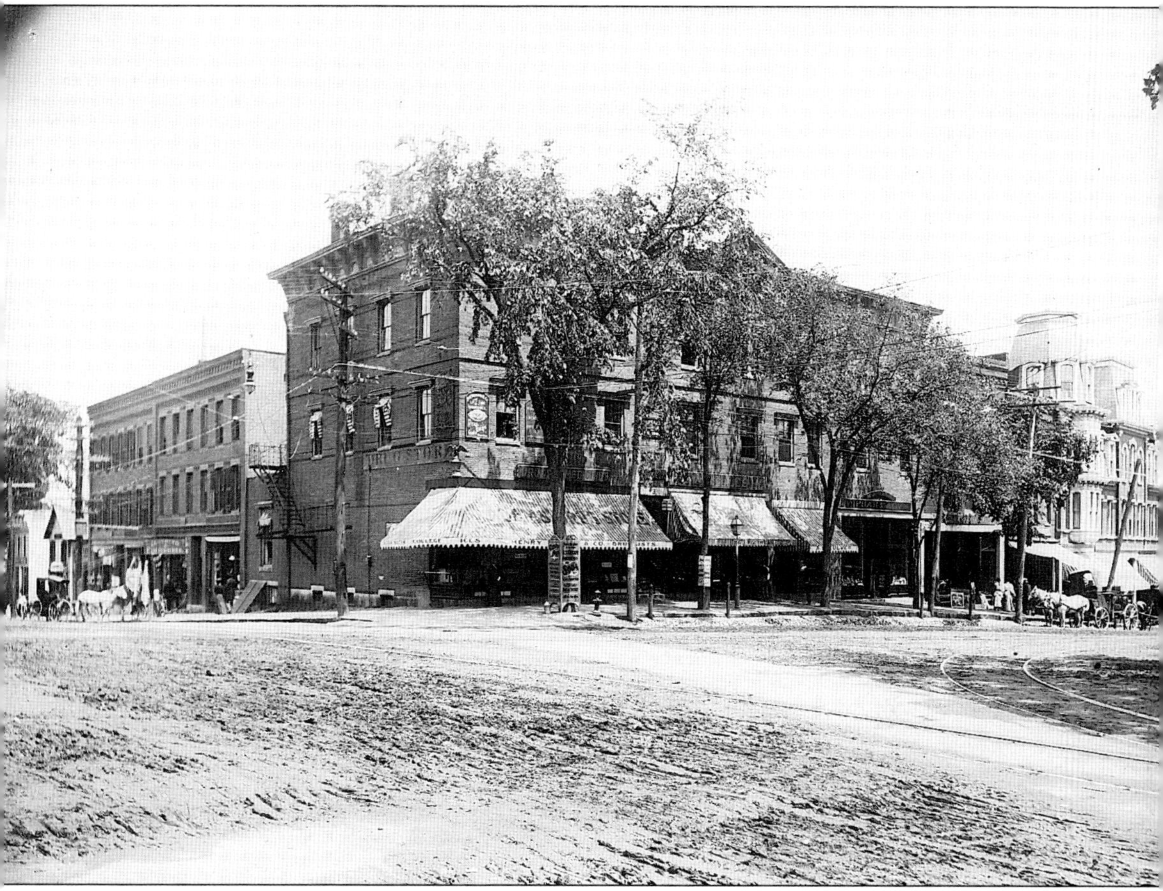

MAIN AND NORTH PLEASANT STREETS IN AMHERST. As commencement approached, Amherst students sometimes went wild and painted the town red. In June of 1884, after a classic Amherst vs. Williams College baseball game, the editors of *The Amherst Record* reported, "We have carefully scanned the annual catalogues issued by Amherst and the Agricultural colleges, but have as yet failed to discover the slightest allusion to the department of red paint. There are pages devoted to departments that teach most of the isms and ologies that go to make up a modern collegiate education, but never a word about red paint."

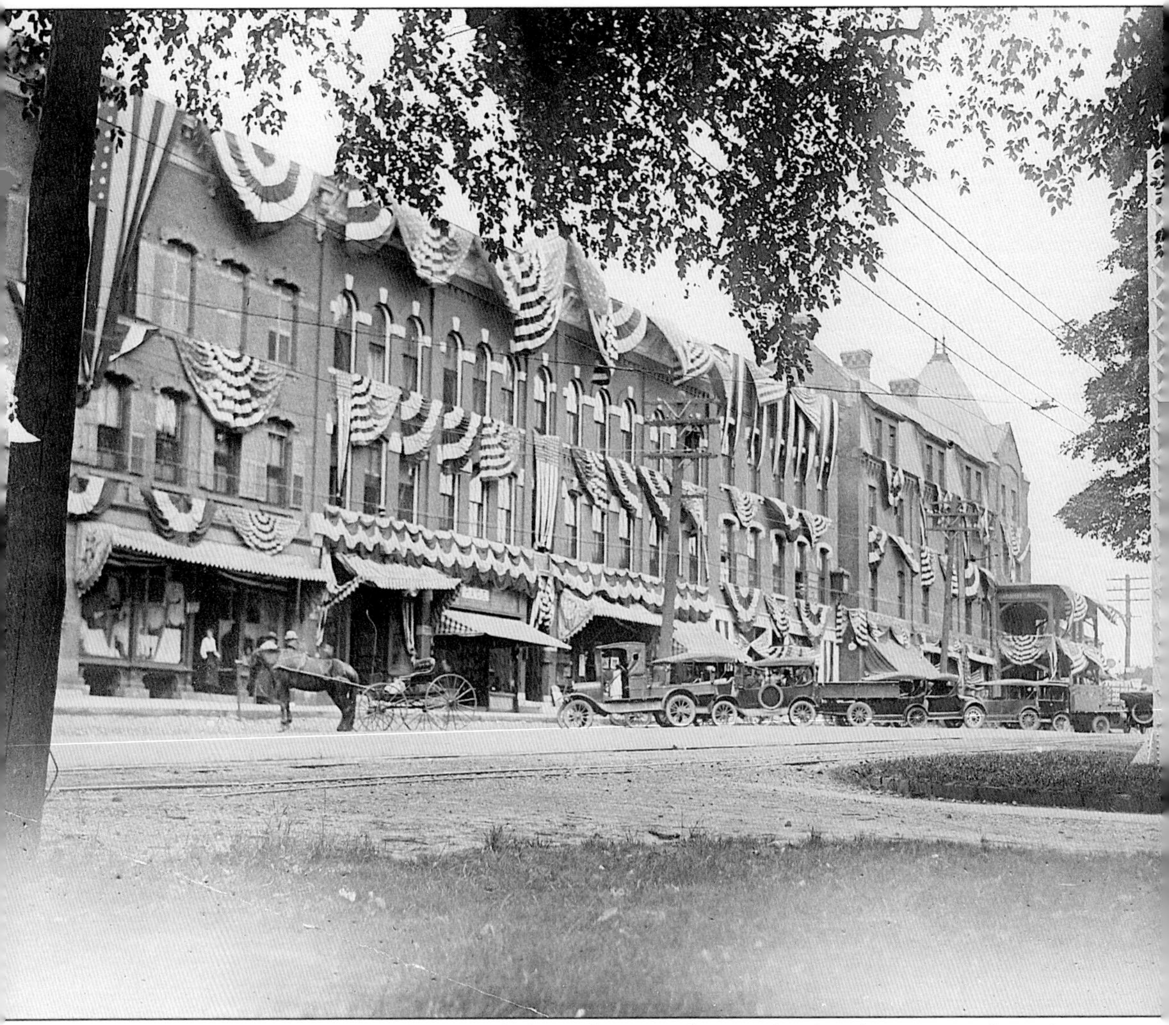

ANNIVERSARY CELEBRATION. Amherst and the colleges within its borders have gone through times of mutual aggravation and celebration. In this photograph from June 1921, all of the shops and the Amherst House hotel on South Pleasant Street are decked out to mark the 100th anniversary of the founding of Amherst College.

An Amherst High School graduation program, June 25, 1869.

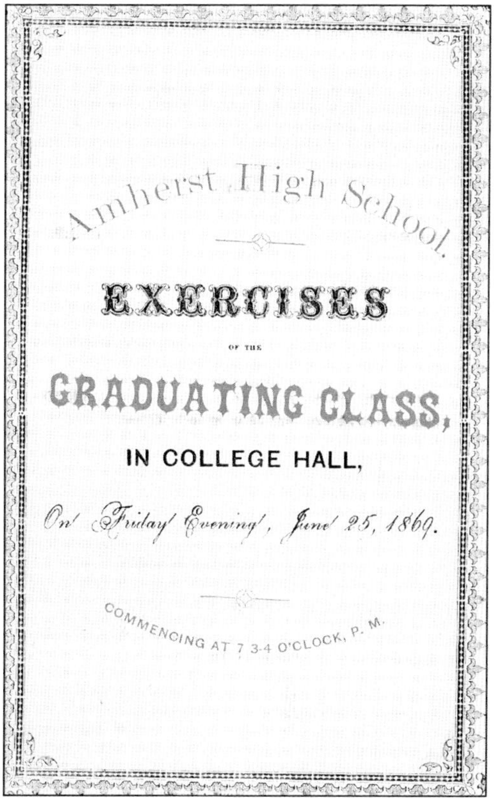
Amherst High School.

EXERCISES

OF THE

GRADUATING CLASS,

IN COLLEGE HALL,

On Friday Evening, June 25, 1869.

COMMENCING AT 7 3-4 O'CLOCK, P. M.

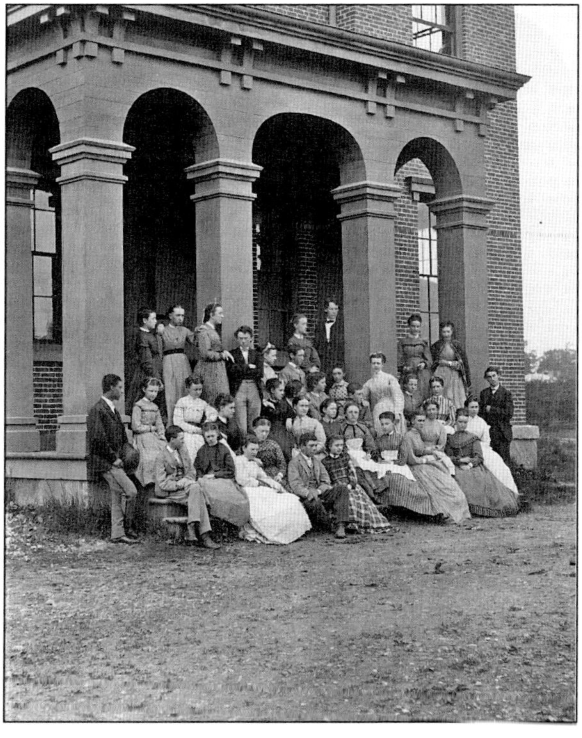

A graduating class of Amherst High School, photographed at the school on Spring Street in about 1868.

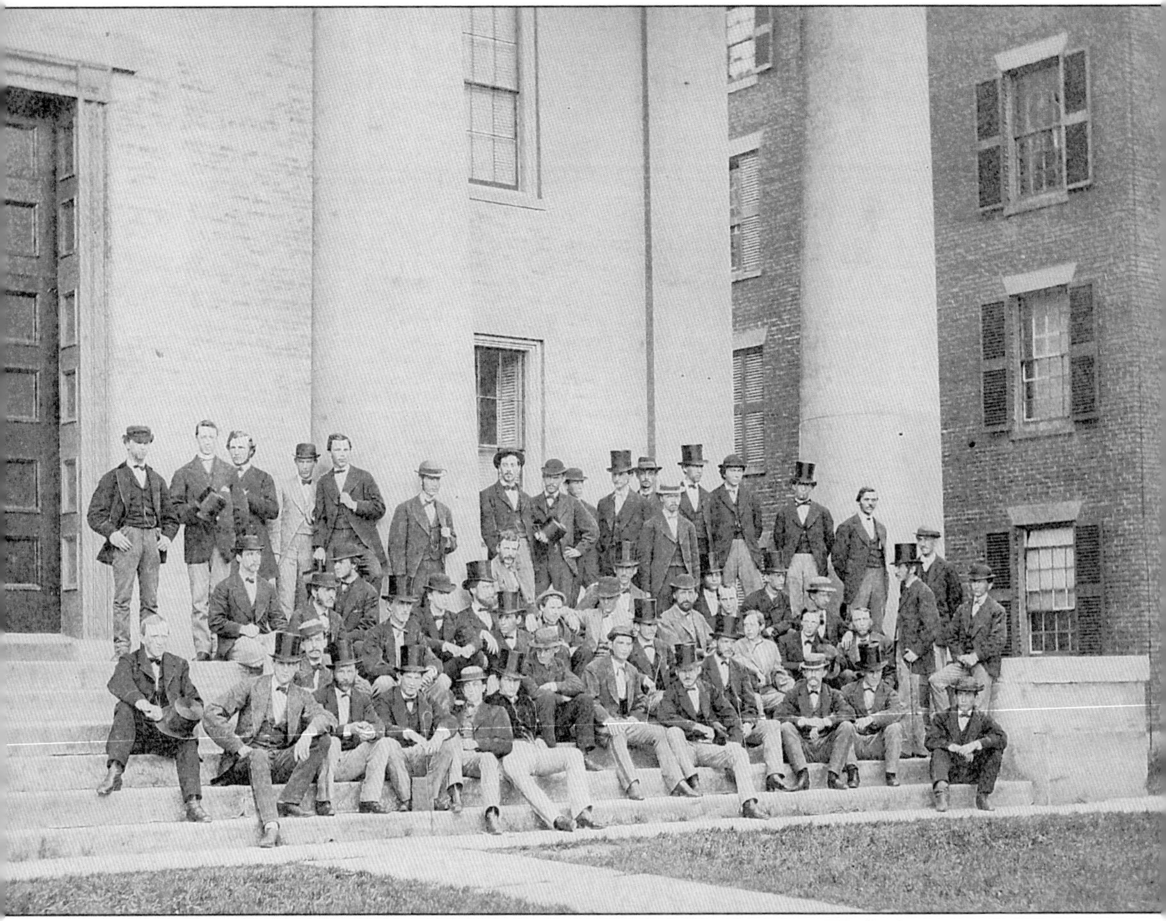

AMHERST COLLEGE CLASS OF 1869. "With June came Commencement. With Commencement came high hats and cockades, blaring bands, and 'epaulets and swords.' In those days the ritual of graduation was more splendid than it is to-day. Feats, reunions and callow boys declaiming the obvious in terms of the infinite. . . . Then the summer with its hush, its wistful lethargy that those of us who know and love New England always feel. This, then, was Amherst." (MacGregor Jenkins, *Emily Dickinson, Friend and Neighbor*, p. 16.)

Three

Summertime

"We lived drunk with the romance of childhood."

—MacGregor Jenkins

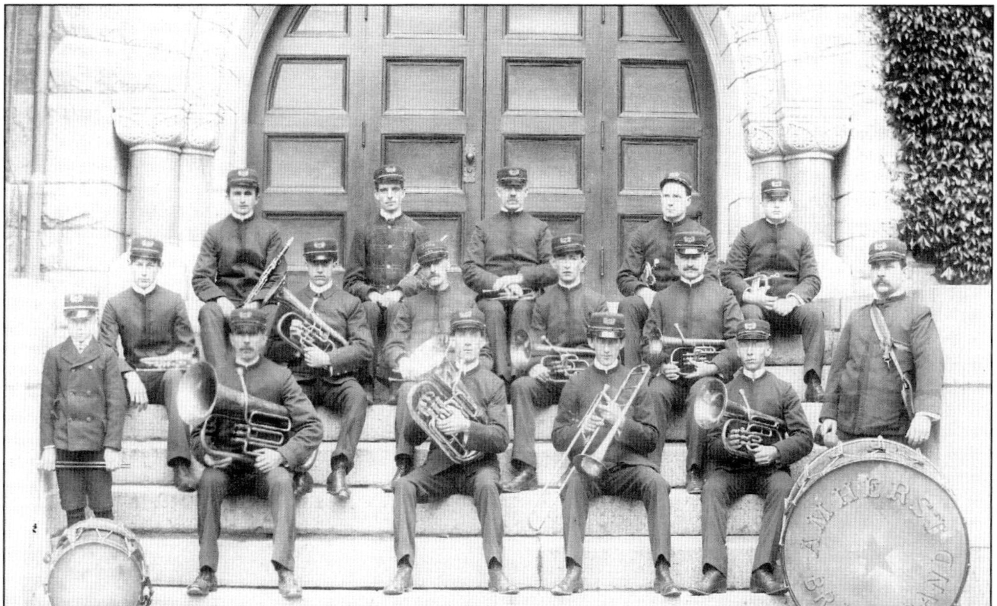

THE AMHERST BRASS BAND AT TOWN HALL IN THE SUMMER OF 1901. The first official town band performed on Fast Day, April 8, 1875, to terrible reviews. Amherst College students hooted and blew fish horns. Undaunted, the band sponsored a Strawberry and Cream Festival the following June and raised money for a bandstand on the common. That August they played to a large audience of mediums and spiritualists at the Lake Pleasant Band Festival in Montague.

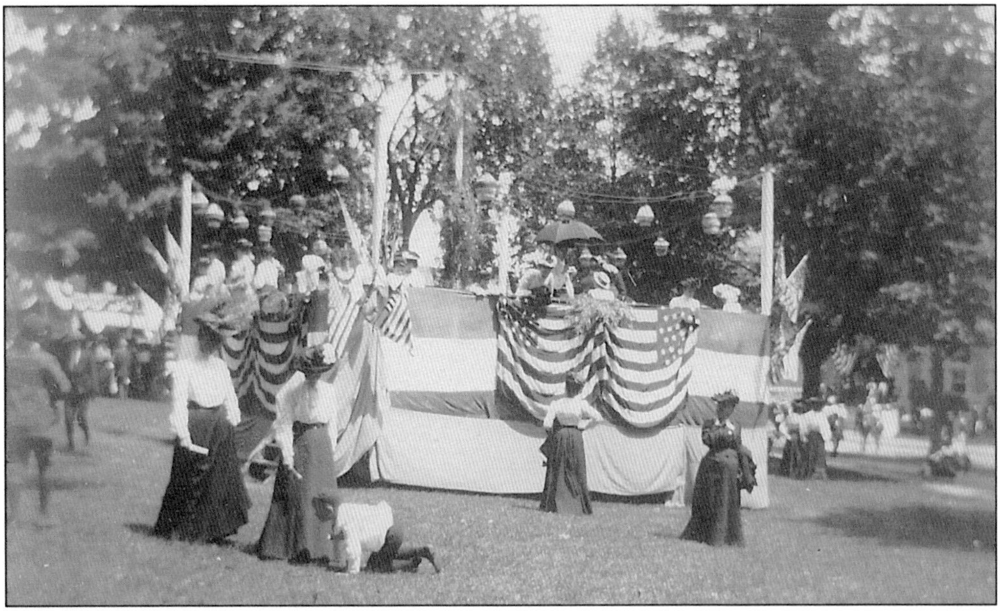

THE BANDSTAND ON THE AMHERST COMMON IN 1903, STRUNG WITH BUNTING AND LIGHTS DURING OLD HOME WEEK. The Amherst Brass Band had performed many summer evenings on makeshift bandstands. Their first was set up at the end of the summer of 1875, but was described as "not so pleasing as we had hoped for." In 1877, students tipped it over one night, and it was later burned down. In 1903, another bandstand was built on the Common, painted green, and strung with Chinese lanterns.

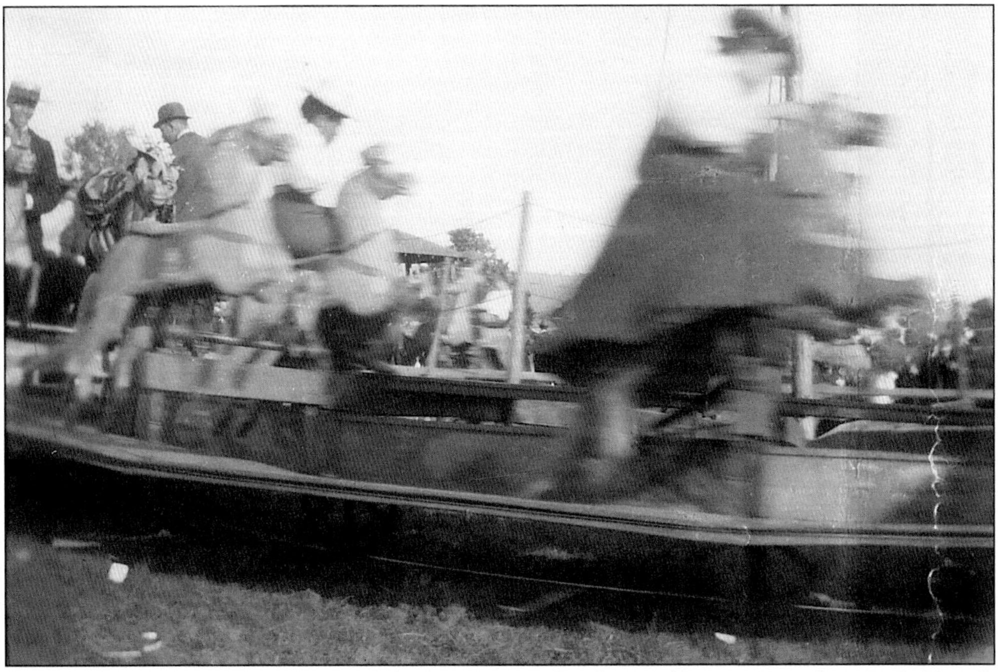

MERRY-GO-ROUND RIDE, C. 1901. Winifred Carpenter flies by in a blur at Hampshire Park. Fourth of July celebrations in Victorian Amherst and Hadley included horse racing at Hampshire Park in Amherst, parades, carousels, stirring speeches, and picnics.

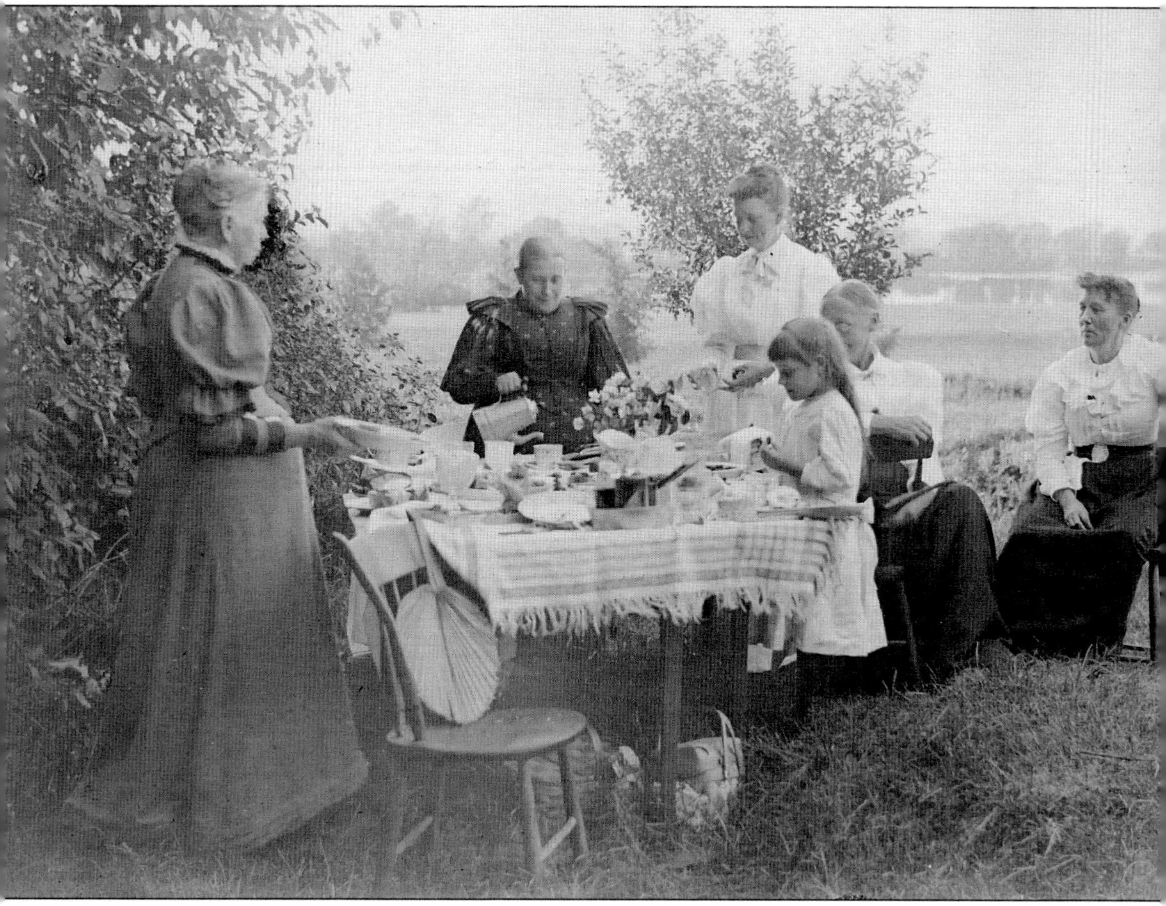

THE THAYER FAMILY, PHOTOGRAPHED PICNICKING IN HADLEY BY CLIFTON JOHNSON. For such occasions Holland & Gallond's store on Main Street in Amherst offered "pickles, plain, mixed and chow chow; Olives, plain and stuffed; Fresh Fruit jams; Smoked Sardines; Salad Dressings and Table Condiments, Saltines and Fancy Wafers, Shrimps, Lobster, Canned Fruit and Meats of all kinds."

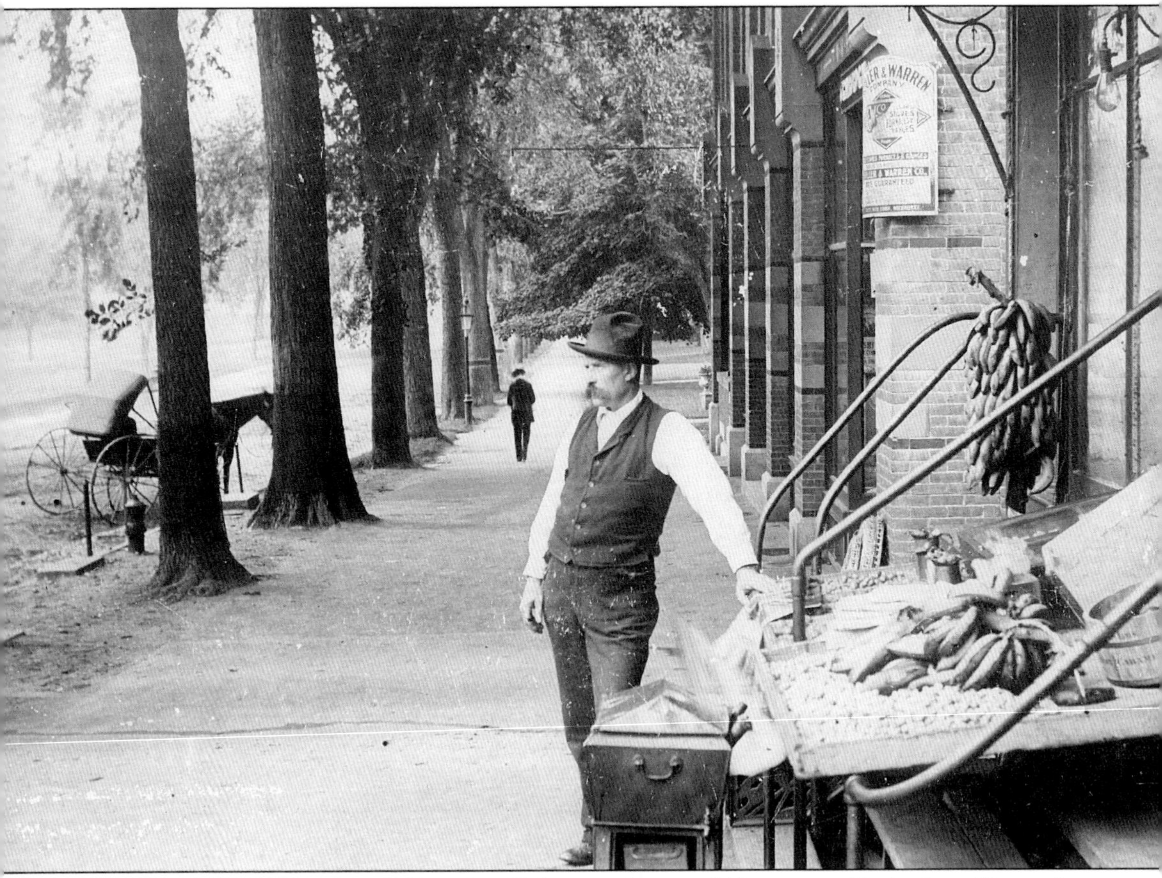

INDEPENDENCE DAY MERCHANDISE. Fourth-of-July picnickers could by nuts and fruits from "Peanut" John Musante on South Pleasant Street. Nearby, John Pettis sold fireworks: "The Fireworks I sell are reliable quality—the kind that go off. . . . Torpedoes, Fire Crackers, Roman Candles, Colored Stars, Sky Rockets, Mines, Flower Pots, Pin Wheels, Colored Triangle Wheels, Cannon Crackers, Cap Pistols, Combination Revolvers, Blank Cartridges, Crescent and Duck Head Canes with ammunition, Repeating Marbles, Whistling Crackers, Dewey Bombs, Flags and Horns of all kinds . . ."

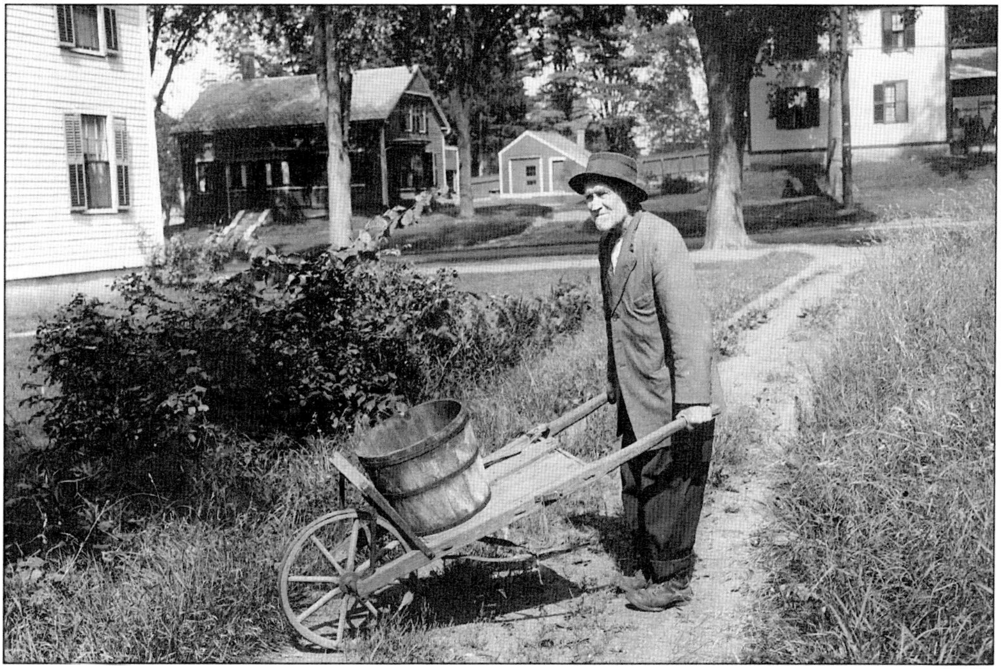

JOHN MCLEAN, A HOMELESS MAN WHO SLEPT IN ARTHUR BARDWELL'S BARN ON NORTH PLEASANT STREET. McLean could often be found telling fortunes in Amherst. After a foolish boy mangled McLean's hand with a lit cannon cracker on July 4, 1901, the town collected donations to pay his hospital bills. "Honest old John," as he was called, fully recovered.

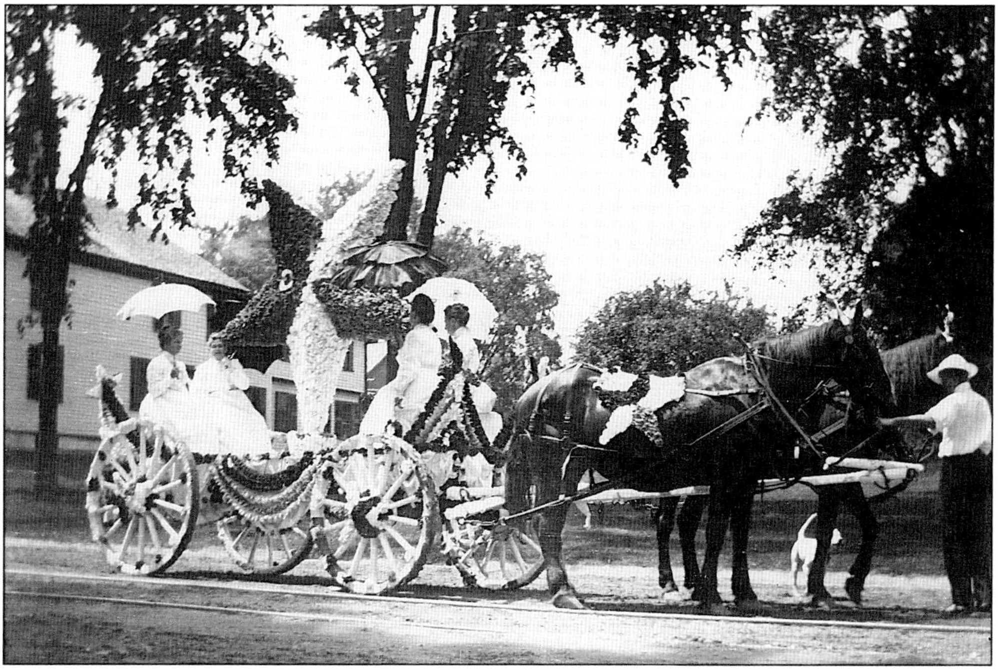

A TURN-OF-THE-CENTURY FOURTH OF JULY PARADE IN AMHERST. Flowers form stars on both the horses and float of the Order of the Eastern Star.

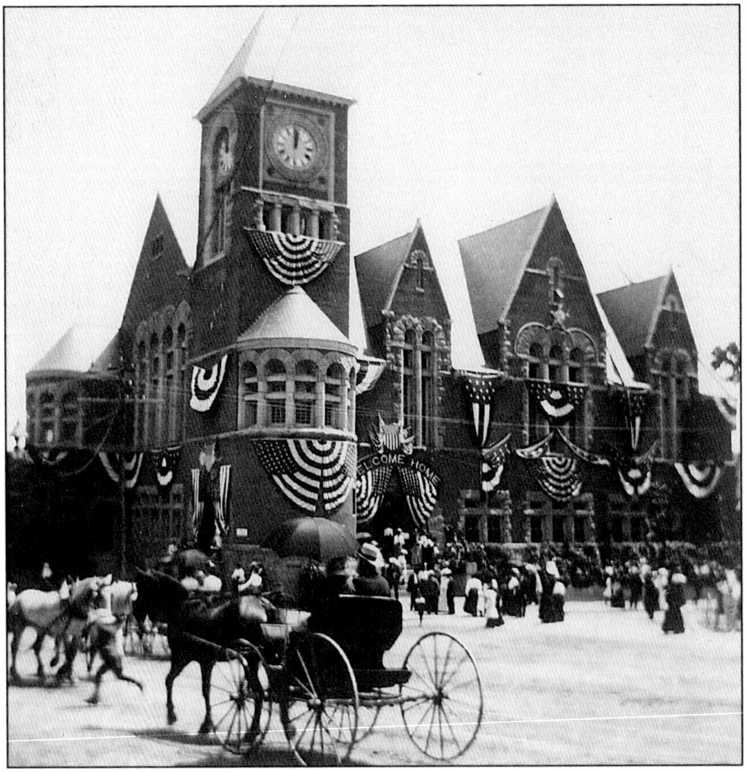

OLD HOME WEEK. Old Home Week became a holiday in Massachusetts in 1902. Everyone who had moved away from their hometown was invited back for a week-long festival. *The Boston Globe* described Amherst's first Old Home Week, held the last week of July 1903: "Thousands Saw Amherst's Parade. They Came by Trolley, by Train and by Team, and All Had a Good Time."

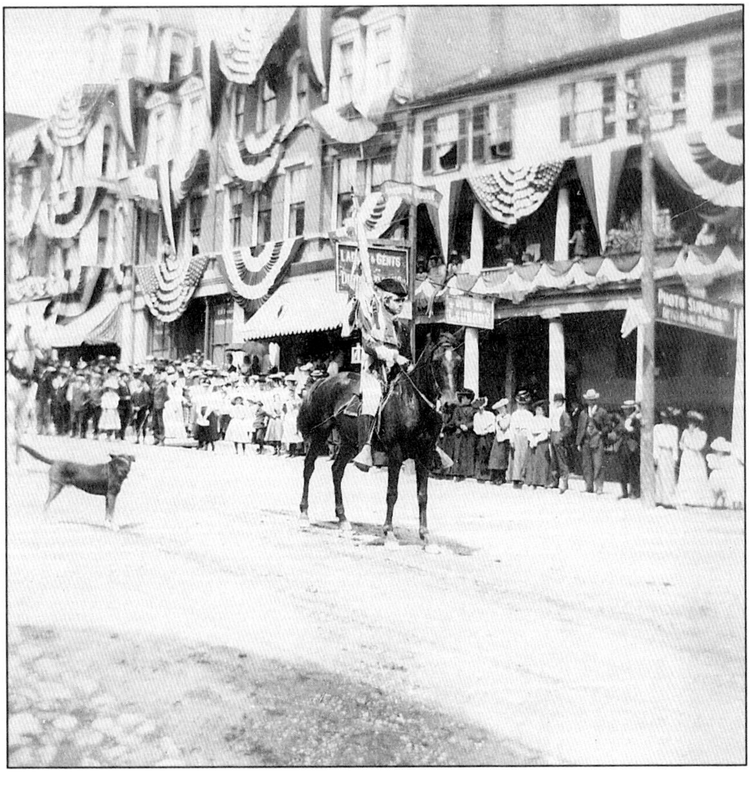

BUTCHER JOHN MULLEN AS LORD JEFFREY AMHERST ON MAIN STREET IN AMHERST. During Old Home Week there were brass band concerts, family reunions, historical arts and crafts exhibits, bell-ringing, and the singing of "Home Sweet Home." The Common was decorated with long rows of brilliant white lights and hundreds of Chinese lanterns. The climax was the parade, attended by more than three thousand people.

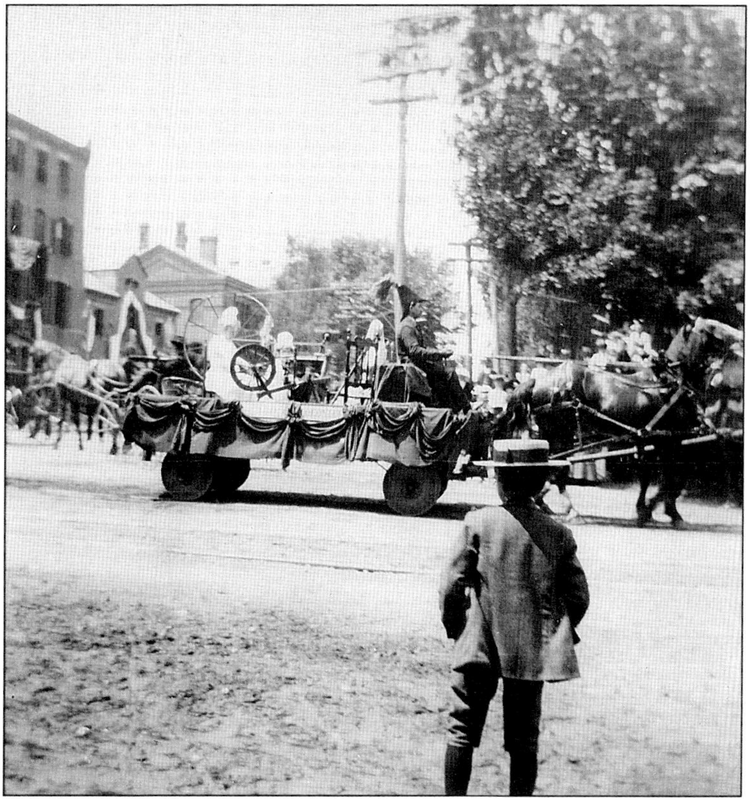

MABEL LOOMIS TODD, EDITOR OF EMILY DICKINSON'S POEMS. Todd, founder of the Amherst Historical Society, demonstrated spinning on an Old Home Week float as it headed up North Pleasant Street.

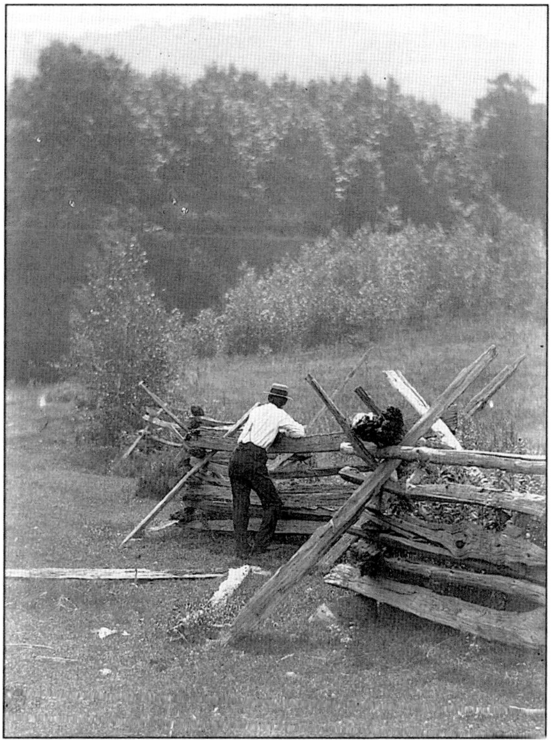

CLIFTON JOHNSON LEANING ON A SPLIT-RAIL FENCE IN HADLEY. "Now is the heyday of summer: everything voluptuously in growth. It is the full, warm, robust middle age of the year, with good health and thriving normal life. The earth, ripe with products as well as promise, smiles on with full contentment. The corn in my field is even with my shoulder, the rowen alfalfa, freshly green, has come eagerly to the second blossoming." (David Grayson, *The Countryman's Year*, July 21.)

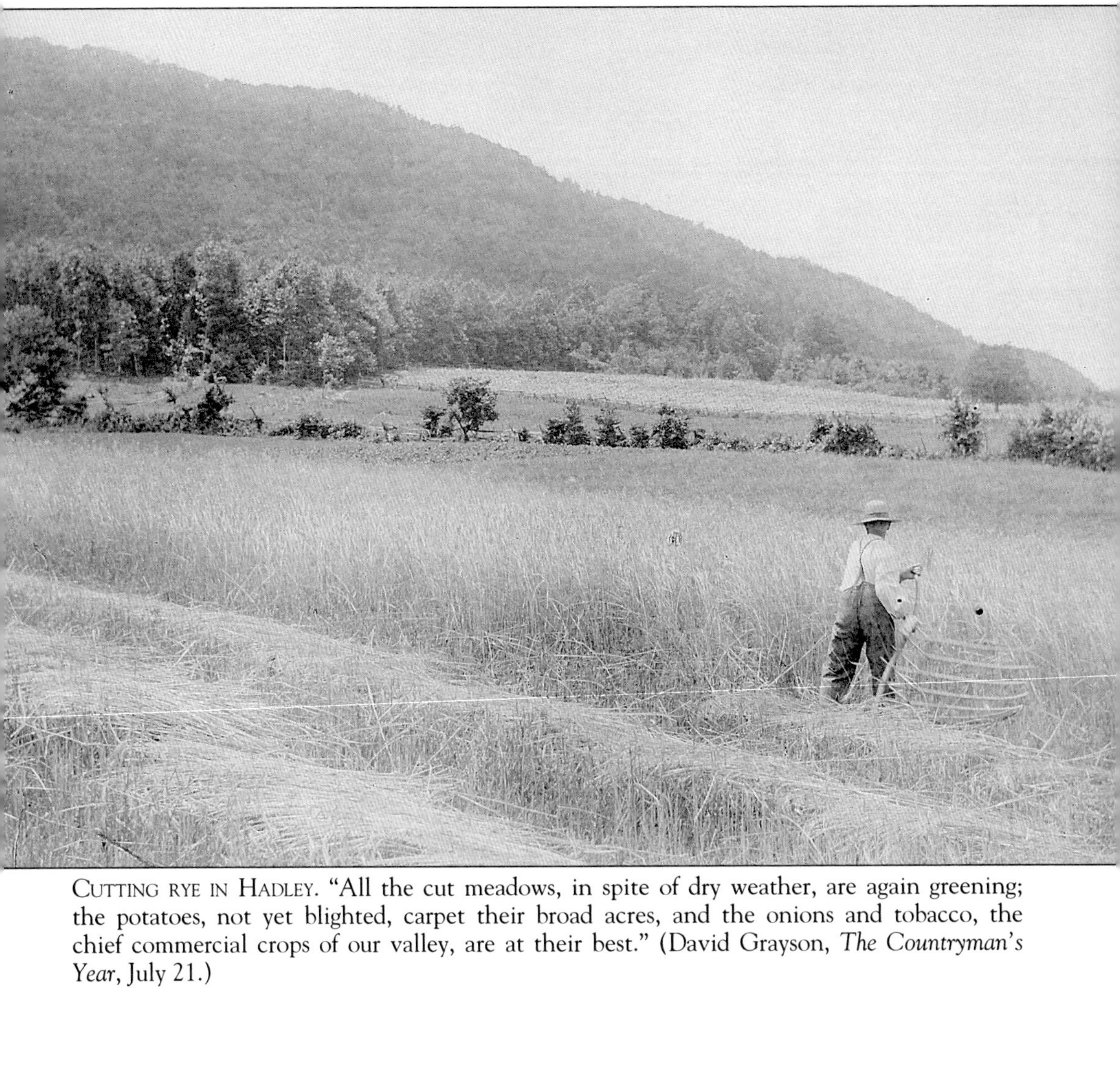

CUTTING RYE IN HADLEY. "All the cut meadows, in spite of dry weather, are again greening; the potatoes, not yet blighted, carpet their broad acres, and the onions and tobacco, the chief commercial crops of our valley, are at their best." (David Grayson, *The Countryman's Year*, July 21.)

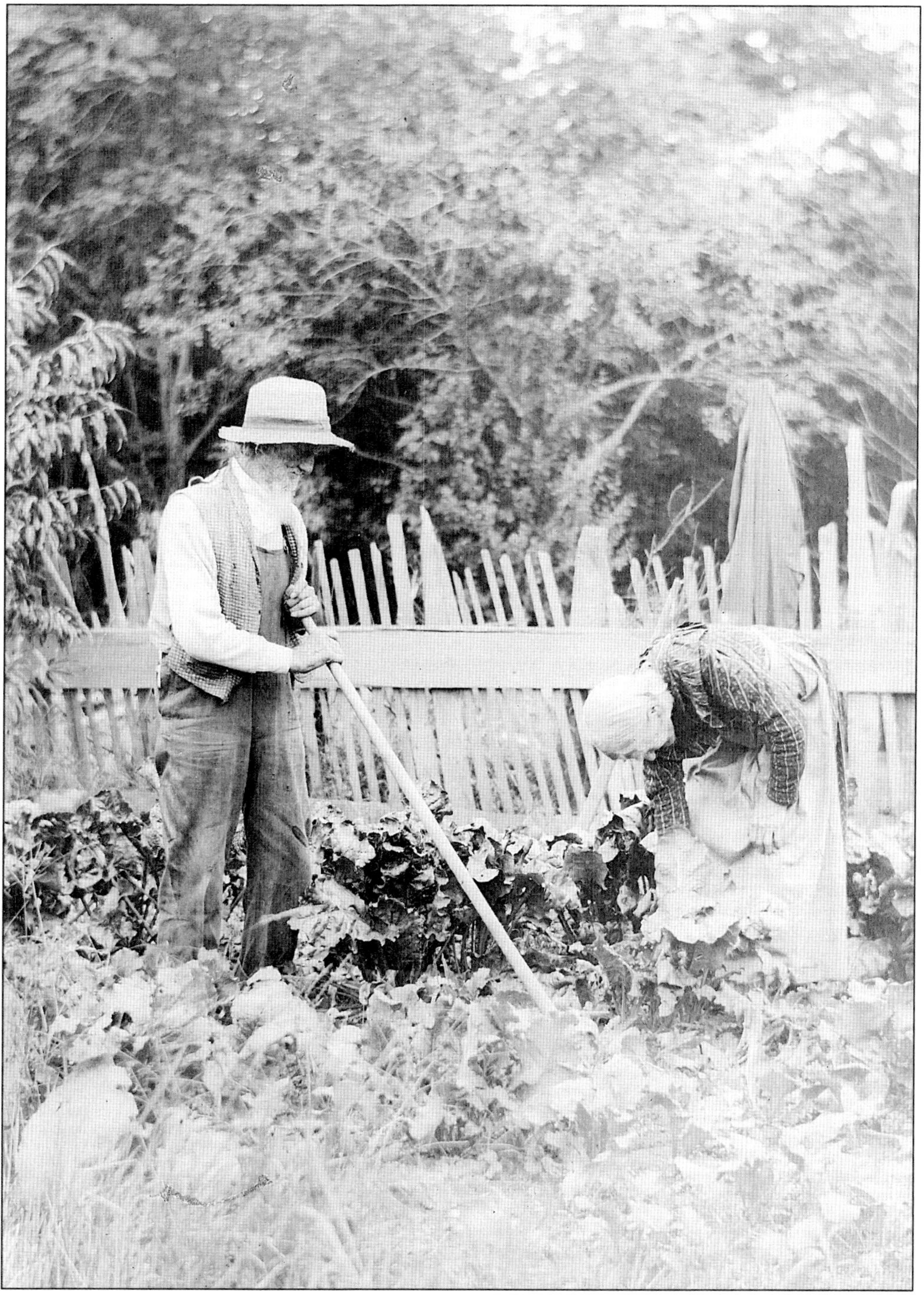

"GRANDPA" LOREN PEASE AND LUCRETIA IN THEIR HADLEY GARDEN, BY CLIFTON JOHNSON. "The early peaches in my orchard—the Mayflower—hang loaded with red-ripening fruit, never so abundant as this year. The raspberries are past . . . The early apples—the Yellow Transparent—are full-grown, nearly ready to use, but the later apples, especially the Spies, are backward. All the hives are filling with honey . . ." (David Grayson, *The Countryman's Year*, July 21.)

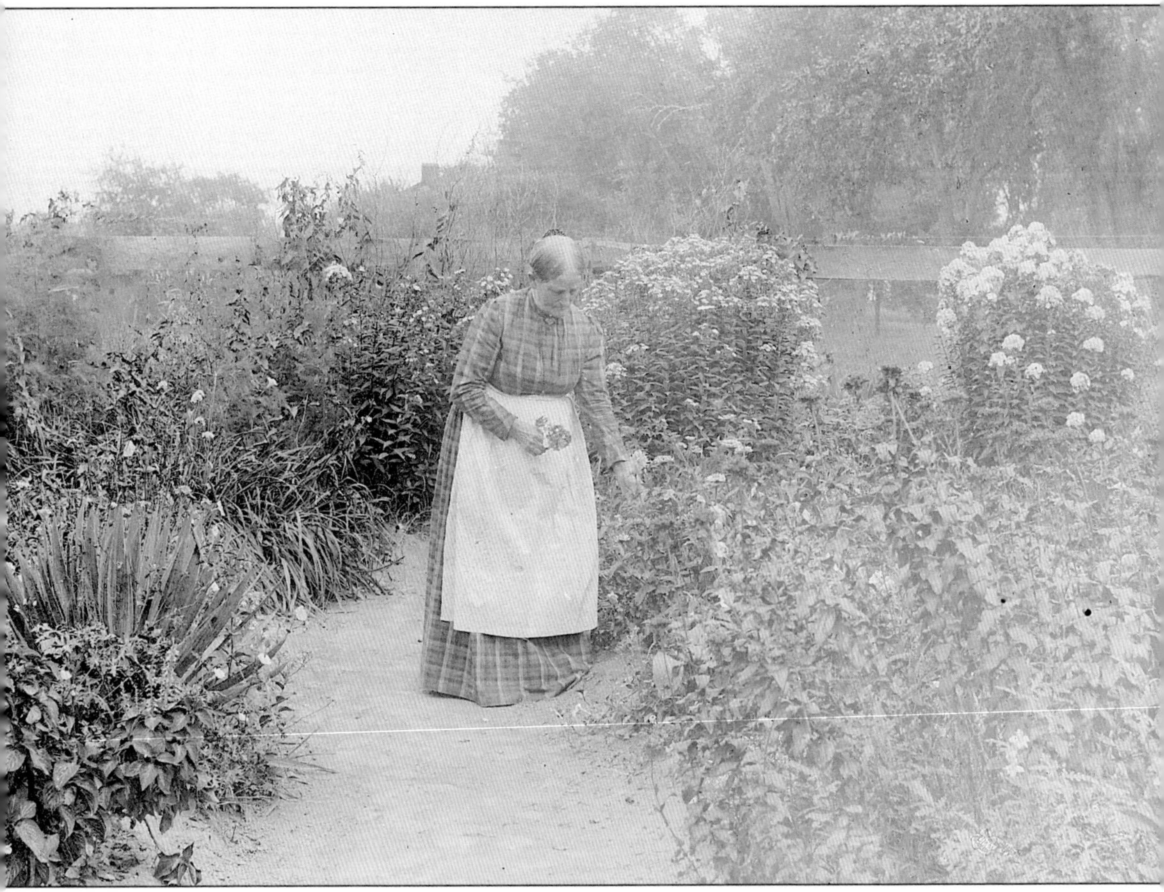

A HADLEY GARDEN IN FULL BLOOM, BY CLIFTON JOHNSON. "In the garden we have zinnias and calendulas and hollyhocks at their best, and great red and white roses. Surely, a good, abundant, smiling time of the year!" (David Grayson, *The Countryman's Year*, July 21.)

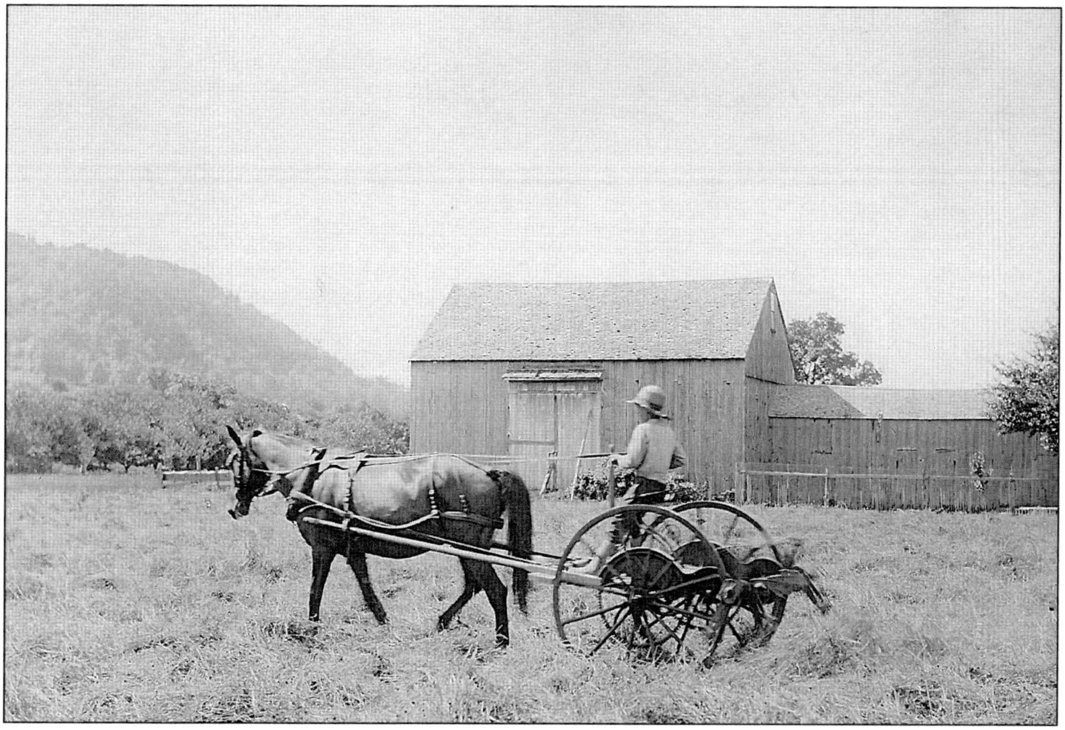

A BOY RIDING A HAY TEDDER ON A HADLEY FARM, BY CLIFTON JOHNSON.

The Sound I Listened For

What I remember is the ebb and flow of sound
That summer morning as the mower came and went
And came again, crescendo and diminuendo,
And always when the sound was loudest how it ceased
A moment while he backed the horses for the turn,
The rapid clatter giving place to the slow click
And the mower's voice. That was the sound I listened for.
The voice did what the horses did. It shared the action
As sympathetic magic does or incantation.
The voice hauled and the horses hauled. The strength of one
Was in the other and in the strength was no impatience.
Over and over as the mower made his rounds
I heard his voice and only once or twice he backed
And turned and went ahead and spoke no word at all.

—Robert Francis, *Collected Poems*, p. 125.
(Amherst: University of Massachusetts Press, 1976.)

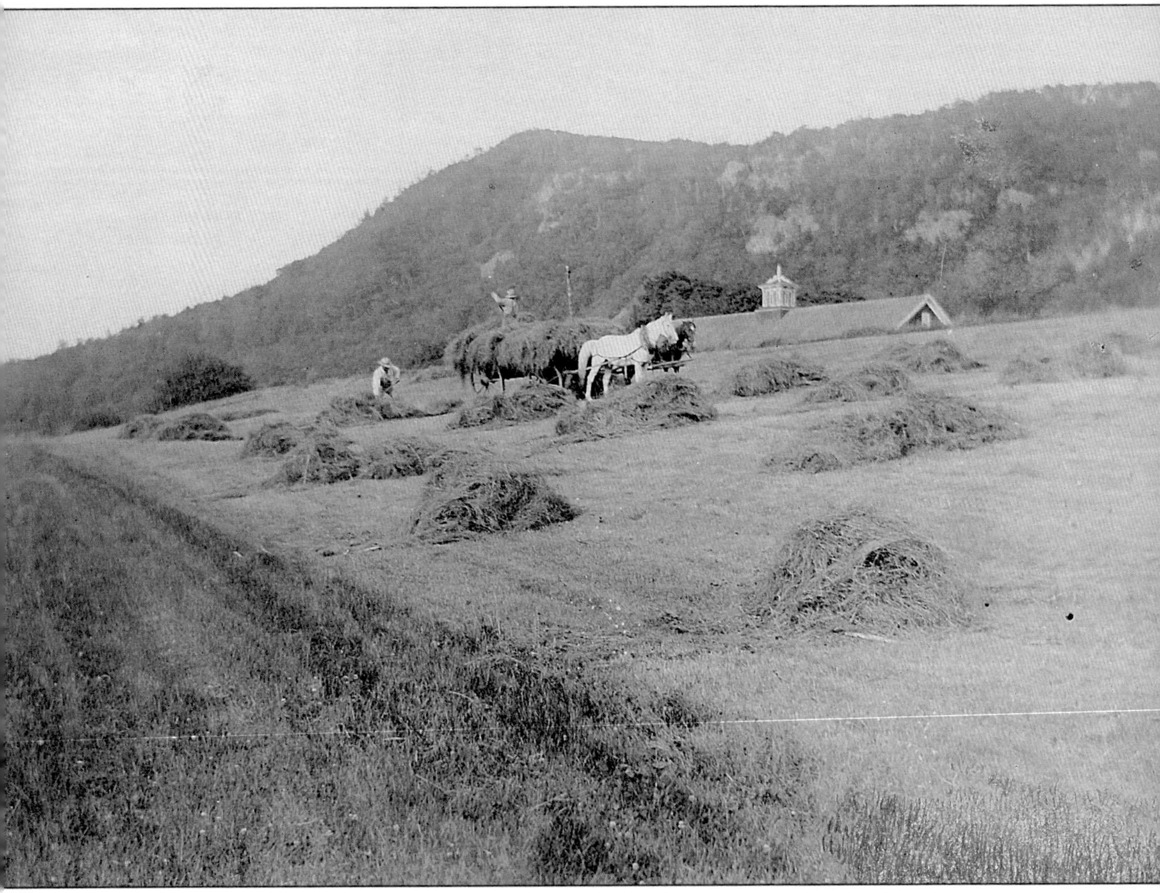

HAYING ON THE THAYER FARM IN HADLEY, BY CLIFTON JOHNSON. "In the summer the men were out before sun up, swinging their scythes through the dewy grass, and leaving long windrows behind them. . . . Mowing, turning, and raking were all done by hand . . . In the busiest times the women and girls of the family often helped in the fields 'tending' hay, or loading it, or raking after." (Clifton Johnson, *The New England Country*, p. 16.)

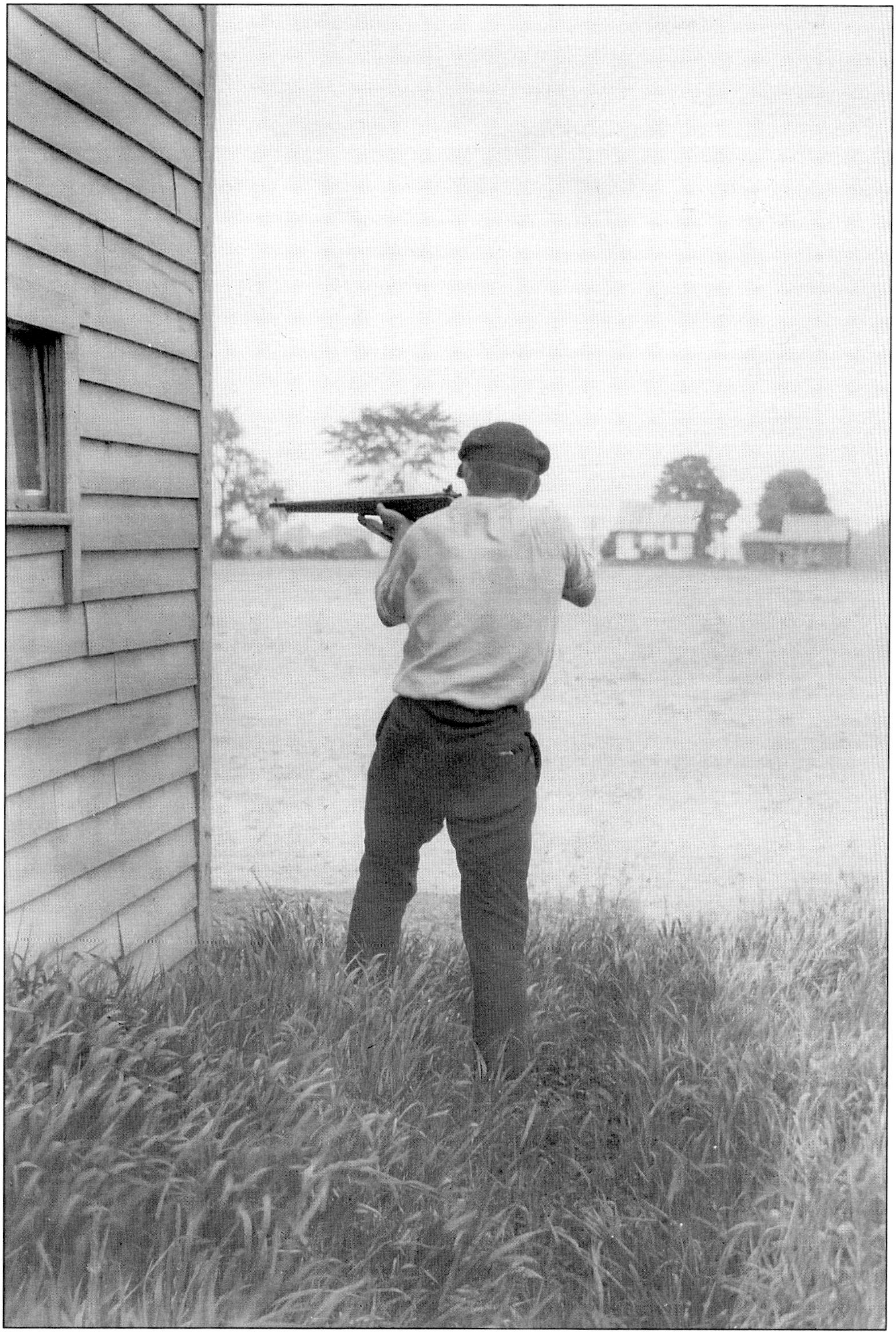

IRVING JOHNSON. Clifton Johnson photographed his son defending the cornfield from crows in Hadley.

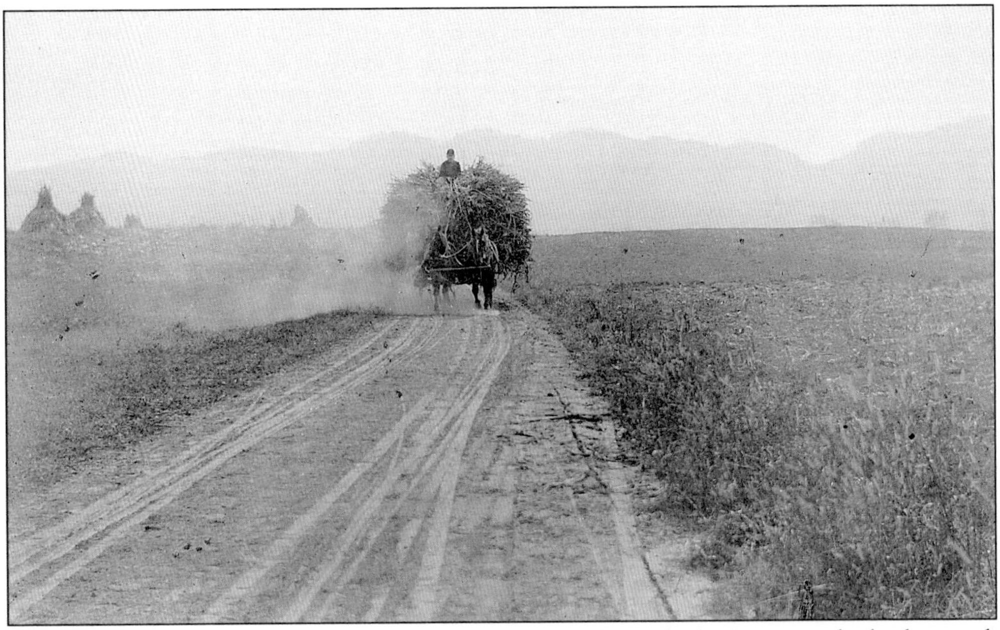

HAULING IN THE CORN. With corn shocks on the left and the Holyoke Range in the background, a load of corn is seen being hauled in from the fields on a dusty summer day. "I have rarely known hotter days in New England. Parching winds from the South, all the earth dry and hot. At evening we went for a plunge off the rocks into the Connecticut River at Whitmore's." (David Grayson, *The Countryman's Year*, August 3.)

Remind Me of Apples

When the cicada celebrates the heat,
Intoning that tomorrow and today
Are only yesterday with the same dust
To dust on plantain and on roadside yarrow—
Remind me, someone, of the apples coming,
Cold in the dew of deep October grass,
A prophecy of snow in their white flesh.

In the long haze of dog days, or by night
When thunder growls and prowls but will not go
Or come, I lose the memory of apples.
Name me the names, the goldens, russets, sweets,
Pippin and blue pearmain and seek-no-further
And the lost apples on forgotten farms
And the wild pasture apples of no name.

—Robert Francis, *Collected Poems*, p. 178.
(Amherst: University of Massachusetts Press, 1976.)

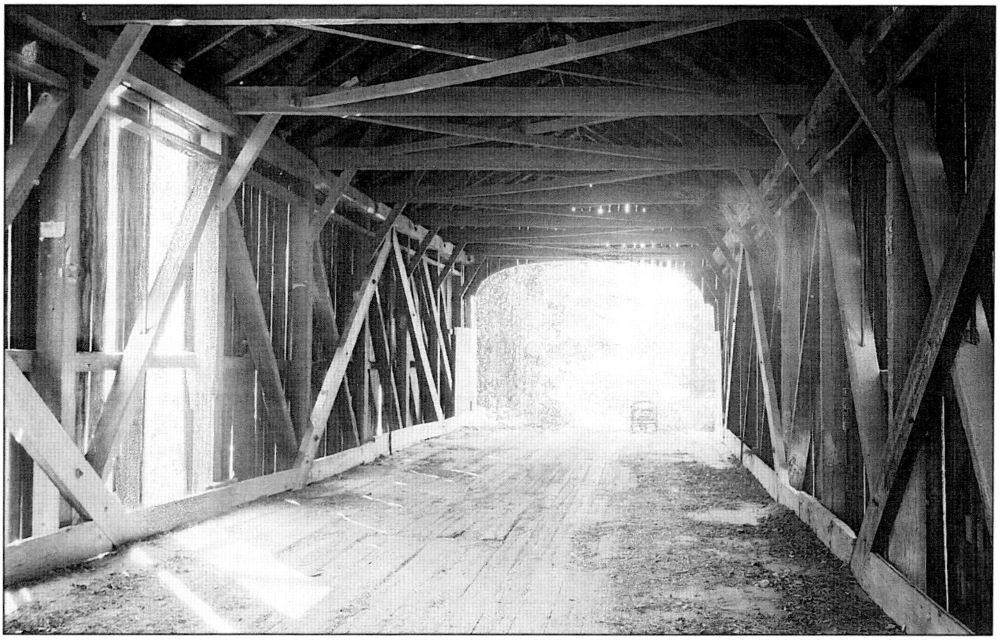

THE COVERED BRIDGE OVER THE FORT RIVER IN HADLEY, BY CLIFTON JOHNSON. "The Connecticut River was spanned by a dusty, covered bridge through the dark and mysterious interior of which the stage rattled, and less pretentious vehicles crawled. A journey to Northampton was a great event in my boyhood." (MacGregor Jenkins, *Emily Dickinson, Friend and Neighbor*, p. 4.)

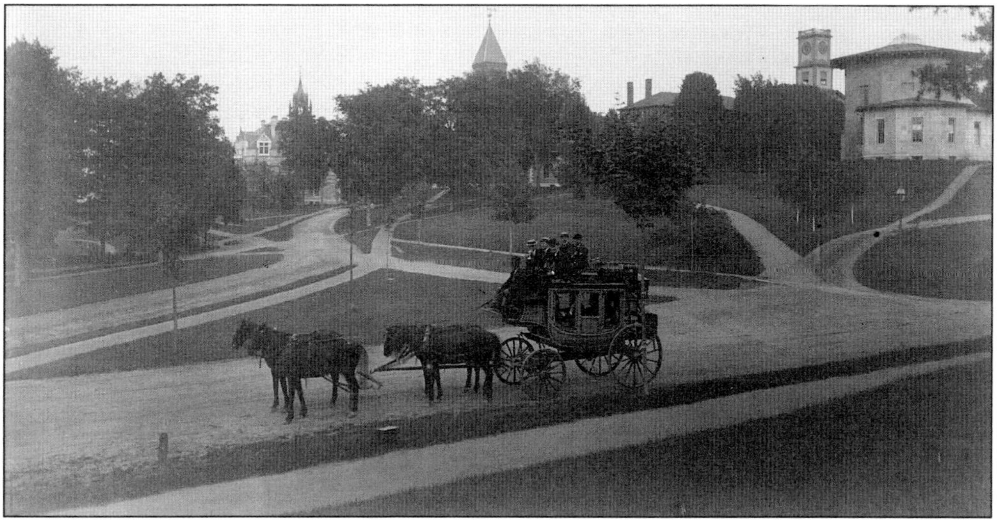

THE AMHERST STAGECOACH AT THE COMMON, BEFORE LEAVING TO CROSS THE BRIDGE TO NORTHAMPTON. ". . . the modest bridge toll was collected by a one-armed war veteran, who [also made] an ambrosial root beer. When he came to the side of the carriage, on his left arm there would be glasses of this delectable beverage, poised precariously, I always thought. But the arm was wood and ingeniously flattened on the top to permit of its use as a serving tray. . . . Each [glass] had a collar of white foam and my mouth would water when I saw it. . . . We rarely went on our way without a delicious, sticky, aromatic flavor lingering on our lips." (MacGregor Jenkins, *Emily Dickinson, Friend and Neighbor*, p. 4–5.)

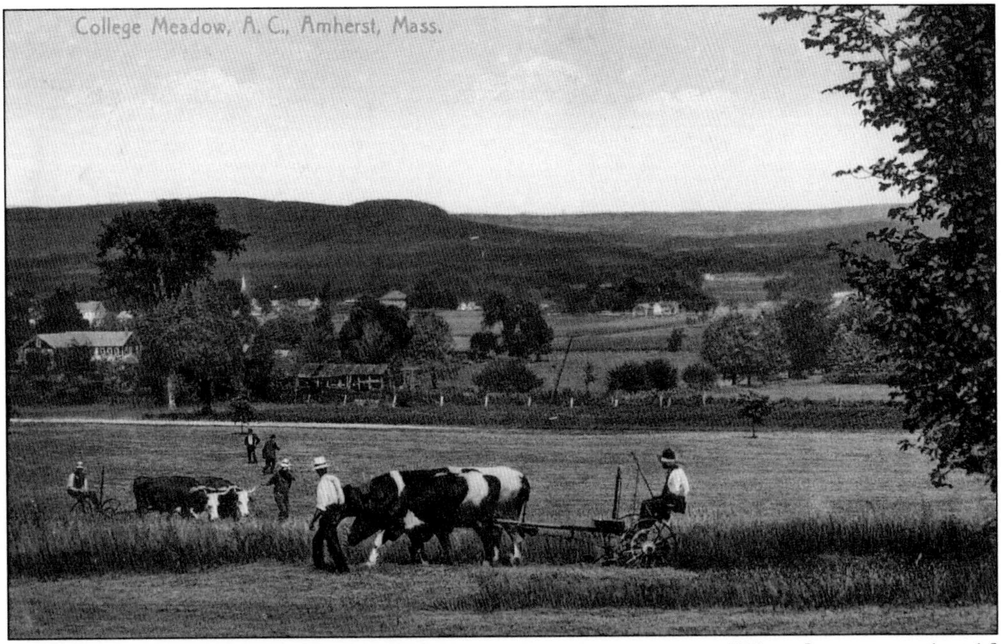

POSTCARD OF FIELDS BEING WORKED BY AMHERST COLLEGE STUDENTS. "They [women and girls] helped, too, in harvesting the grain and flax, and later in picking up apples in the orchard. They did the milking the year round, using clumsy wooden pails, and for a seat, a heavy three-legged stool or a block of wood." (Clifton Johnson, *The New England Country*, p. 16.)

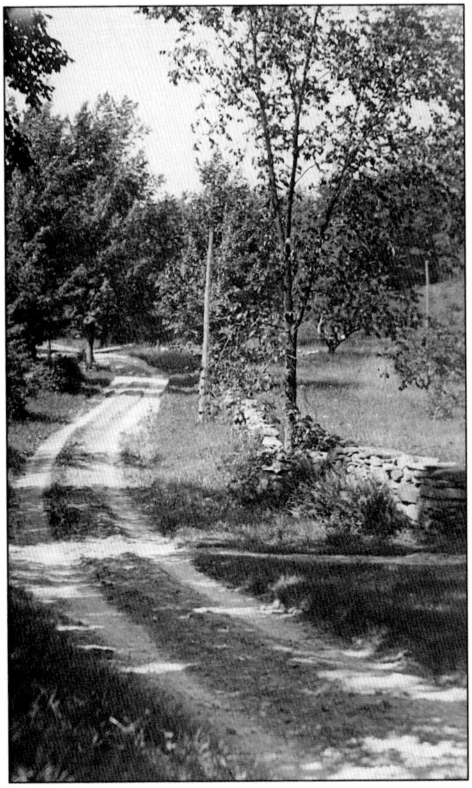

A WINDING AMHERST ROAD AND STONE WALL. "The smaller children drove the cows to pasture in the morning and brought them back at night, often a distance of a mile or two along lonesome roadways or by-paths." (Clifton Johnson, *The New England Country*, p. 16.)

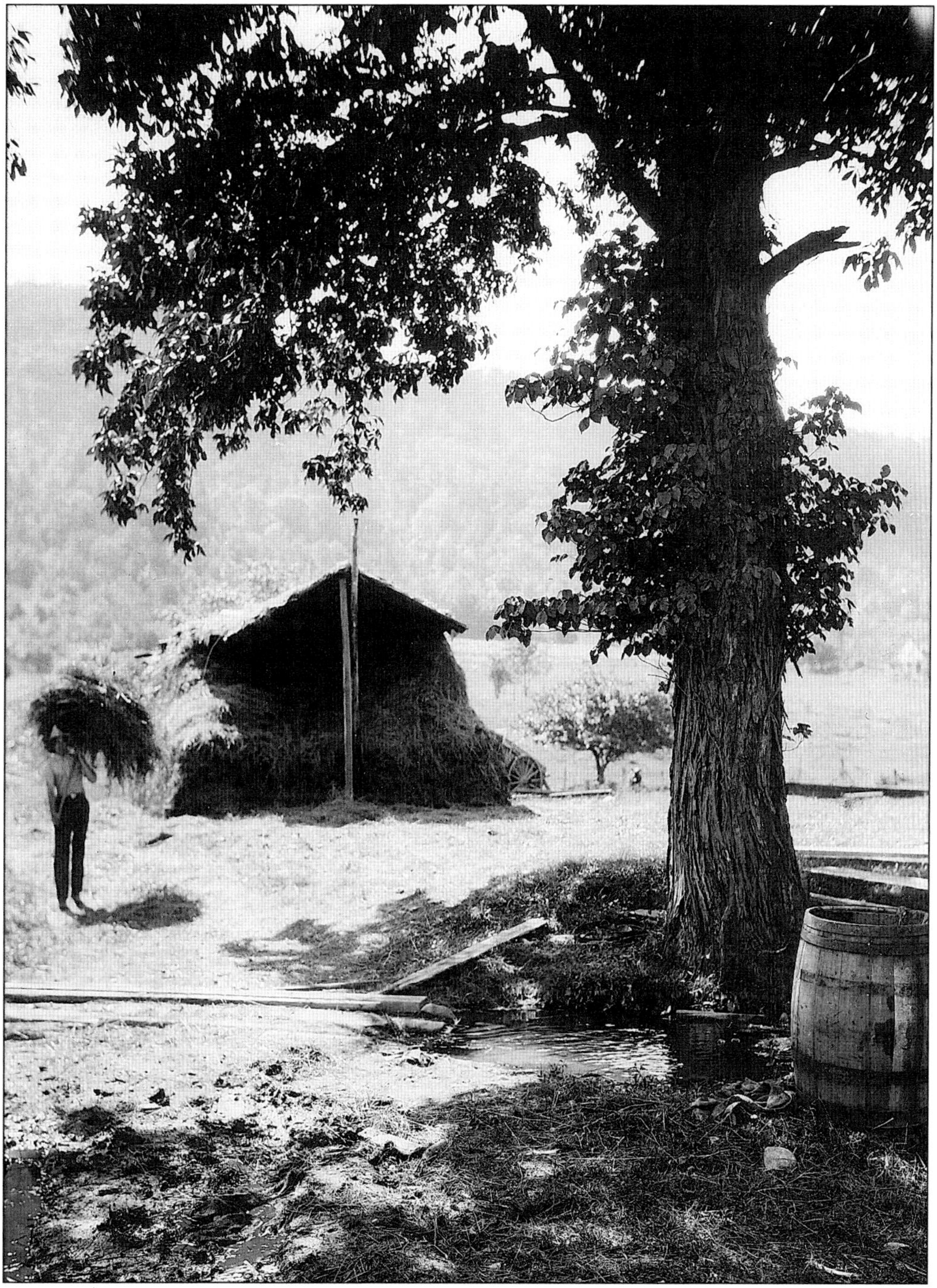

A BOY CARRYING A FORKFUL OF HAY FROM THE HAYSTACK TO THE BARN, BY CLIFTON JOHNSON. "Often on pleasant summer mornings I was up at dawn or earlier. . . . The sun rose higher, the grass put on its spangles of morning dew, and all at once the countryside seemed to awaken gloriously—the birds were singing, the dogs exchanging morning greetings across the fields, and the cows lowing, eager to be milked and turned out to pasture." (Ray Stannard Baker, *American Chronicle*, p. 290.)

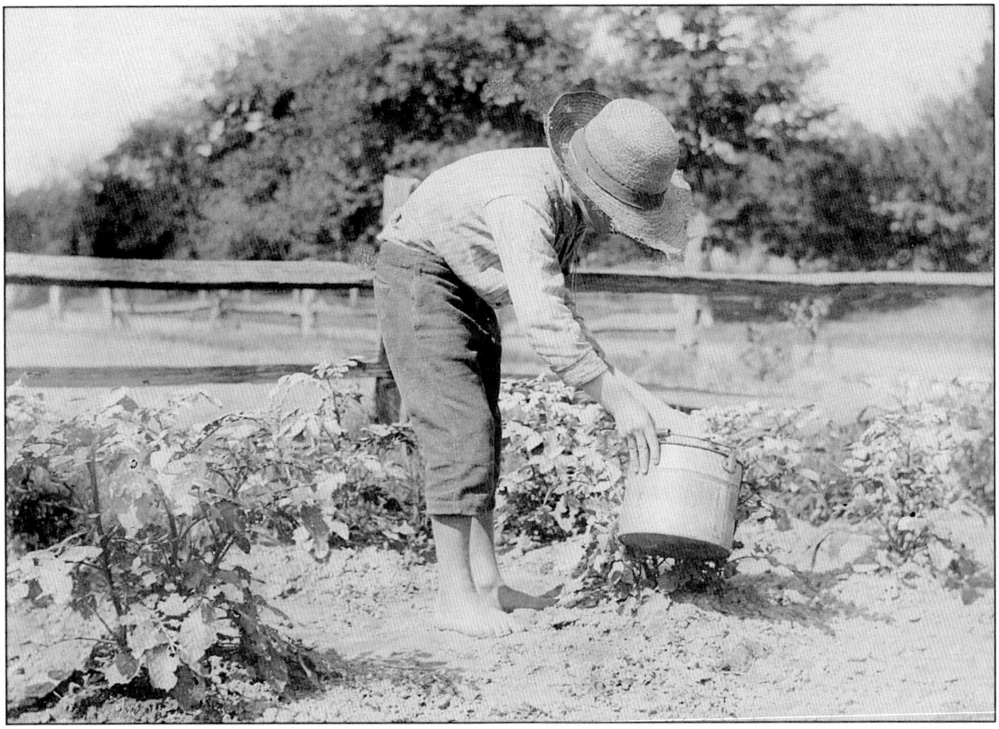

A boy in Hadley knocking potato bugs into a bucket with a paddle.

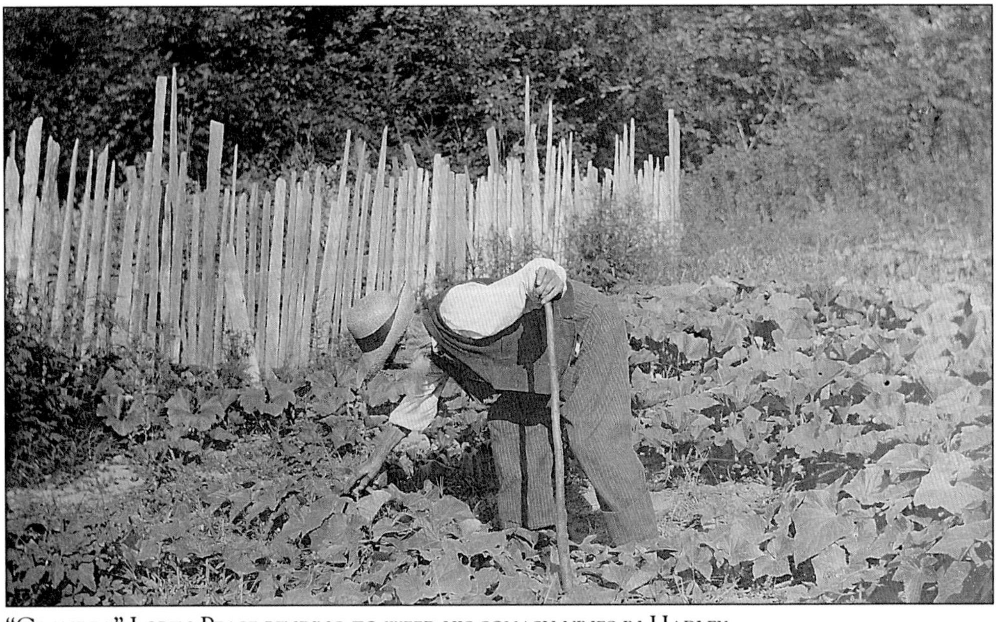

"Grandpa" Loren Pease bending to weed his squash vines in Hadley.

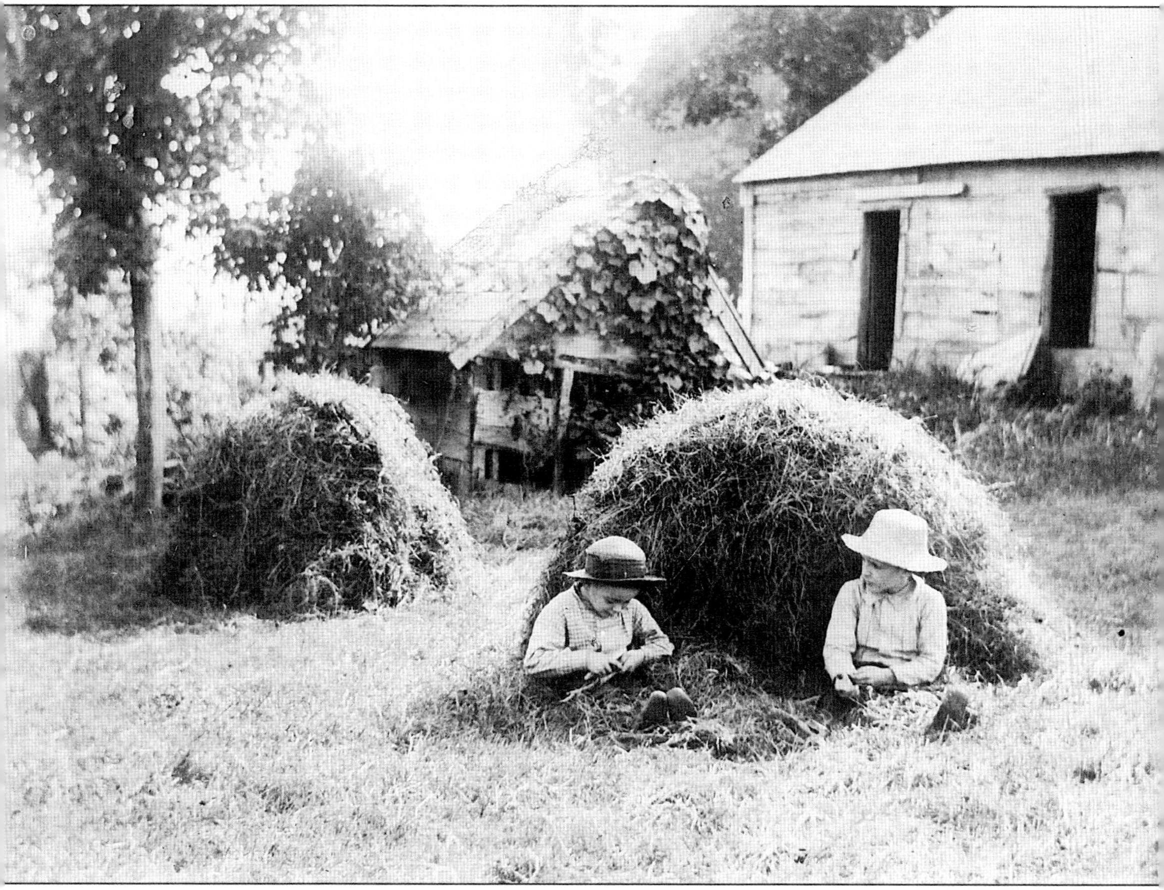

TWO BOYS ENJOYING THEMSELVES ON A SUMMER AFTERNOON, HALF SHELTERED FROM THE SUN BY A HAYCOCK. The icehouse and back of an old farmhouse are behind them. This picture was taken in about 1895 in the Hockanum section of Hadley by Clifton Johnson.

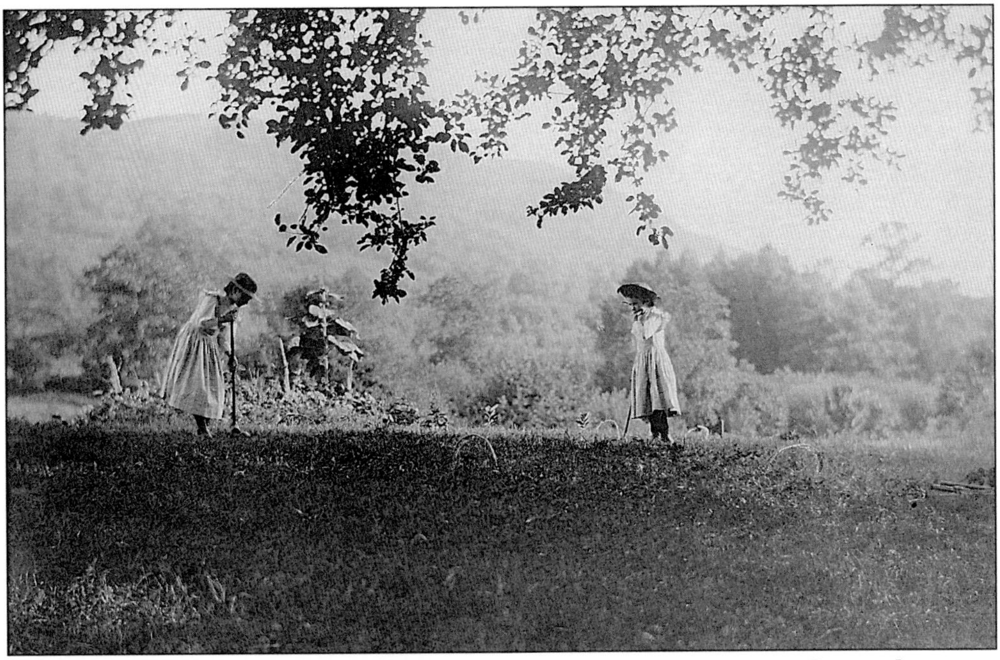

Two girls playing croquet in the yard in front of their Hadley house, by Clifton Johnson.

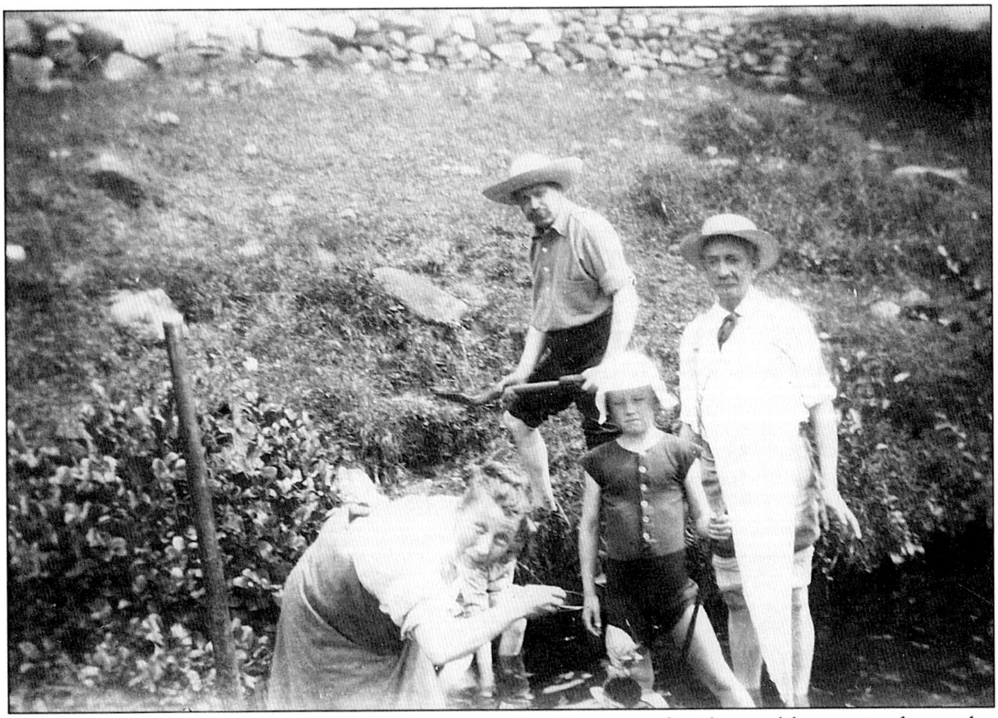

Escaping the sun's rays. In the heat of summer, the Carpenter family would camp in the cooler hills of Pelham. Here, they swim in a brook, in modest swimwear.

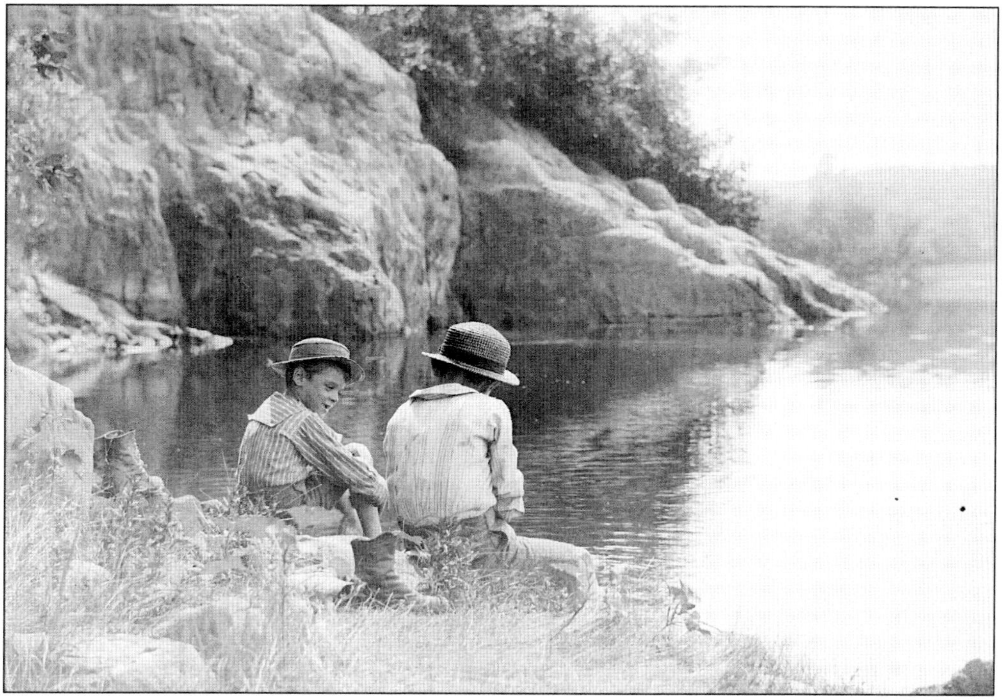

A MOMENT'S RELIEF. At rockbound Russell's Cove, boys took off their boots and dangled their feet in the water. Near this spot used to be a ferry to take travelers across the Connecticut River. It was said that Lafayette crossed the river here on his last visit to America. This photograph was taken by Clifton Johnson about 1894.

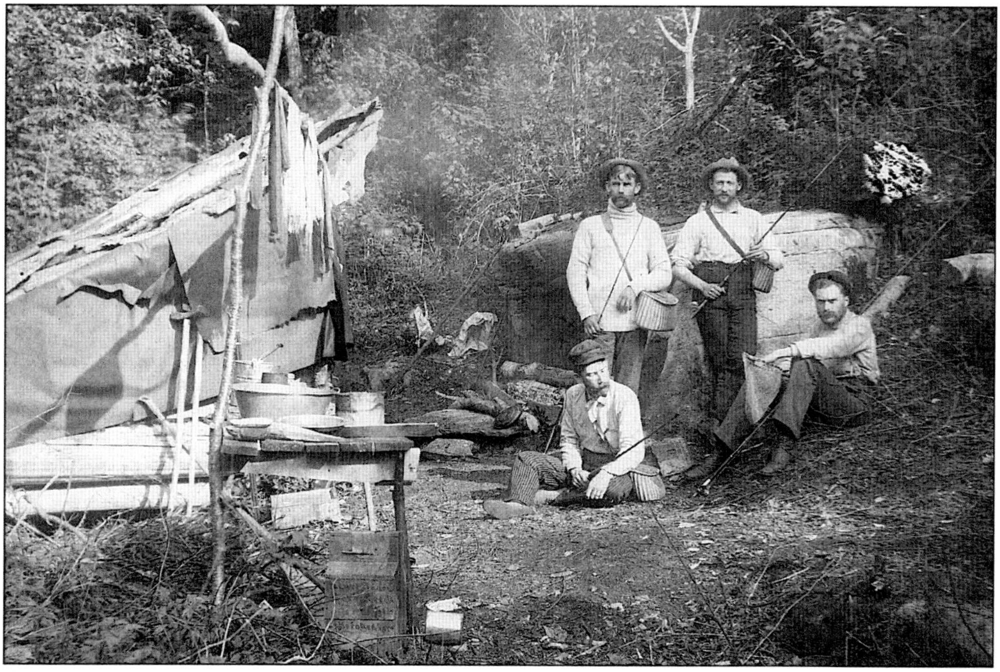

A GROUP OF FISHERMEN POSING WITH THEIR RODS, BASKETS, A NET, AND A GUN. Their tarpaper lean-to is surrounded by various fry pans, wash basins, and clothes hung up to dry.

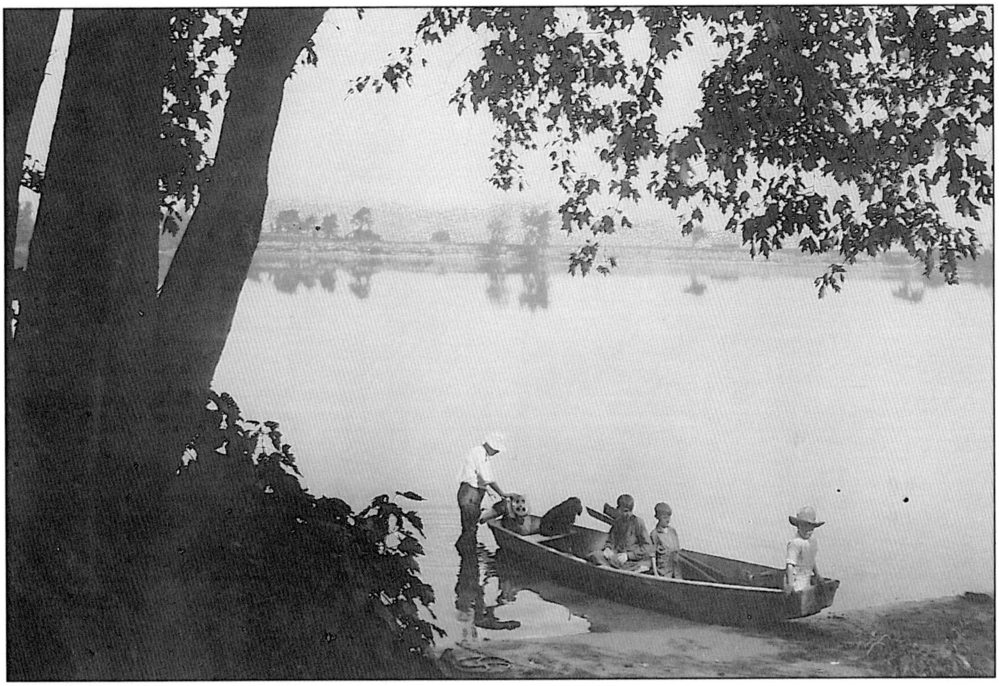

ROGER JOHNSON TAKING HIS BOYS AND THE FAMILY DOG FOR A SUMMER VOYAGE ON THE CONNECTICUT RIVER. This photograph was taken by Clifton Johnson.

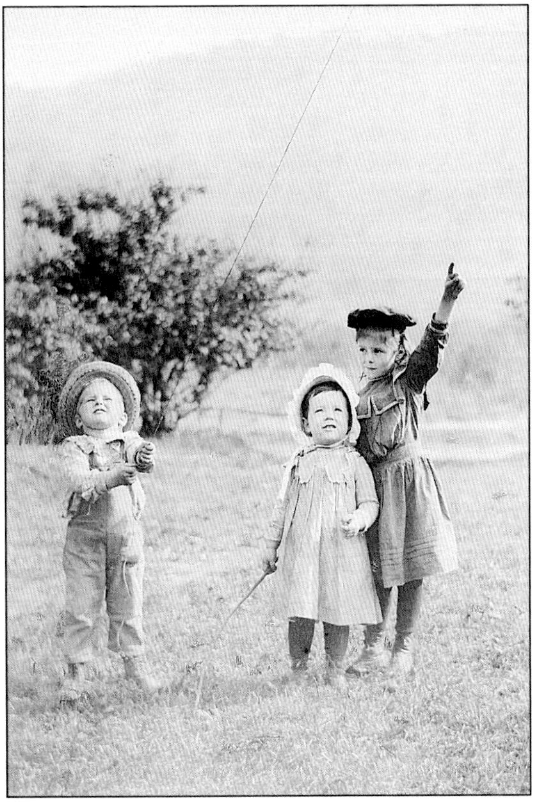

ARTHUR, ROGER, AND MARGARET JOHNSON FLYING A KITE IN A HOCKANUM FIELD. Clifton Johnson took the photograph about 1904.

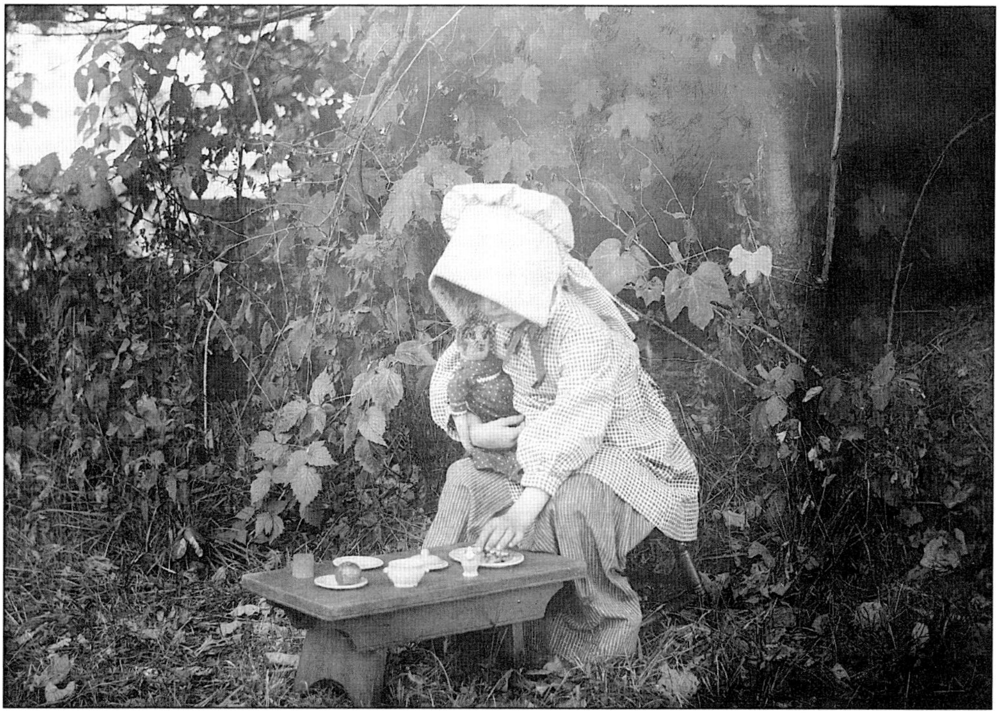

A CHILD SETTING UP A TEA PARTY WITH HER DOLL IN A NEGLECTED CORNER OF THE GARDEN. The image was captured by Clifton Johnson.

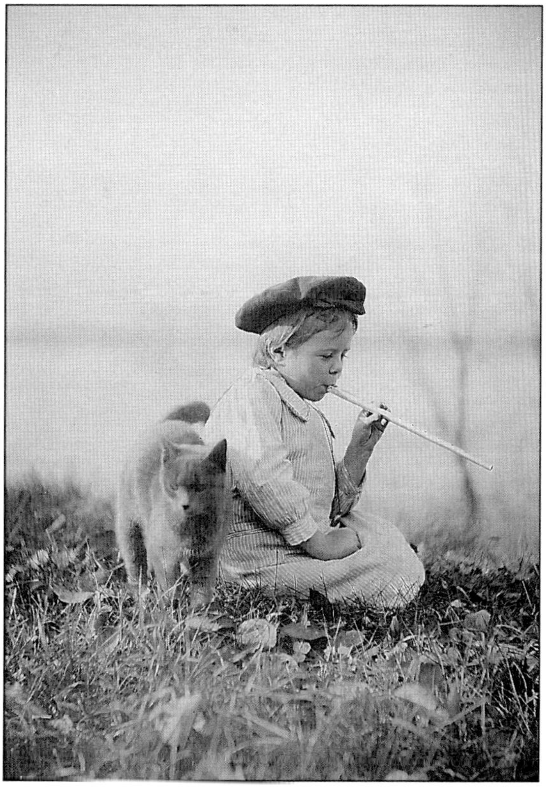

PORTRAIT OF CLIFTON JOHNSON'S DAUGHTER MARGARET PLAYING A WOODEN FLUTE ABOUT 1903. "Emily Dickinson was the child of Amherst, of its whimsicality and culture and its freedom, the child of Amherst when she mused in her garden and asked the Pelham Hills 'What is morning?' and when she admitted the children to her confidence and when she was borne over the green fields to the cemetery by men who had been faithful servants in her father's household." (MacGregor Jenkins, *Emily Dickinson, Friend and Neighbor*, p. 11.)

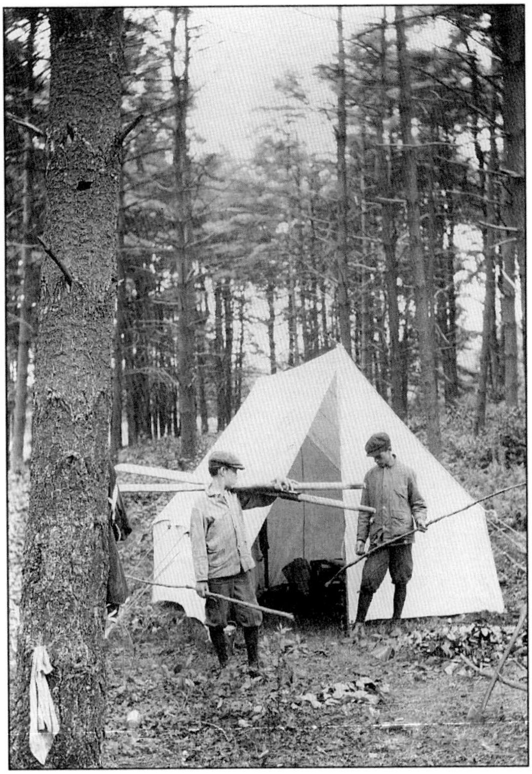

ROGER AND ARTHUR JOHNSON PREPARING FOR A DAY'S EXCURSION WHILE CAMPING. The photograph was taken by Clifton Johnson in 1913. "We roamed and quarreled, sailed the high seas, hunted buffalo and split into hostile groups, only to swear a new and more vehement allegiance. We lived drunk with the romance of childhood." (MacGregor Jenkins, *Emily Dickinson, Friend and Neighbor*, p. 20.)

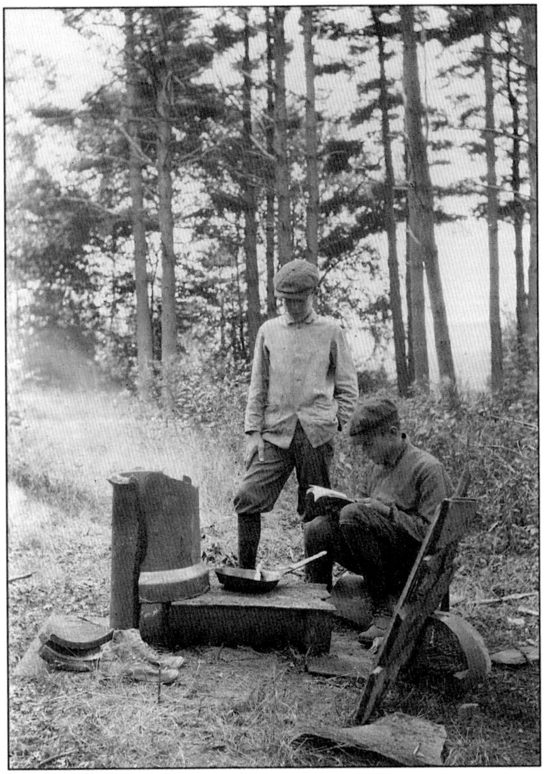

FEASTING ON NATURE'S BOUNTY, BY CLIFTON JOHNSON. After a day out on the Connecticut River, Roger and Arthur Johnson built a campfire and prepared dinner back at camp. "Several of the young men from the village, including students, are camping out on an island in the Connecticut. . . . They are expected to live during their stay on herring and bluefish and possibly bass, salmon-trout and shad." (*The Amherst Record*, July 1879.)

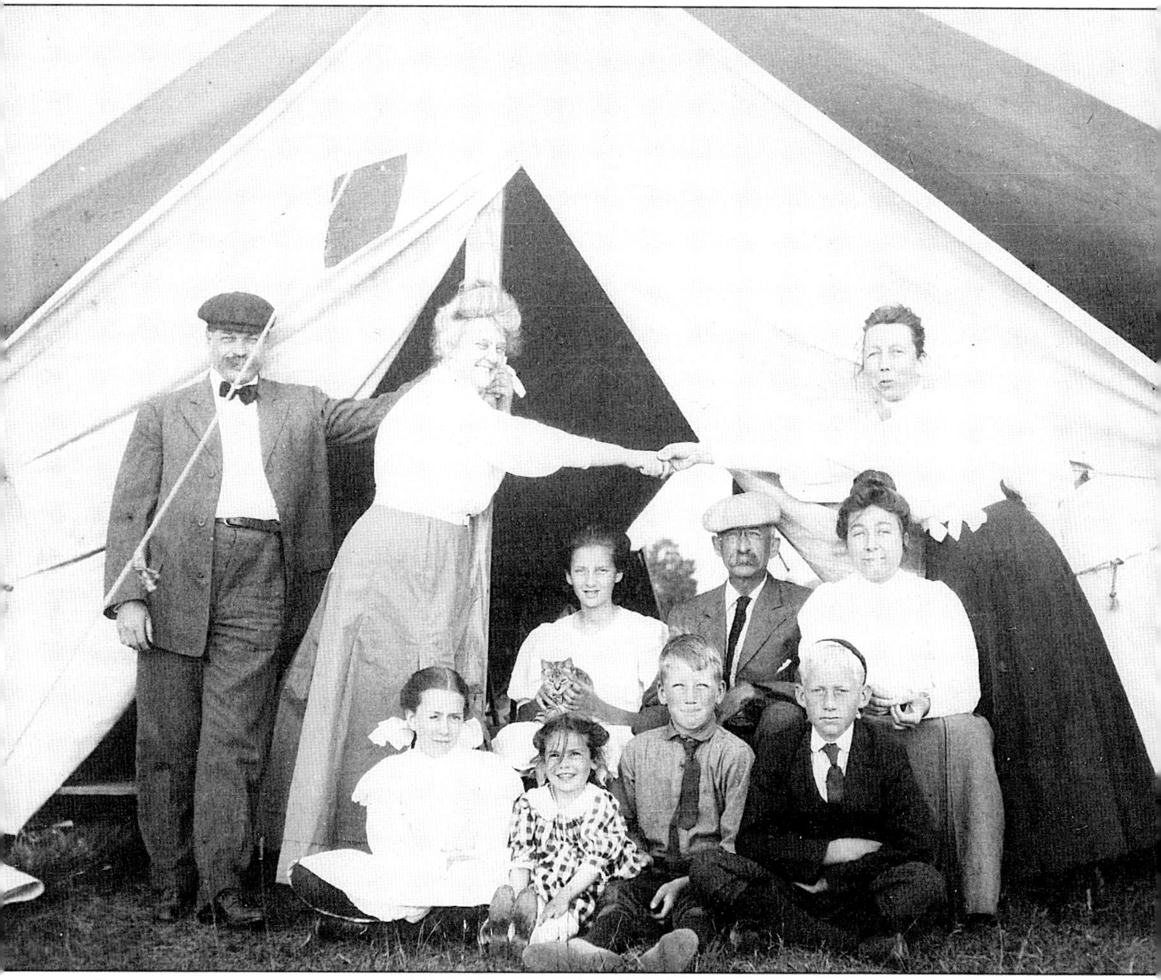

RELAXING IN THE COUNTRYSIDE. The Carpenter family of Amherst camped for several summers in Pelham. Here, they pose in front of their tent on Butter Hill in 1907.

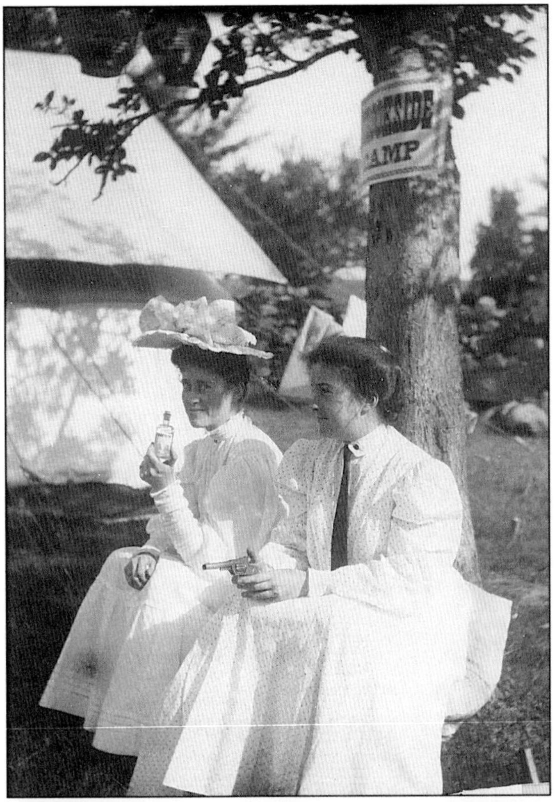

Dangerous characters. Two Carpenter family members pose with a bottle of liquor and a revolver on the camping trip of 1907.

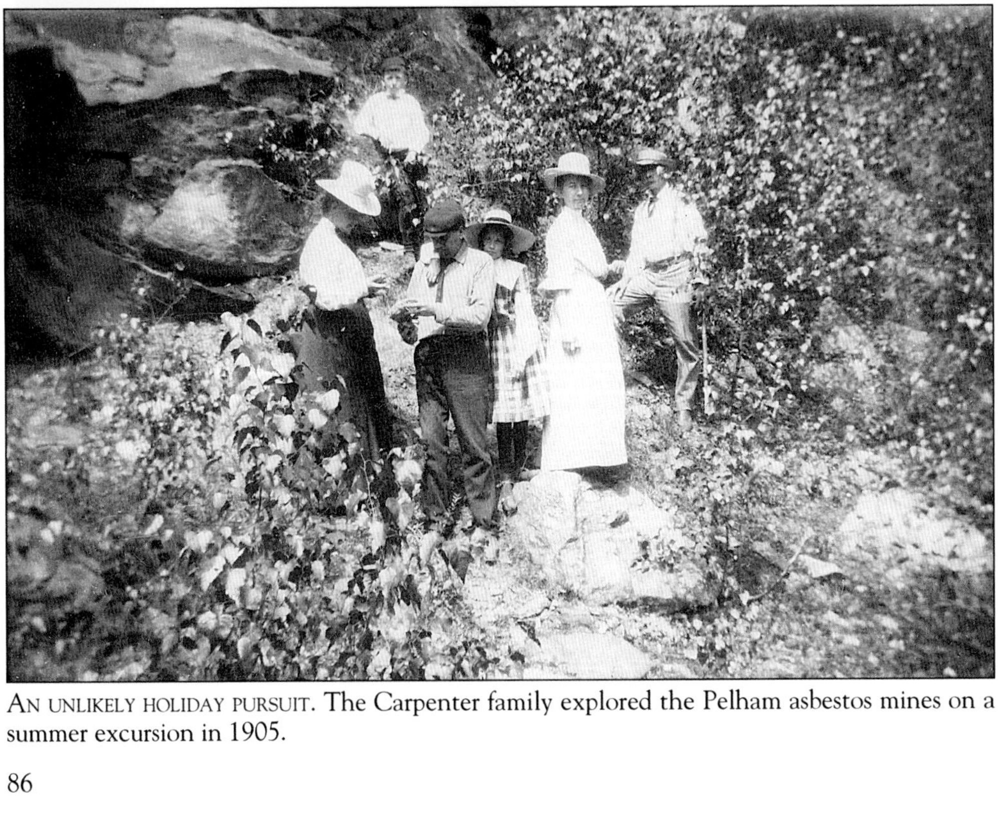

An unlikely holiday pursuit. The Carpenter family explored the Pelham asbestos mines on a summer excursion in 1905.

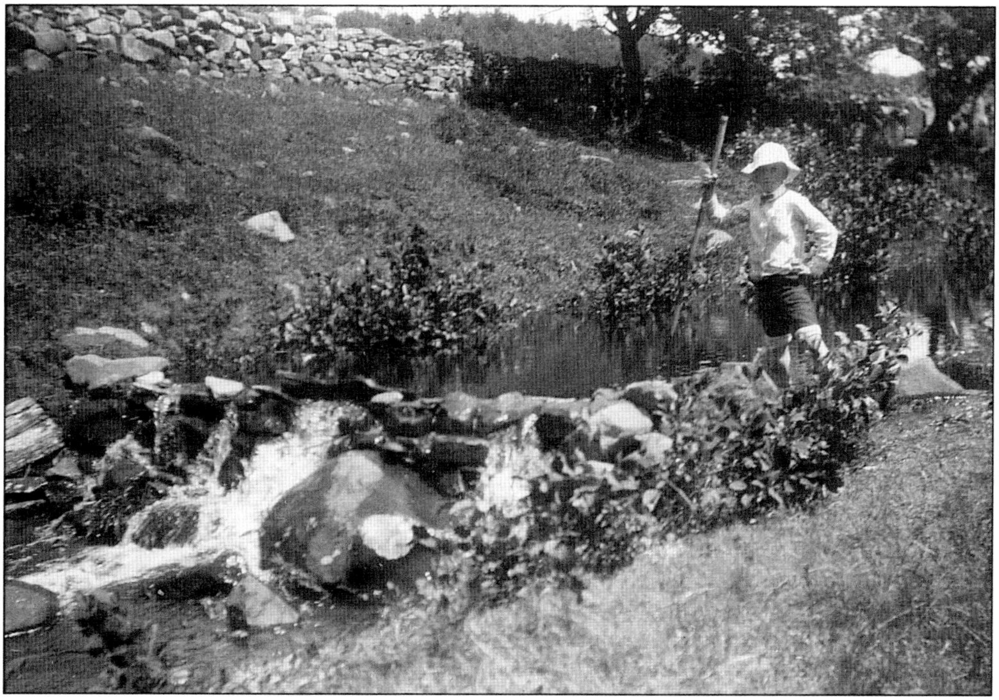

COOLING OFF IN A DAMMED BROOK—A 1905 CARPENTER FAMILY CAMPING TRIP. "There are various ways of expressing it but they all mean the same thing. The man of few words says—Hot. One a little more intense says—Very hot. The next fellow has it—Fearfully hot . . . Still another blurts out—Blarsted hot. Then there are those who prefix some very hot adjectives to the word hot, to convey how hot the hotness is." (*The Amherst Record*, July 1876.)

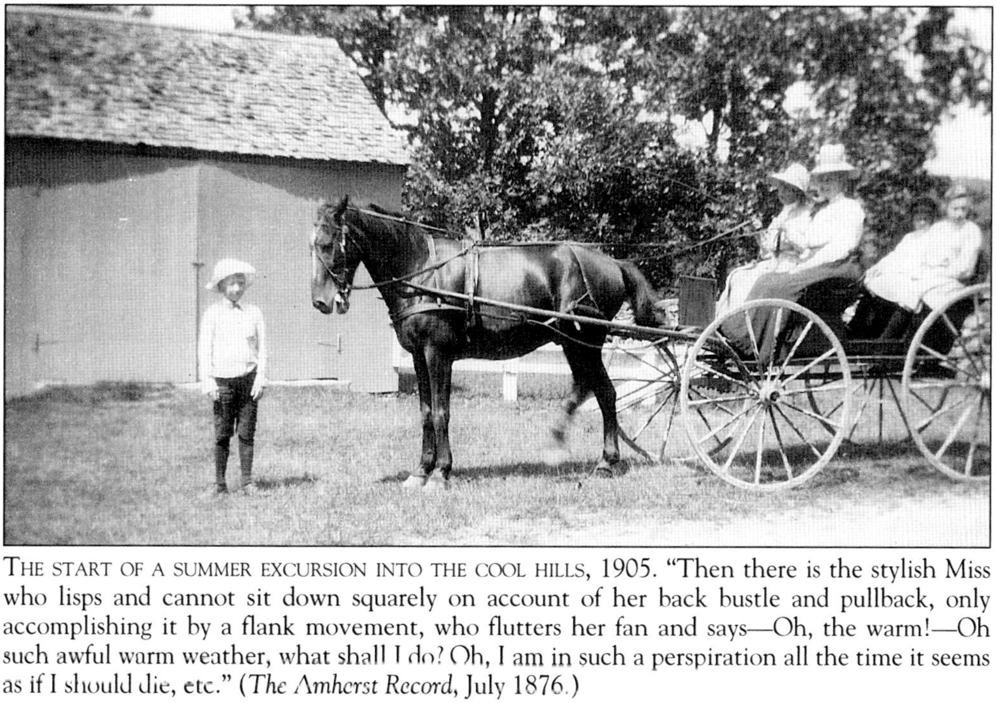

THE START OF A SUMMER EXCURSION INTO THE COOL HILLS, 1905. "Then there is the stylish Miss who lisps and cannot sit down squarely on account of her back bustle and pullback, only accomplishing it by a flank movement, who flutters her fan and says—Oh, the warm!—Oh such awful warm weather, what shall I do? Oh, I am in such a perspiration all the time it seems as if I should die, etc." (*The Amherst Record*, July 1876.)

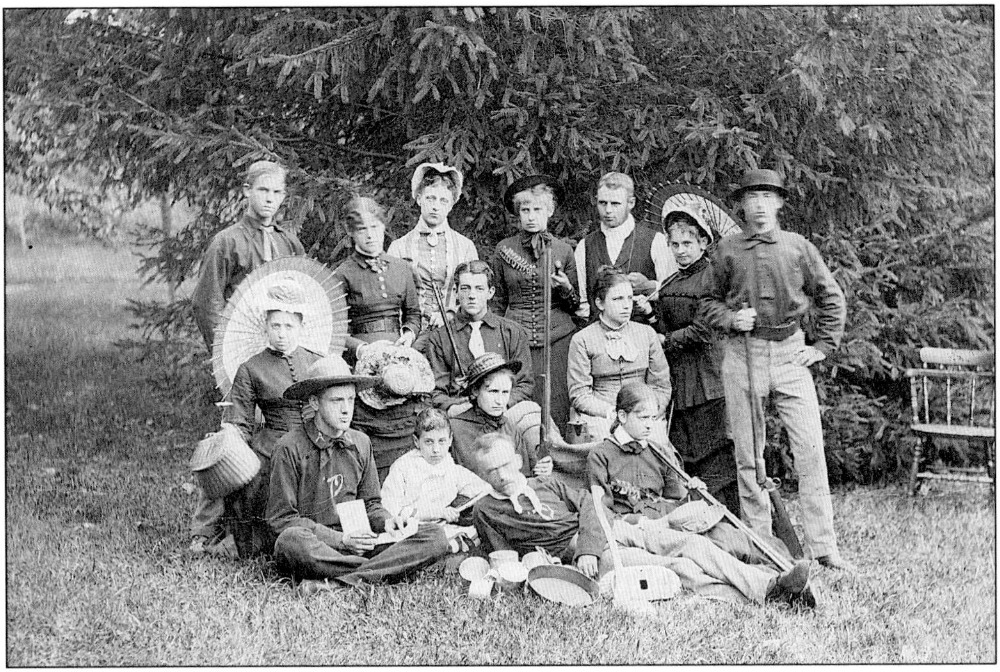

WELL-EQUIPPED. This group of Amherst campers went up to the Pelham Hills for a week in July 1879 with a full array of campers' necessities: guns, fishing tackle, an ax, cups, a frying pan, parasols, writing paper, and a wooden flute.

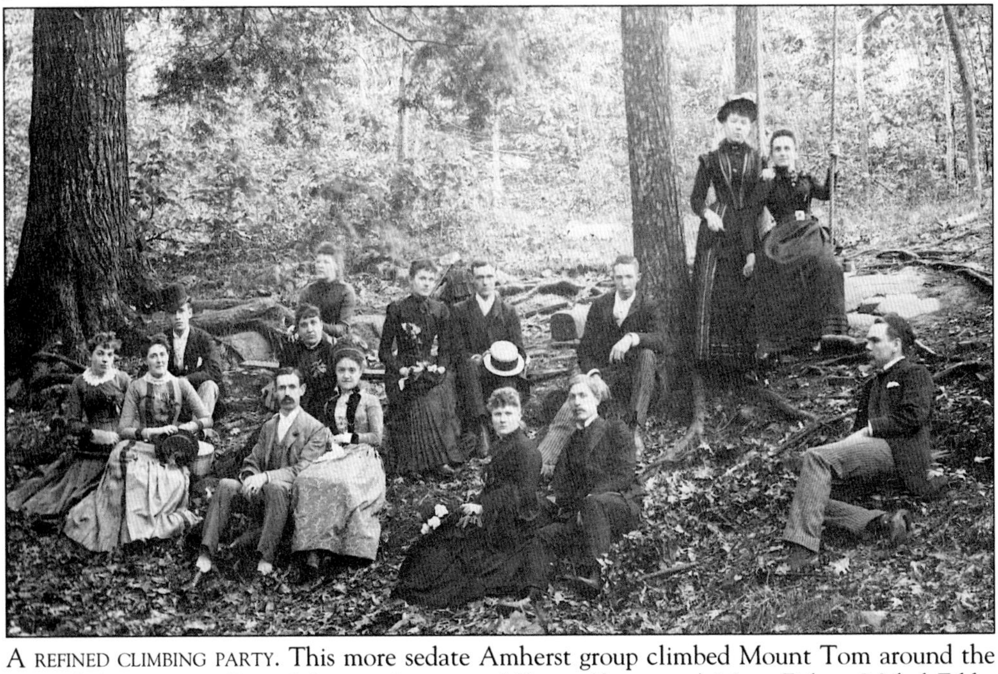

A REFINED CLIMBING PARTY. This more sedate Amherst group climbed Mount Tom around the turn of the century. From left to right are as follows: (front row) Mary Fisher, Mabel Eddy, Reverend and Mrs. Holden, Mr. and Mrs. Utley, and Charles King; (middle row) Truman Thayer, Kate Eddy, Edna McCloud, unknown, and W.A. Hyde; (back row) Harriet Wiley, Ida Fuller, and Flora Libert (on a swing).

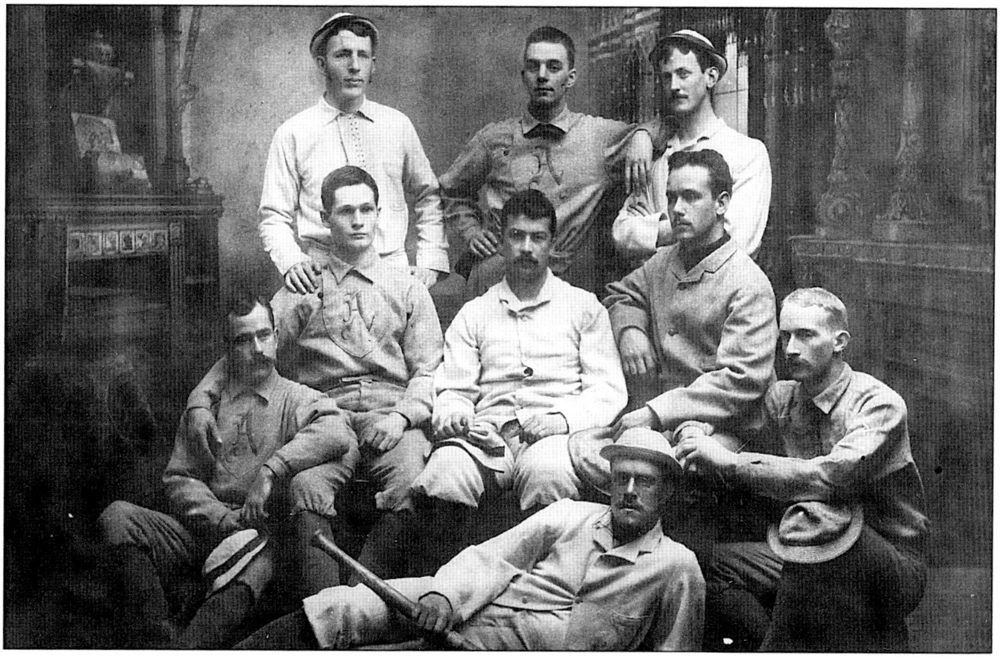

PRIDE IN SPORT. Amherst College baseball teams took the sport very seriously from early on. Both college and town erupted into riotous joy in 1886 after a famous win over Yale: "The tall man embraced the short man, the lean man the fat . . . and all tried to waltz to the fish horn racket. The fat man was hardly a thing of beauty with his hat stove in and torrents of perspiration streaming down his enflamed visage." (*The Amherst Record*, May 1886.)

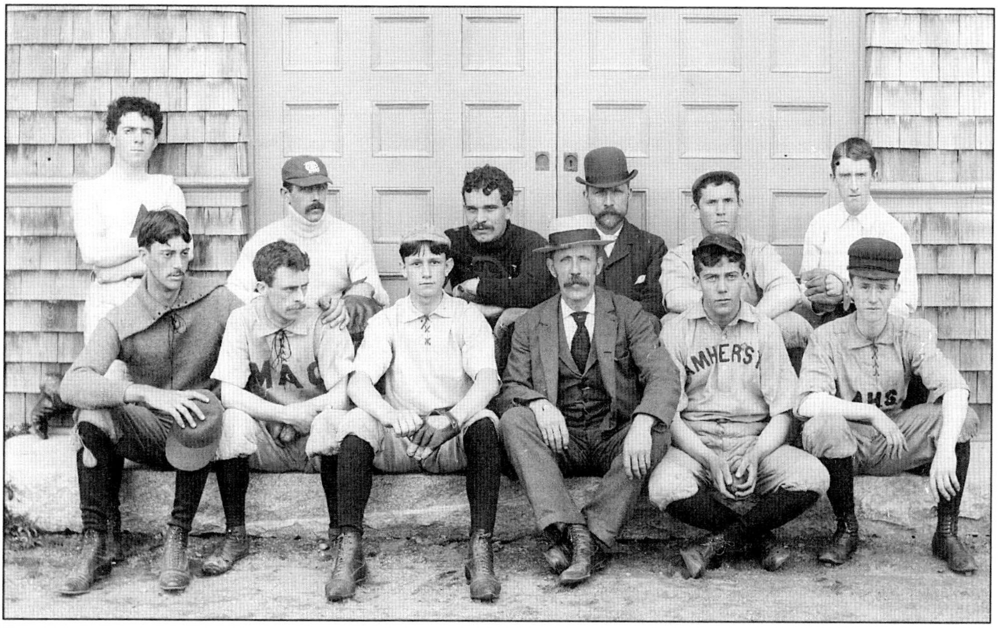

THE PHOENIX ROW BALL TEAM IN 1895. When the Merchants Row (South Pleasant Street) and Phoenix Row (Main Street) baseball teams challenged each other it was sandlot baseball at its best. The dry goods clerks, boot makers, jewelers, and druggists played one wild game each year around the Fourth of July.

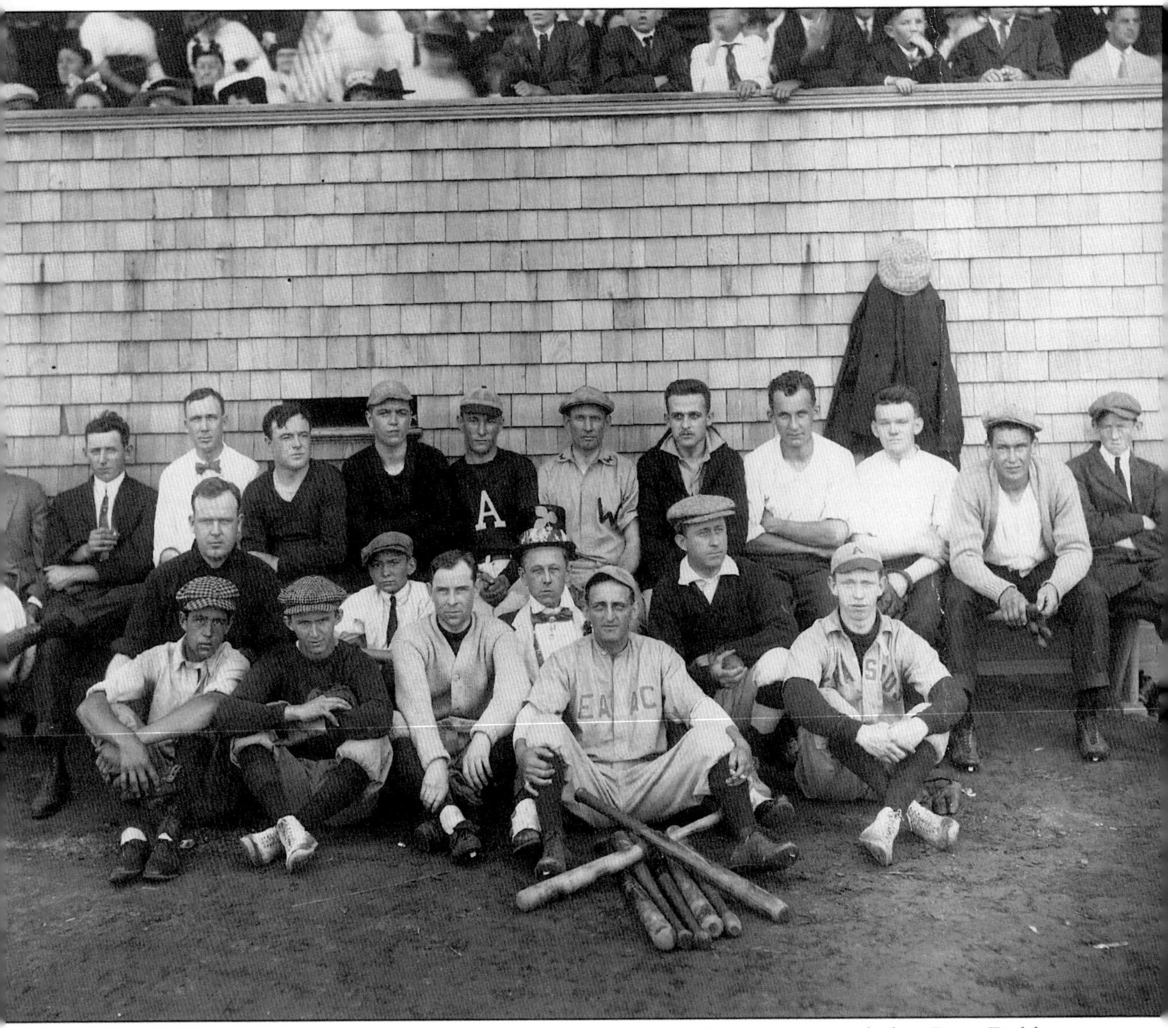

THE PHOENIX ROW AND MERCHANTS ROW BALL TEAMS, 1914. The teams were led to Pratt Field at Amherst College by the Amherst Brass Band (described as "a band possessed of good intentions but lacking in team work"). *The Amherst Record*, whose offices were on Phoenix Row, wryly described the scene: "It was a surprise to many to find how much superlative baseball talent has been loafing around Amherst and escaping the eagle eyes of the big league scouts. Phoenix Row, by the way that's where we hang out, had things pretty much its own way."

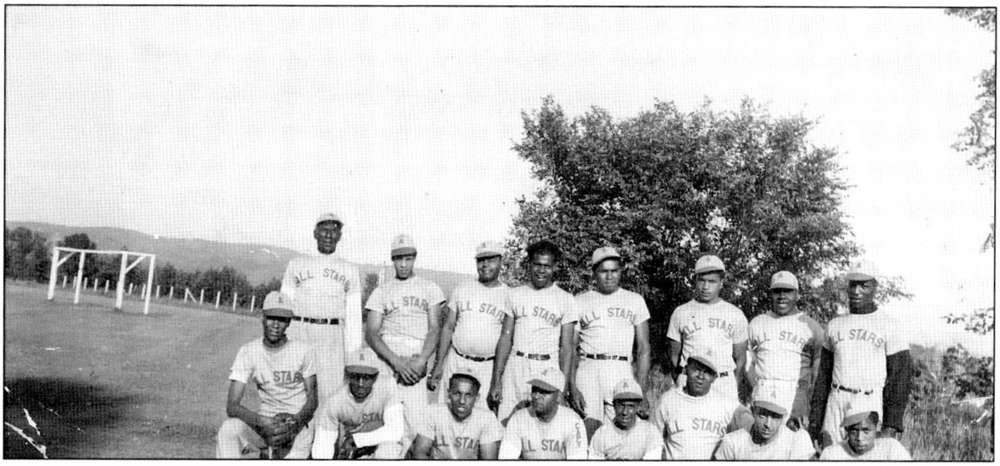

THE ALL STARS, A LOCAL AFRICAN-AMERICAN BASEBALL TEAM, ON PRATT FIELD AT AMHERST COLLEGE IN A RARE PHOTOGRAPH. From left to right they are as follows: (front row) Ray Coles, Fred Till, (?) Clark, Brownie Roberts, Louie Bias, Skinny Roberts, unknown, and Arthur Andrews; (back row) Edgar Brown (or Ned Newport), Elliot Newport, Gil Roberts, Bob Bias, Bob Bosworth, Charles Roberts, Pop Ward, and unknown.

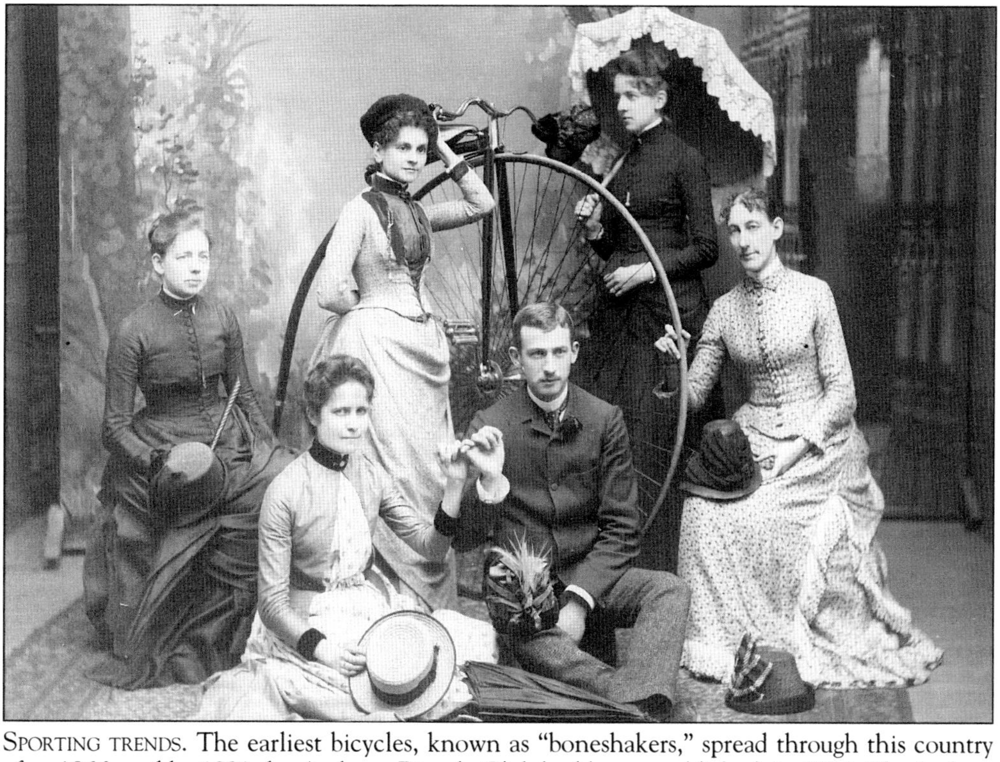

SPORTING TRENDS. The earliest bicycles, known as "boneshakers," spread through this country after 1866, and by 1881 the Amherst Bicycle Club had been established. In 1884, *The Amherst Record* noted, "Bicycling is beginning to be the rage among Amherst boys, and the last bicycle to arrive at the express office is a fine machine, coming to the order of George Cutler, Jr., and costing $150. Now George rises at 3:30 am. and takes a 'header' before any of his fellows are up." Here George links fingers with Mary Scott, surrounded by Fanny Cutler (left), Kittie Burnell, Susie Cutler, Mame Clark, and his prized cycle.

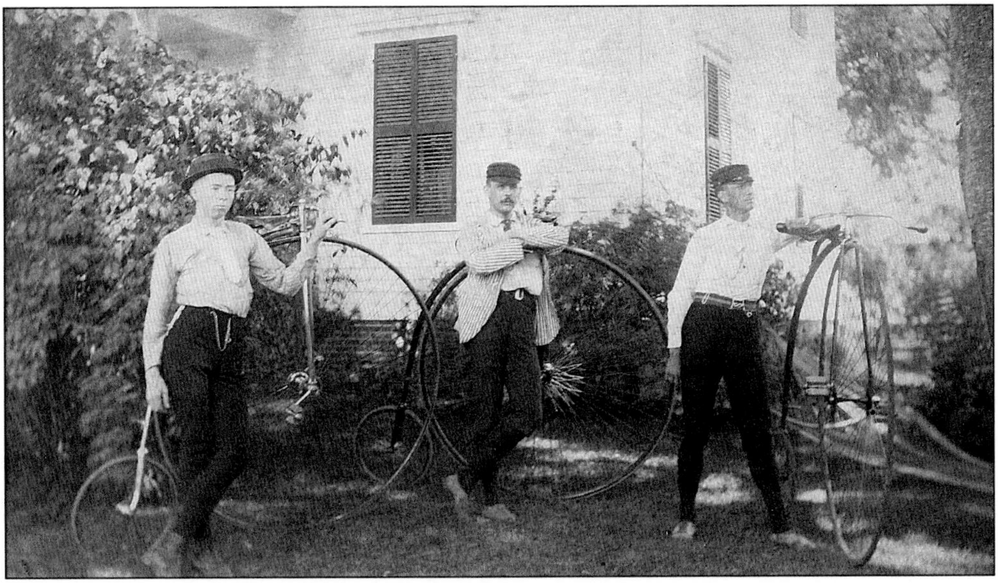

BICYCLE RACES. The Nonotuck Bicycle Club drew crowds of nearly five hundred to races held in Hampshire Park in the 1890s. The cyclists were so slow that judges put time limits on the races. In 1895, it was reported, the time limit "seemed to have no effect on the racers, for they all loafed around the track, Bugbee of Southbridge coming in first." The race was run over again because no one came in on time, but Bugbee, having just ridden the 5-mile race, refused to race again.

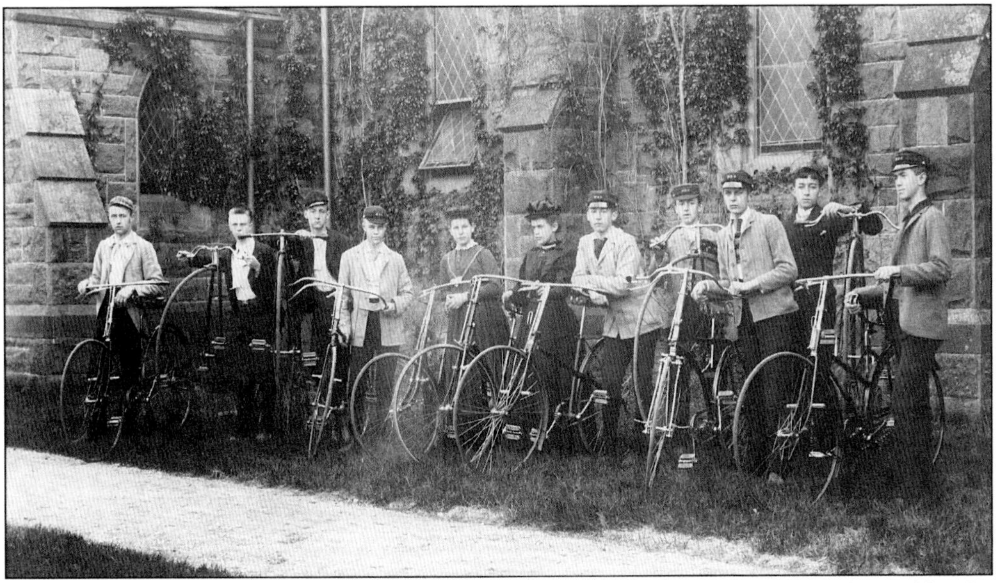

CHAOS ON THE STREETS. The local bicycle craze aggravated some and led to accidents, like the one in the following description from 1890: "A well-known citizen was traveling along the sidewalk, not many miles from the depot, when he saw a bicycle with human attachment, also on the sidewalk. The wind was abeam, but the cycle was tacking rapidly and gathering in all the sidewalk, so the pedestrian sought safety in the street; straight as a stone thrown by a cross-eyed woman at a hen the bicycle came on, struck the foot passenger amidships, and all hands went to earth with a dull thud." (*The Amherst Record*, May 1890.)

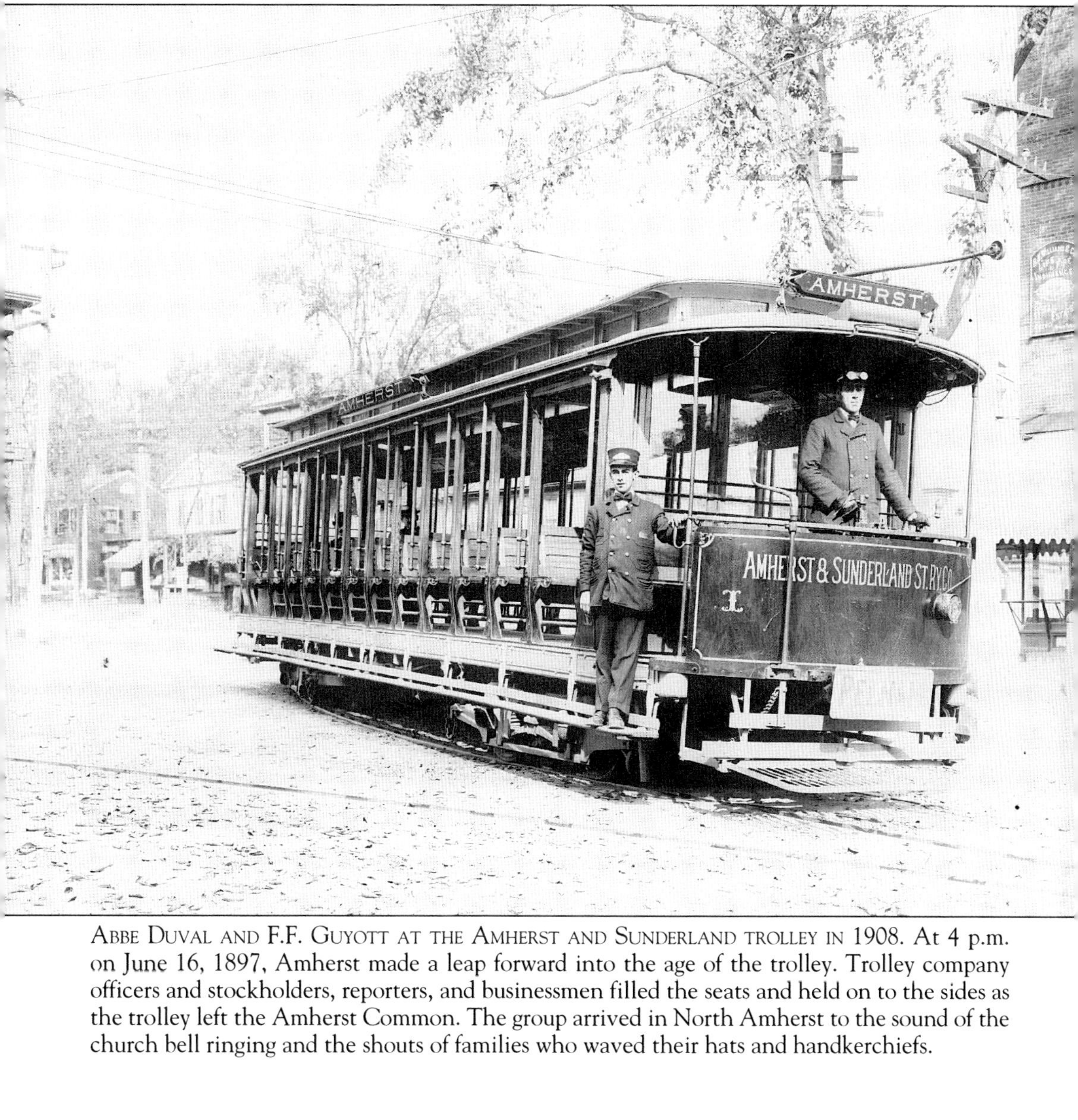

ABBE DUVAL AND F.F. GUYOTT AT THE AMHERST AND SUNDERLAND TROLLEY IN 1908. At 4 p.m. on June 16, 1897, Amherst made a leap forward into the age of the trolley. Trolley company officers and stockholders, reporters, and businessmen filled the seats and held on to the sides as the trolley left the Amherst Common. The group arrived in North Amherst to the sound of the church bell ringing and the shouts of families who waved their hats and handkerchiefs.

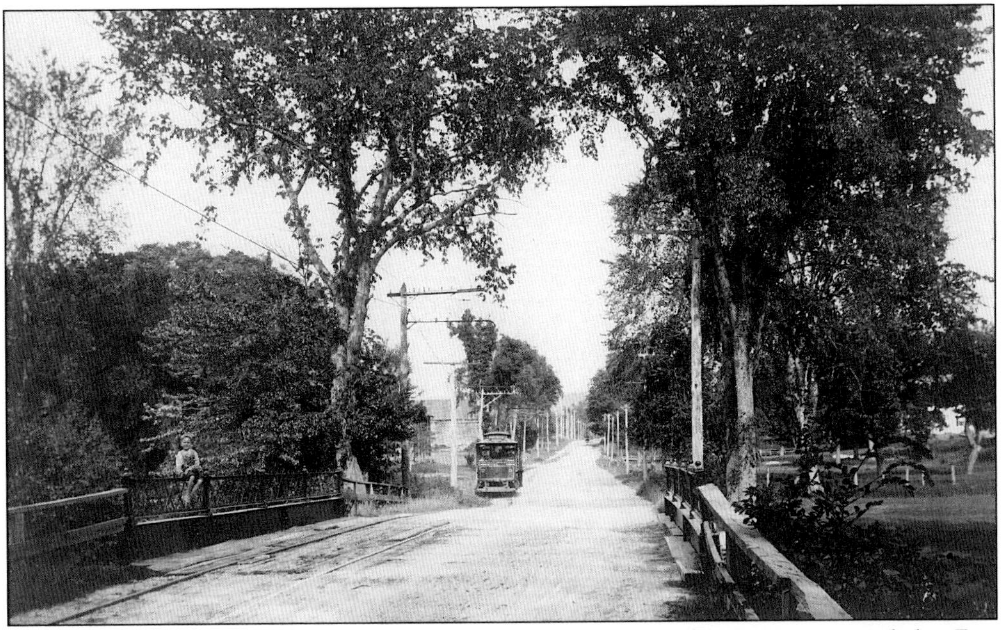

TROLLEY PASSING A BOY ON A PELHAM ROAD BRIDGE. In 1897, the trolley line was extended to East Amherst along Pelham Road. The link through Hadley to Northampton came in 1900. The ride took 45 minutes and included a crossing of the Connecticut River Bridge in large wagons.

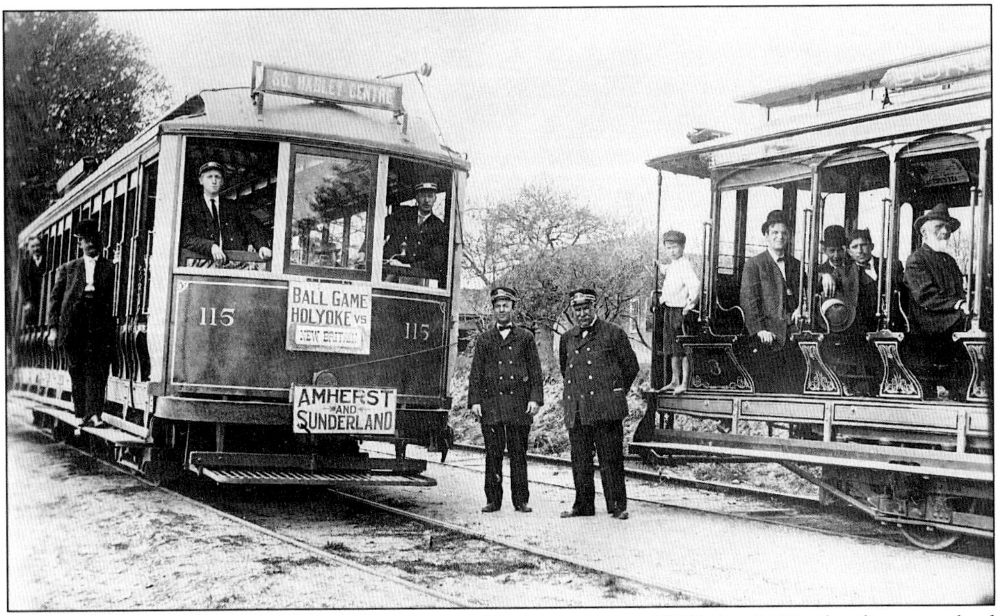

TROLLEYS CONNECTING AMHERST AND SOUTH HADLEY, AFTER 1907. In 1901 the line reached Sunderland, and the next year it was extended south to Granby. The trolley on the left advertises a baseball game between teams from Holyoke, Massachusetts, and New Britain, Connecticut.

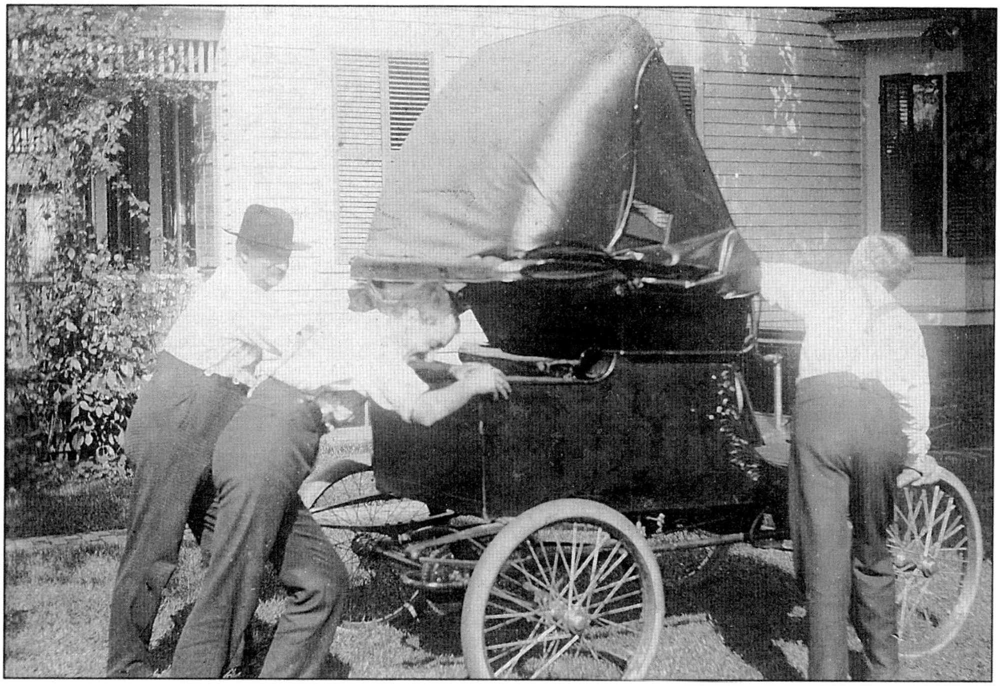

Elmer Staples and his Stanley Steamer, one of the earliest cars in the Amherst and Hadley area. By 1915 automobiles became the rage in Amherst. Over 100 were registered in that year. The *Springfield Republican* reported: "All the efforts of the Amherst Board of Health, the regular practicing physicians, and of the overseers of the poor to check the automobile fever have ignominiously failed."

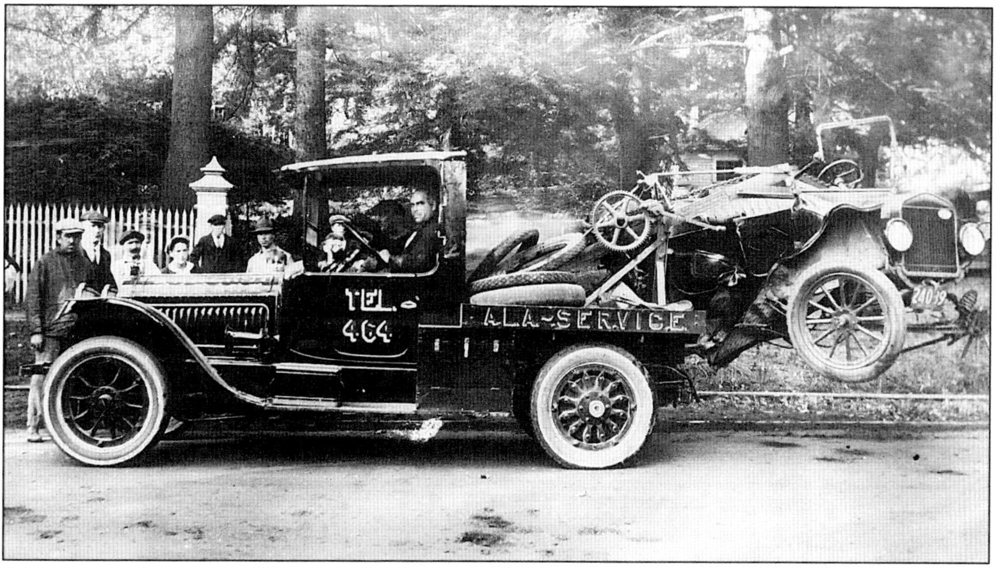

A frightening wreck. This barely recognizable car was in an accident in front of Emily Dickinson's house on Main Street in the 1920s. In 1914, *The Amherst Record* noted, "The auto, since coming into general use, has acquired a deserved reputation as a remarkably efficient agency in keeping down the surplus of population. Both to the man in the body of the car and the man who gets in front of it the auto is an agent of swift destruction."

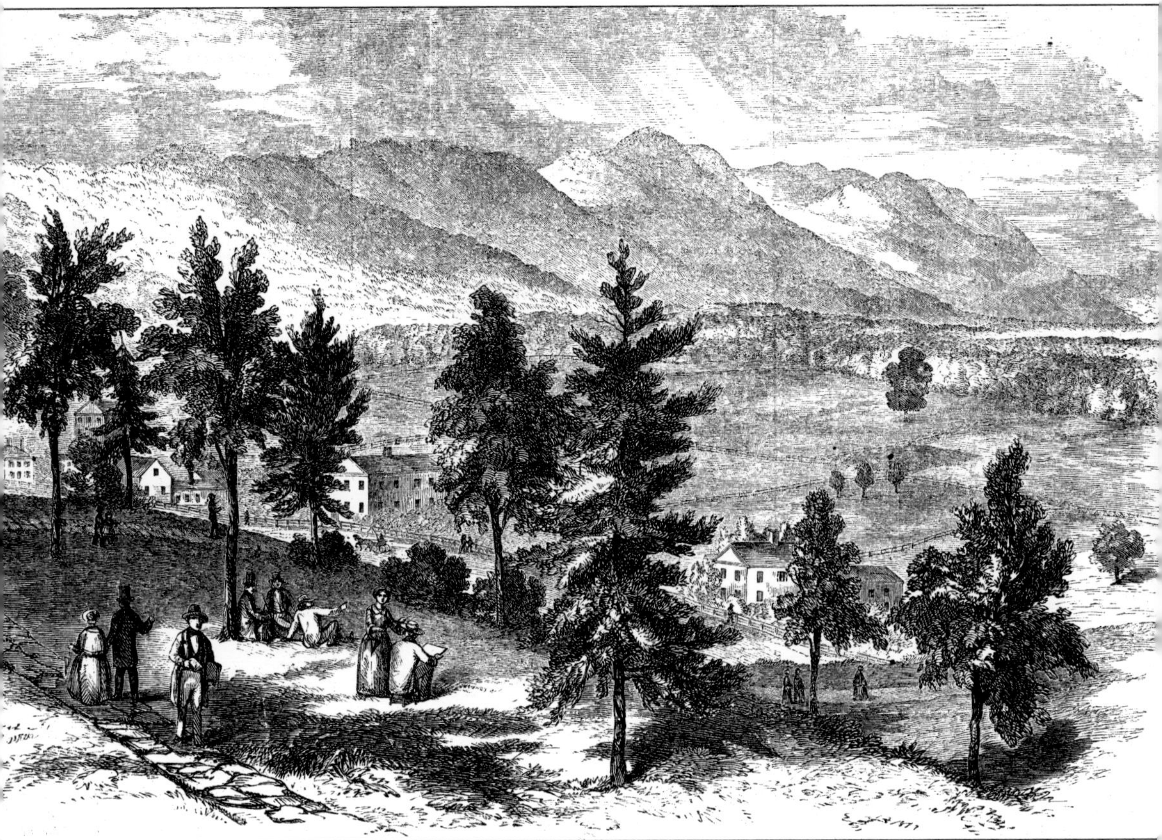

ENGRAVING OF THE VALLEY FROM AMHERST COLLEGE TO THE HOLYOKE RANGE, C. 1855. "After spending three days very pleasantly at Mrs Shepard's [in Amherst], among orators, botanists, mineralogists, & above all, Ministers, I set off on Friday Morning with Thos Greenough & another little cousin in a chaise to visit Mount Holyoke. . . . The prospect repays the ascent and although the day was hot & hazy so as to preclude a distant prospect, yet all the broad meadows in the immediate vicinity of the mountain through which the Connecticutt winds, make a beautiful picture seldom rivalled." (Ralph Waldo Emerson's journals, August 4, 1823.)

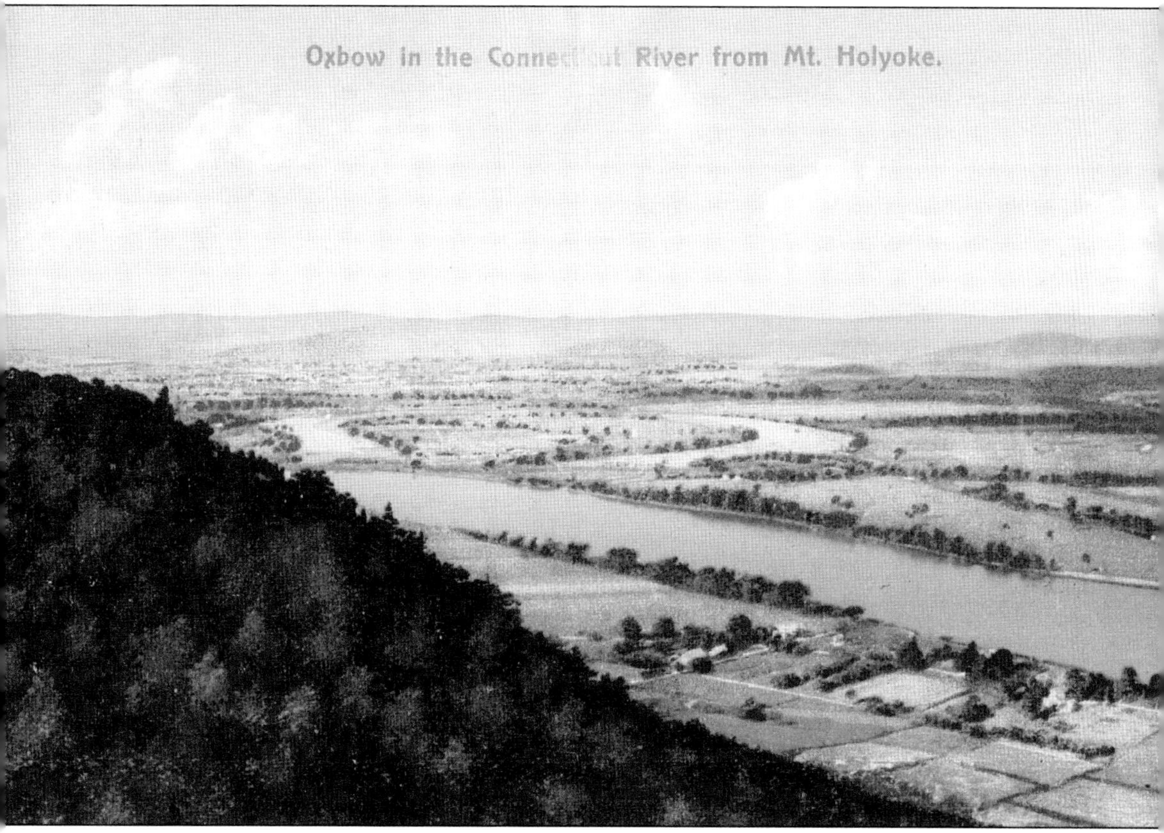

Above the Oxbow

Here in this valley of discreet academies
We have not mountains, but mounts, truncated hillocks
To the Adirondacks, to northern Monadnock
Themselves mere rocky hillocks to an Everest.
Still, they're our best mustering of height: by
Comparison with the sunken silver-grizzled
Back of the Connecticut, the river-level
Flats of Hadley farms, they're lofty enough
Elevations to be called something more than hills.
Green, wholly green, they stand their knobby spine
Against our sky . . .
They mound a summer coolness in our view . . .

—Sylvia Plath, *The Collected Poems of Sylvia Plath*, p. 87.
(New York: HarperCollins, 1959.)

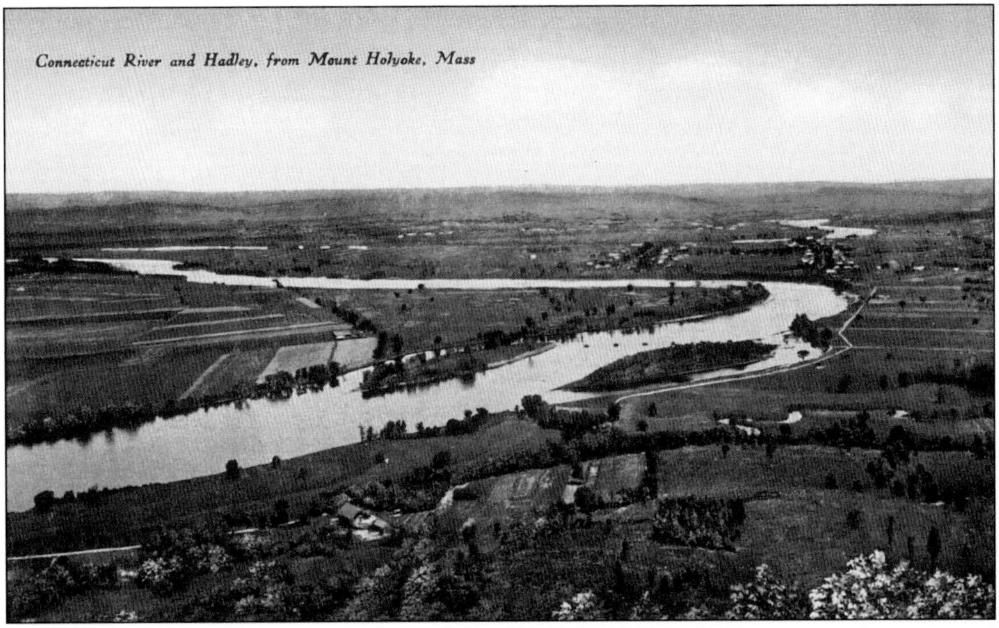

"After adding our names in the books to the long list of strangers whom curiosity has attracted to this hill we descended in safety without encountering rattlesnakes or viper that have given so bad fame to the place. We were informed that about 40 people ascend the mountain every fair day during the summer. After passing through Hadley meadows, I took leave of my companions at Northampton bridge, and crossed for the first time the far famed Yankee river." (Ralph Waldo Emerson's journals, August 4, 1823.)

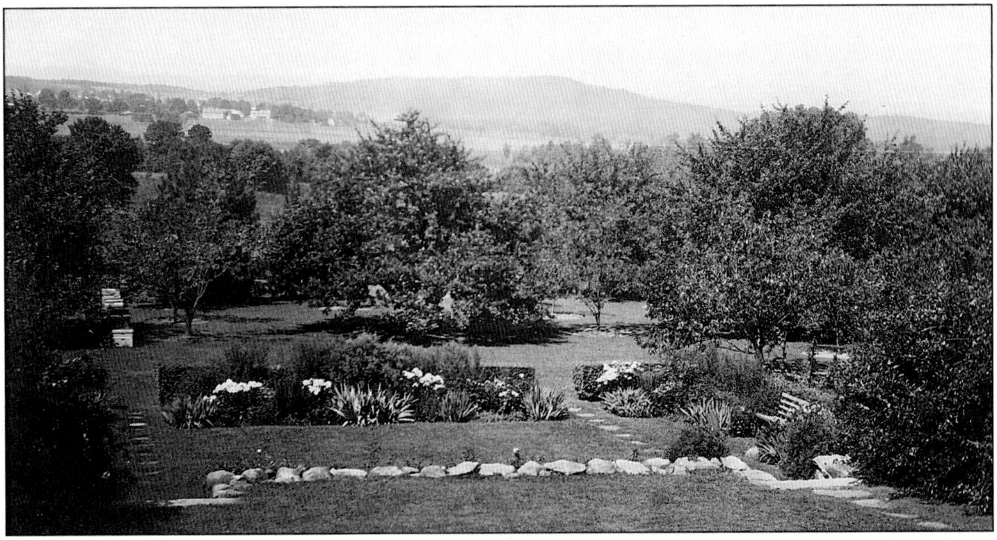

MOUNT WARNER FROM DAVID GRAYSON'S GARDEN. "These long quiet summer days I have been much alone. . . . I walk alone across the fields, I climb Mt. Warner and sit in the still woods, I tramp onward to the wide meadow above the Hadley ponds and sit there on the hillside . . . the white steeple of the church and the roofs of the little town among the foliage. The tobacco cutters are at work in the fields below me. It seems to me I want now to be quiet for a century or so to consider all the things I have ever seen." (David Grayson, *The Countryman's Year*, August 28.)

Four

Autumn

"We go to sleep with the peach in our hand and wake with the stone, but the stone is the pledge of summers to come."

—Emily Dickinson

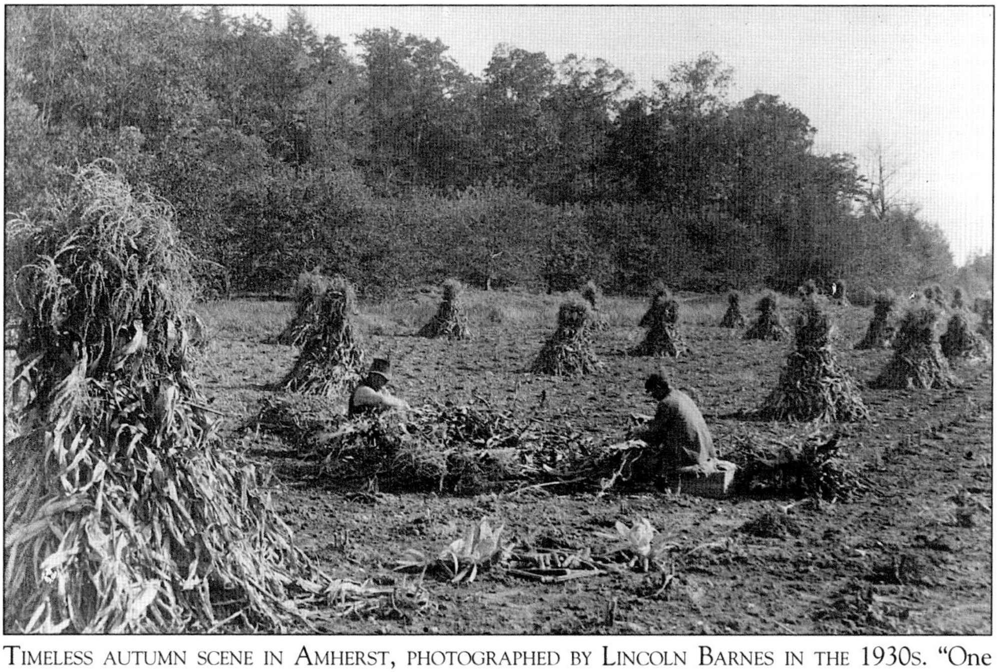

TIMELESS AUTUMN SCENE IN AMHERST, PHOTOGRAPHED BY LINCOLN BARNES IN THE 1930S. "One perfect October week-end, with sunshine and clear cool air, the best New England knows, I visited an old and dear college friend . . . in Amherst. On Saturday afternoon we climbed to the top of Mount Lincoln. The leaves were in their full autumn coloring, chestnut burrs were opening and the nuts were falling. Men in the little fields were beginning to husk their corn." (Ray Stannard Baker, *American Chronicle*, p. 289.)

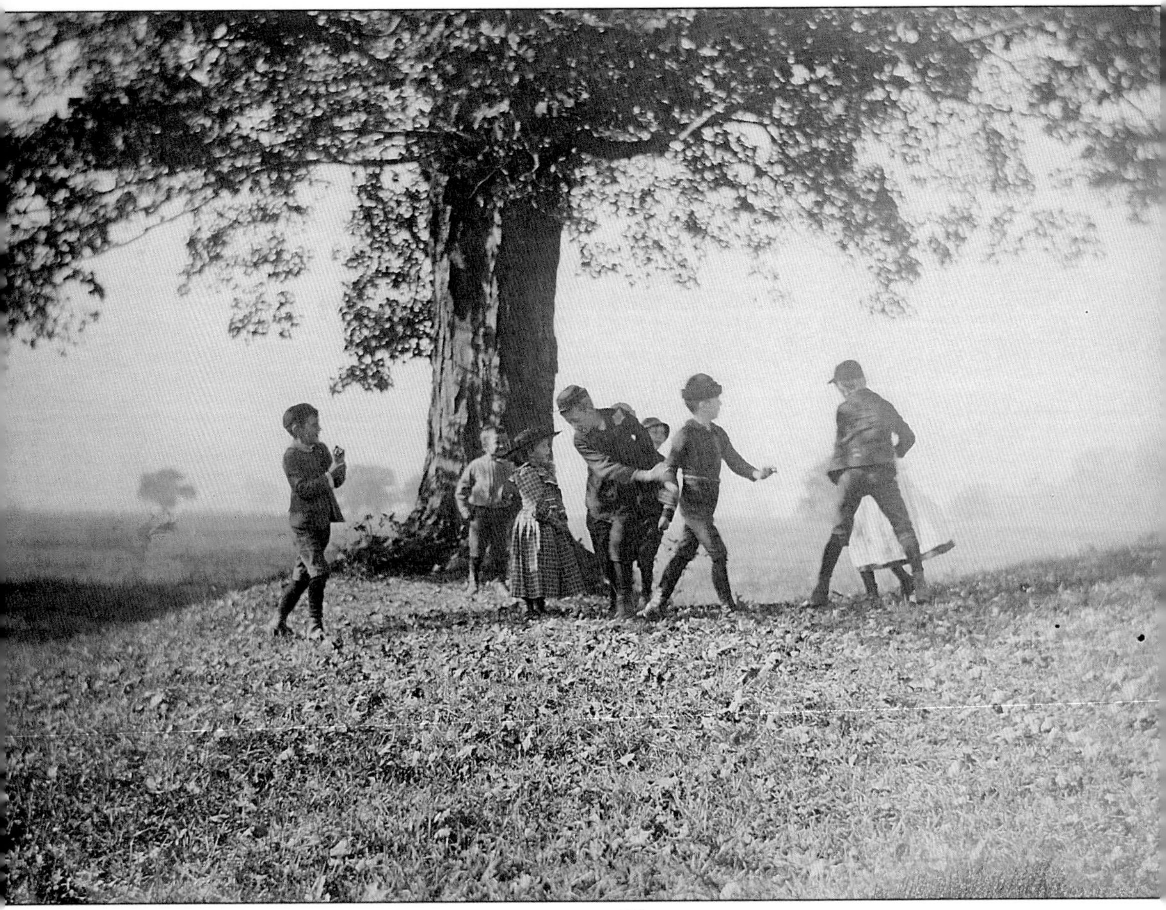

A CLIFTON JOHNSON SCENE OF CHILDREN PLAYING IN HADLEY AS SUMMER TURNS TO AUTUMN IN THE 1890S.

. . . like late revellers at dawn, the chance
of one sweet, mad, last hour, all things assail,
And conquering, flush and spin; while, to enhance
The spell, by sunset door, wrapped in a veil
Of red and purple mists, the summer, pale,
Steals back alone for one more song and dance.

—Amherst poet Helen Hunt Jackson's *Verses by H.H.*, p. 84.
(Boston: Roberts Brothers, 1873.)

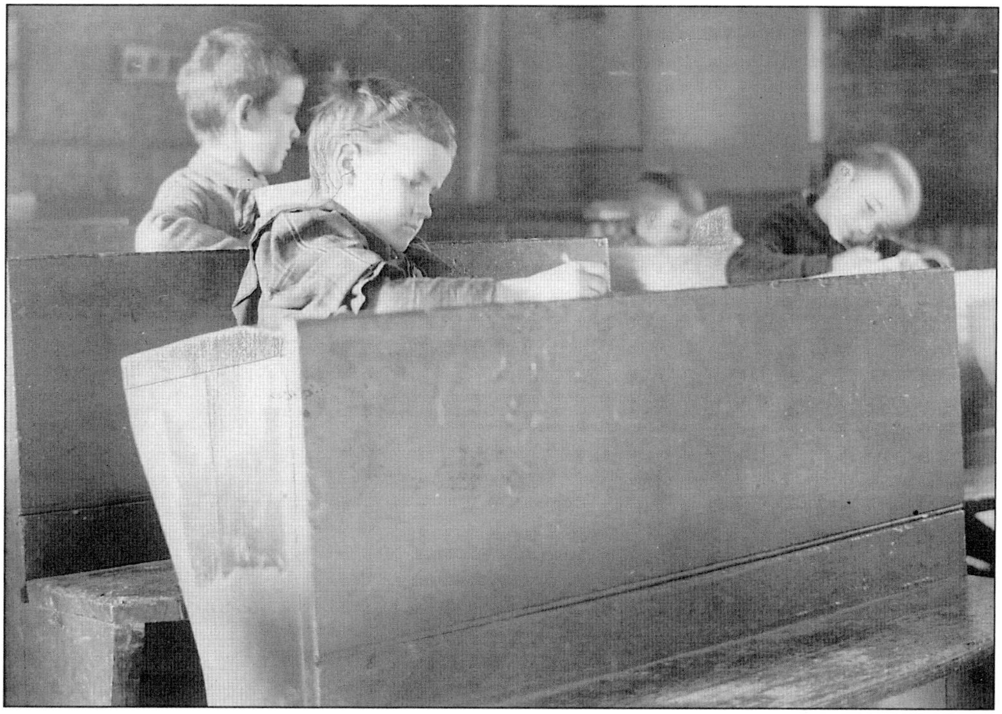

SCHOOLBOY PHOTOGRAPHED IN THE 1890S BY CLIFTON JOHNSON IN THE HOCKANUM SCHOOL IN HADLEY.

Farm Boy after Summer

A seated statue of himself he seems.
A bronze slowness becomes him. Patently
The page he contemplates he doesn't see.

The lesson, the long lesson, has been summer.
His mind holds summer as his skin holds sun.
For once the homework, all of it, was done.

What were the crops, where were the fiery fields
Where for so many days so many hours
The sun assaulted him with glittering showers?

Expect a certain absence in his presence.
Expect all winter long a summer scholar,
For scarcely all its snows can cool that color.

—Robert Francis, *Collected Poems*. p. 184.
(Amherst: University of Massachusetts Press, 1976.)

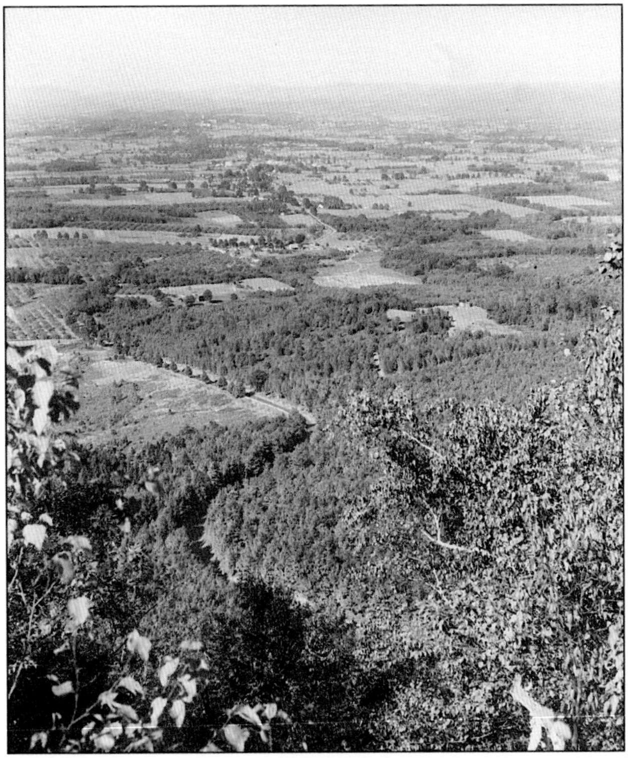

A Donald Lacroix photograph of Amherst farmland from the Holyoke Range. "What a good time of the year is this. The fat land! I spent much of the afternoon and evening gathering peaches, plums and pears, some as fine as ever I saw—ripe from the trees. I brought in a large sample basket containing the best of the Carman peaches . . . ripe Bartlett pears, purple plums, bunches of grapes . . . a few McIntosh apples . . . and two fine muskmelons . . ." (David Grayson, *The Countryman's Year*, September 2.)

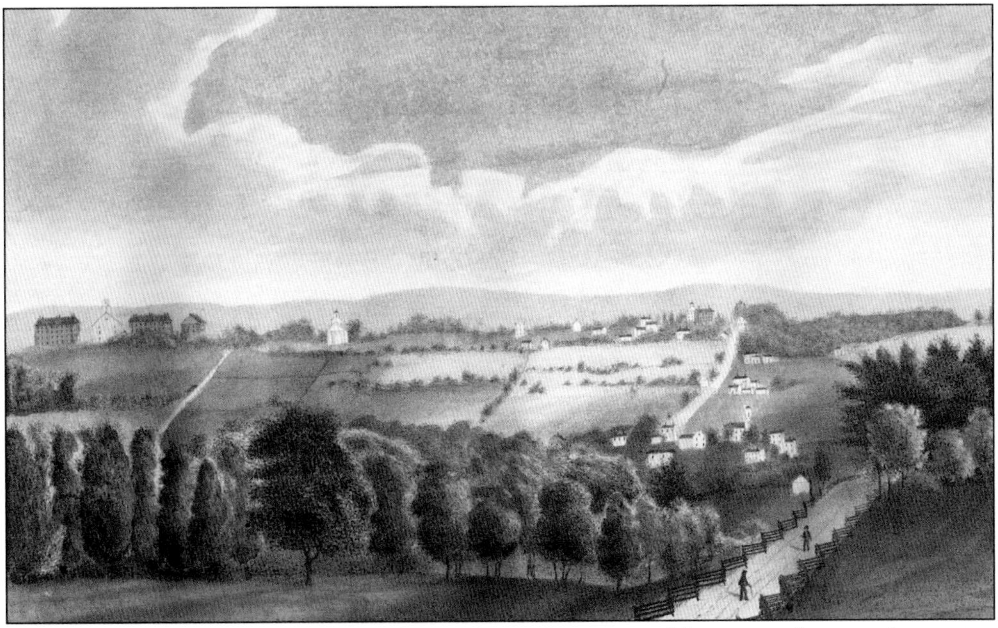

Amherst in autumn about 1833, by Orra White Hitchcock. "Autumn coloring is beginning to show. The elms grow rusty, and the nut trees, but the clematis blooms white by the wall, asters and goldenrod color the countryside, last fading proof of summer. There is such a thing—I have heard of it—as living too long or too much. I do not believe it." (David Grayson, *The Countryman's Year*, Sept. Sunday.)

SO PASSES THE GLORY OF SUMMER. Autumn witnessed a major change in the valley, as local schools opened and students from across the country returned to the colleges. Jennie Cowles is seen on the steps of the Amity Street Grammar School with her class in this stereoscopic print.

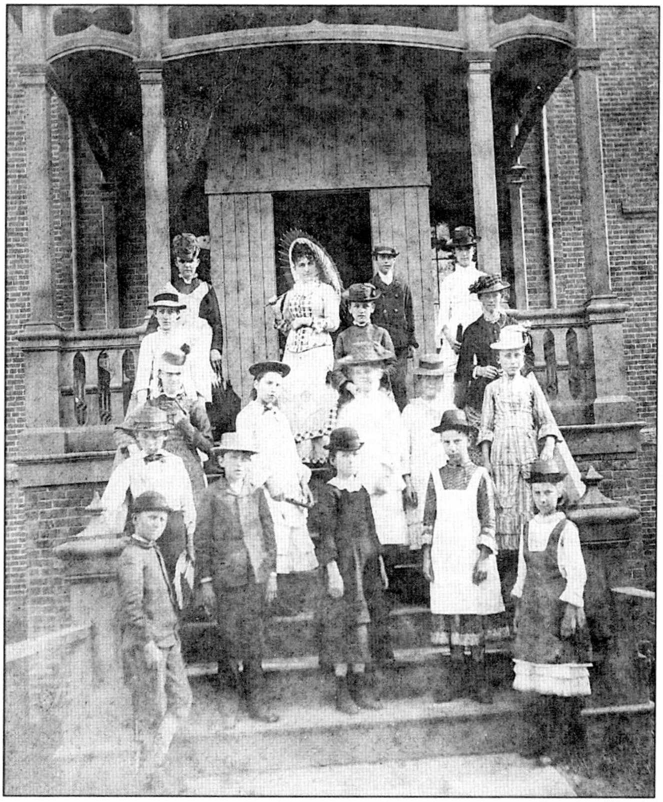

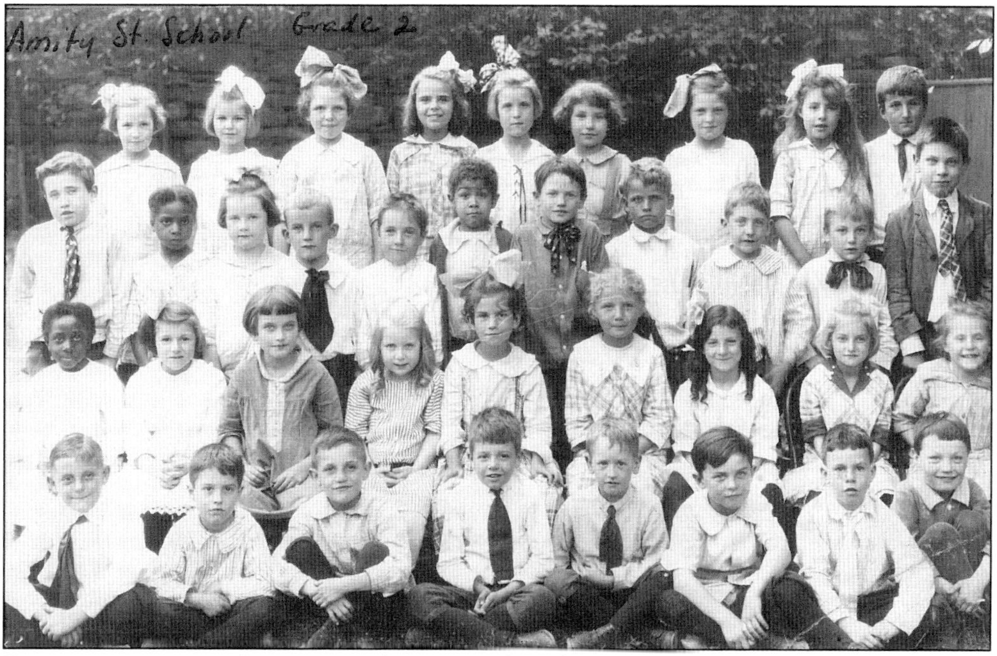

THE CYCLE CONTINUES. A generation later, second-graders pose at the same school in 1915.

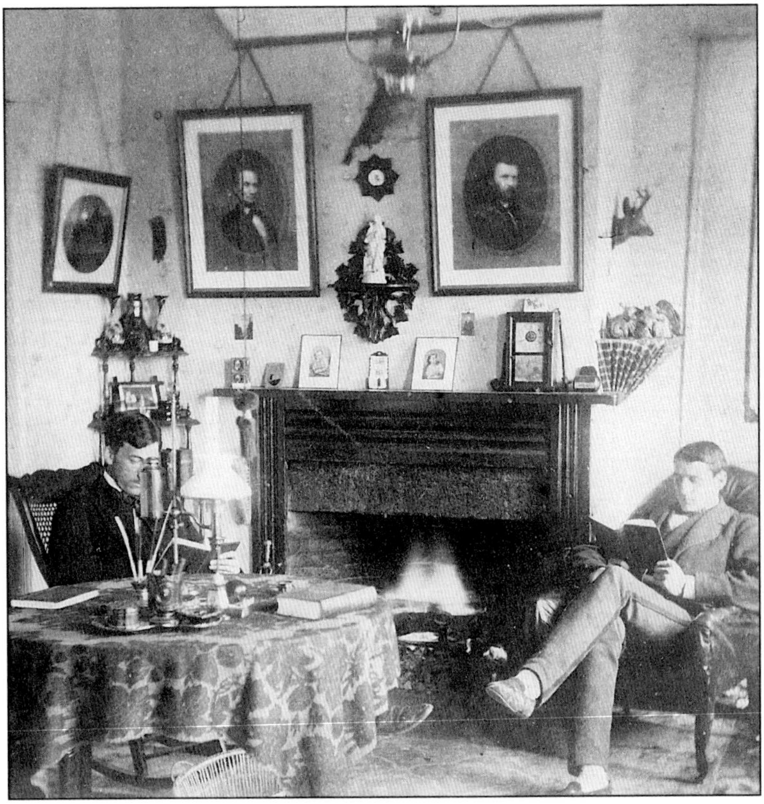

AMHERST COLLEGE STUDENTS OF THE CLASS OF 1869. Julius Sanderson and Henry Field study by the fire of their comfortable Victorian dorm room.

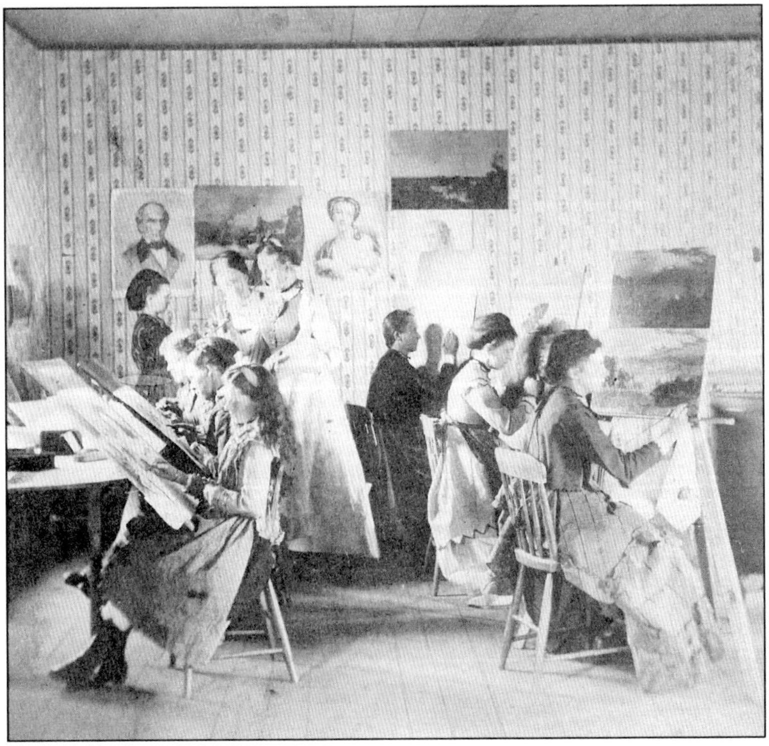

A GIRLS' ART CLASS. Private schools, both small and large, abounded in the valley. John Lovell, one of Amherst's earliest photographers, captured these girls as they painted by the warmth of a wood stove.

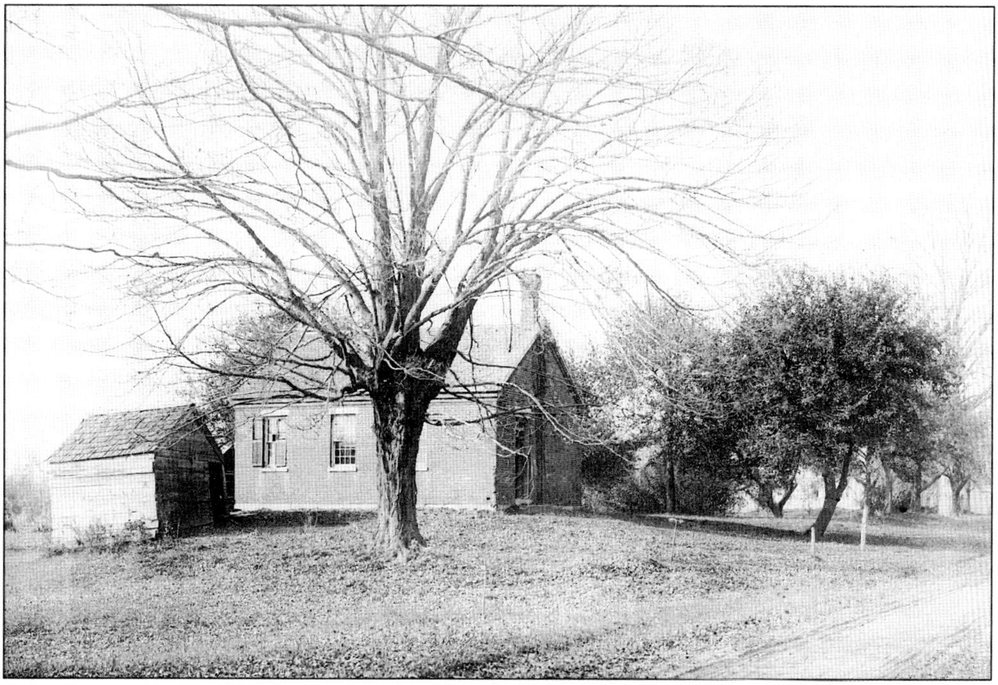

THE HOCKANUM SCHOOL IN HADLEY. "Midway on the single north and south road stood the weather-worn little school building. A narrow, open yard, worn bare of grass for a space about the doorstep, separated the schoolhouse from the dusty road. At one end of the building a big apple tree partly shadowed it. At the other end was a lean-to shed where the wood for the fire was stored." (Clifton Johnson, *The Country School*. New York: Thomas Y. Crowell & Co., 1907, p. 43.)

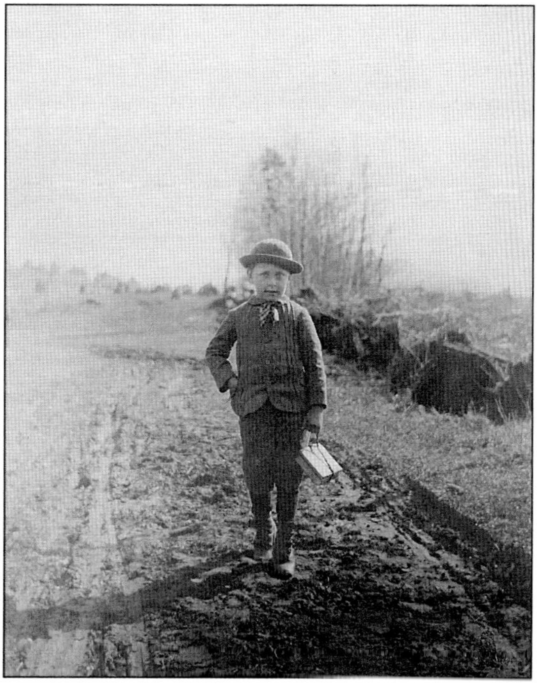

A BOY AND HIS SCHOOLBOOKS ON A MUDDY ROAD TO THE HOCKANUM SCHOOL. Noah Webster, who lived in Amherst from 1812 to 1822, wrote the blue-backed speller used in most schools. "The speller also served as a reader. The first and simplest reading started with, 'No man may put off the law of God.' Farther on were some little stories and fables, accompanied by a few rude pictures. Lastly came the Moral Catechism, starting with the question, 'Is pride commendable?'" (Clifton Johnson, *The Country School*. New York: Thomas Y. Crowell & Co., 1907, p. 10.)

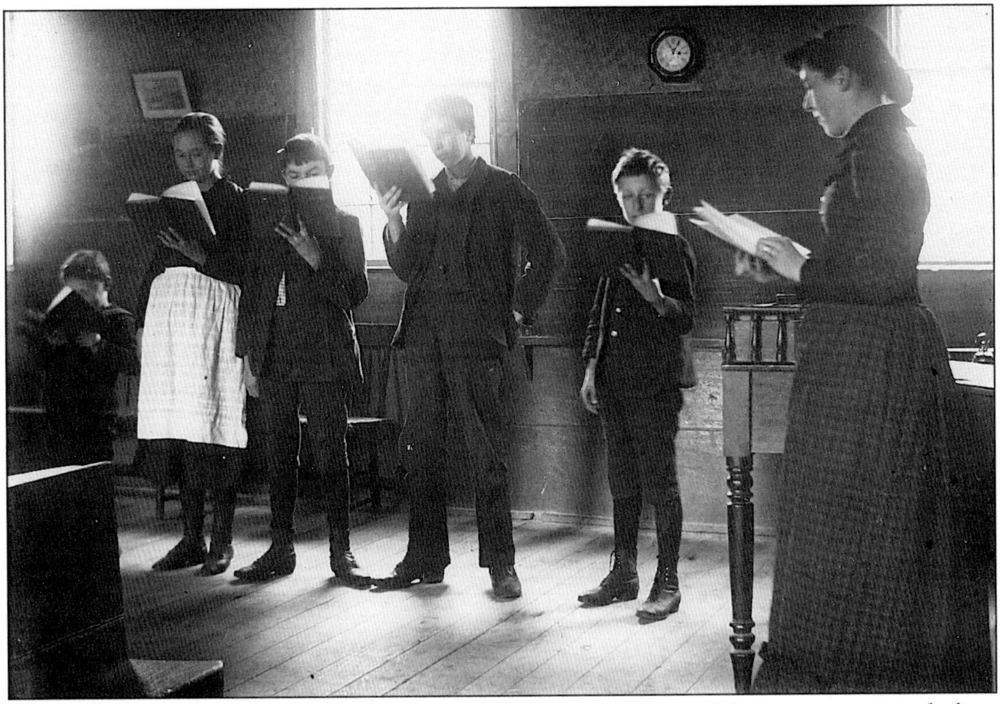

An 1890s image of the Hockanum School, by Clifton Johnson. "The more mature scholars, though almost men and women in size, were no older than fourteen or fifteen. As a rule they left school for good at that age, but a few would attend an academy, and now and then a boy would fit himself for college by studying with the minister." (Clifton Johnson, *The Country School.* New York: Thomas Y. Crowell & Co., 1907, p. 10.)

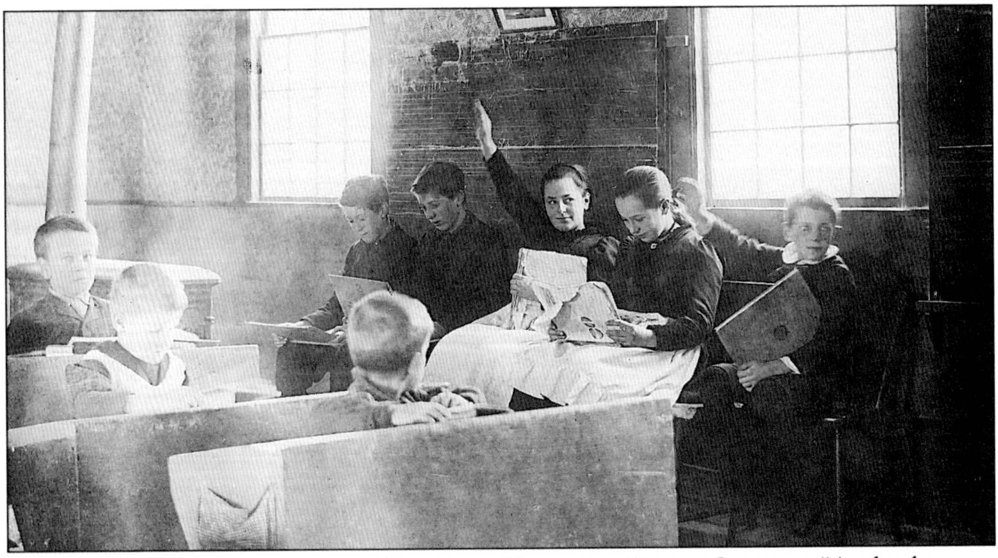

An 1890s geography lesson at the Hockanum School, by Clifton Johnson. "As the day wore on, the weather grew colder; the wind came up and rattled the loose clapboards, and whistled about the eaves and chimney-mouth, and made the branches of the trees back of the schoolhouse sway and shiver." (Clifton Johnson, *The Country School.* New York: Thomas Y. Crowell & Co., 1907, p. 17.)

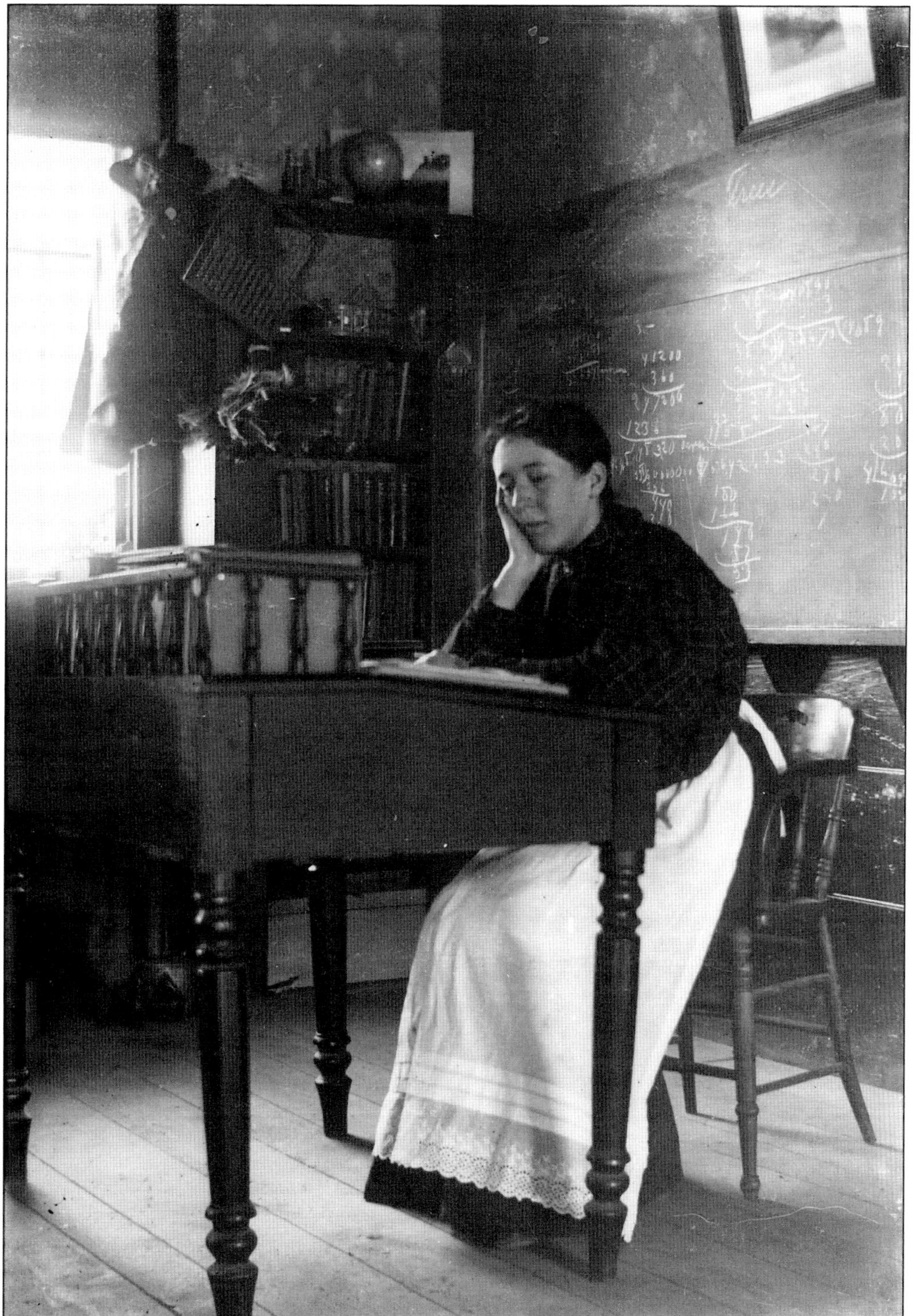

AFTER A HARD DAY'S WORK. This portrait of tired schoolteacher Anna McQueston was taken by Clifton Johnson at the Hockanum School. Johnson and McQueston married in 1896.

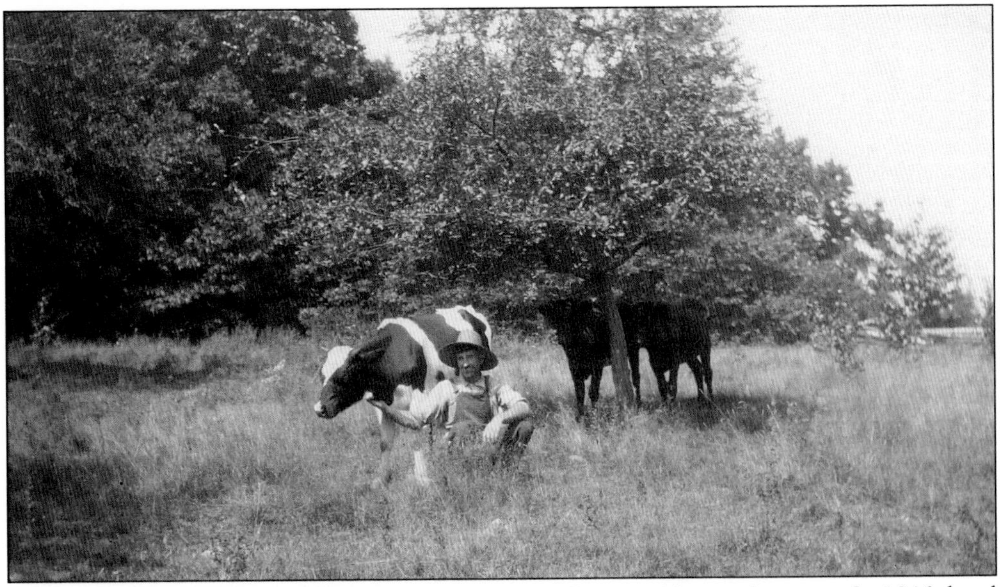

CATTLE ON HERBERT DICKINSON'S FARM ON MONTAGUE ROAD IN NORTH AMHERST. In 1846, local farmers held one of the first cattle shows in the area. It was described as "one of the greatest, if not the greatest, display of cattle ever exhibited in Hampshire County." (*The Hampshire and Franklin Express*, Sept. 1846.) The Amherst Common held 144 yoke of cattle and 40 horses. More than one hundred people sat for dinner at the Amherst House and organized the East Hampshire Agricultural Society.

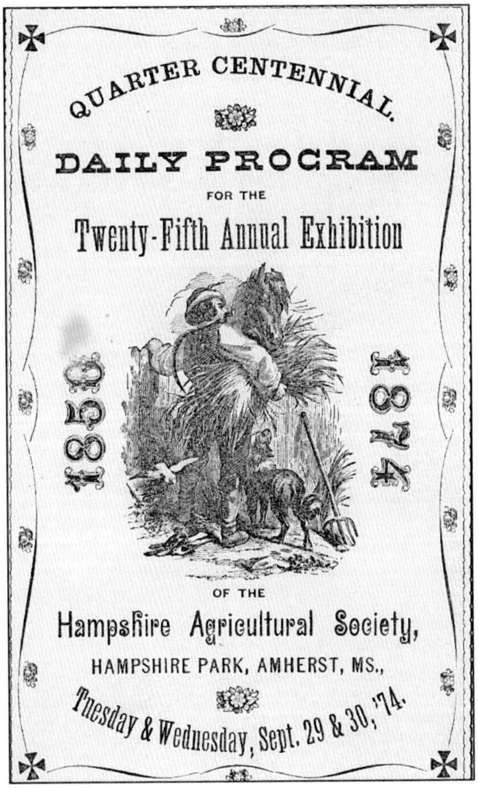

AGRICULTURAL COMPETITION. In October of 1856, Emily Dickinson's rye and Indian bread won second prize at the annual cattle show. In 1866, the East Hampshire Agricultural Society dedicated Hampshire Park, which comprised 16 acres on the Belchertown Road. Local bands "discoursed sweet music at different times throughout the day." Oxen, horses, poultry, products of the harvest, and baked goods competed for ribbons.

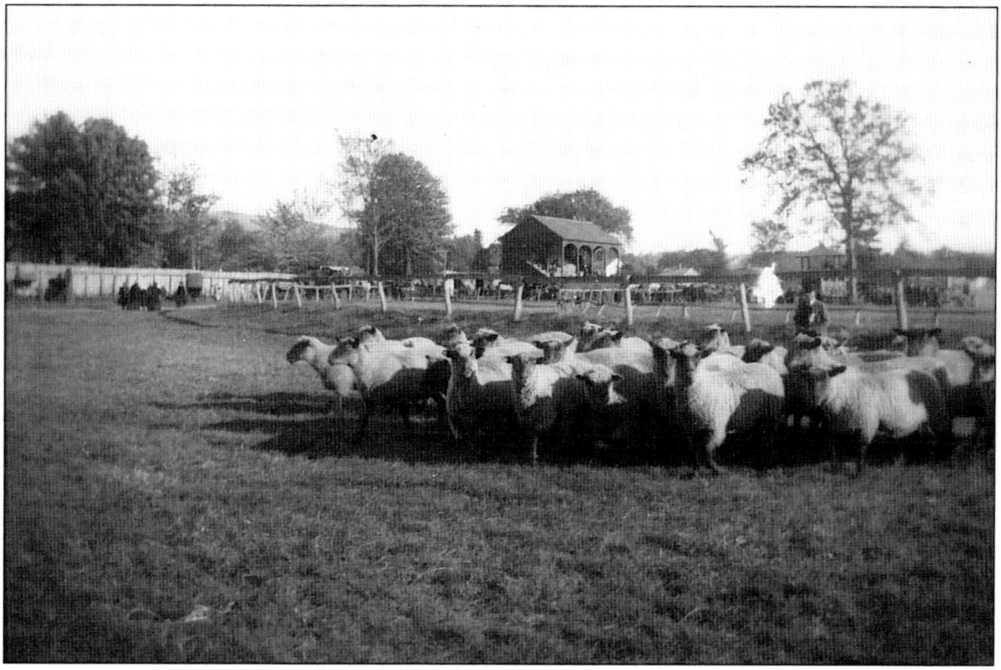

HAMPSHIRE PARK ON THE BELCHERTOWN ROAD, DURING THE CATTLE SHOW OF ABOUT 1898. By the 1890s the great cattle shows declined. Horse racing and entertainment like "Gorman's Wonderful Educated Horses" took over.

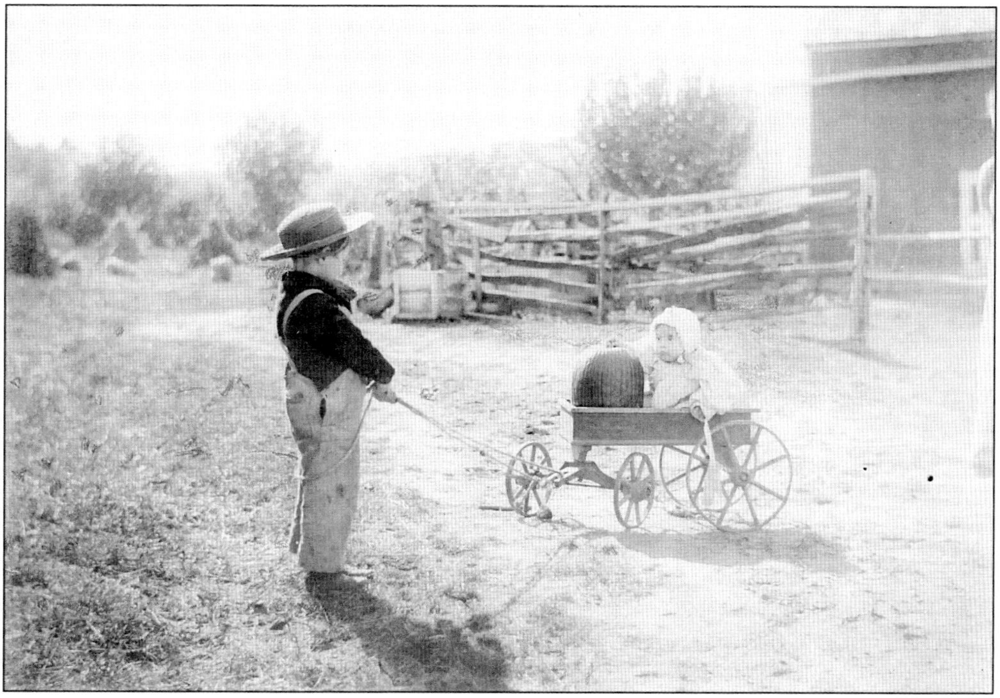

ERNEST AND GRACE RUSSELL WITH THEIR PUMPKIN C. 1899, BY CLIFTON JOHNSON. Halloween originated in medieval Britain and Ireland as All Hallows Eve, celebrated the night before All Saint's Day. It began as a thinly veiled pagan festival of the dead.

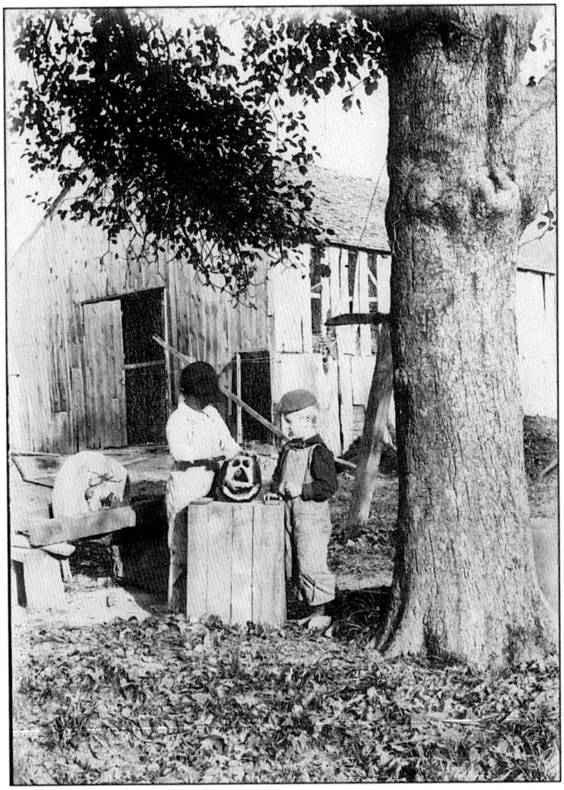

THE SPIRIT OF HALLOWEEN. Oscar and Arthur Johnson carved a jack-o'-lantern near Edward Johnson's barn in Hadley. By the late 19th century mischief-making, dressing as goblins, and demanding treats began to supplant the real fear of the spirits of the dead. The traditional Scottish-carved turnip became our native-carved pumpkin.

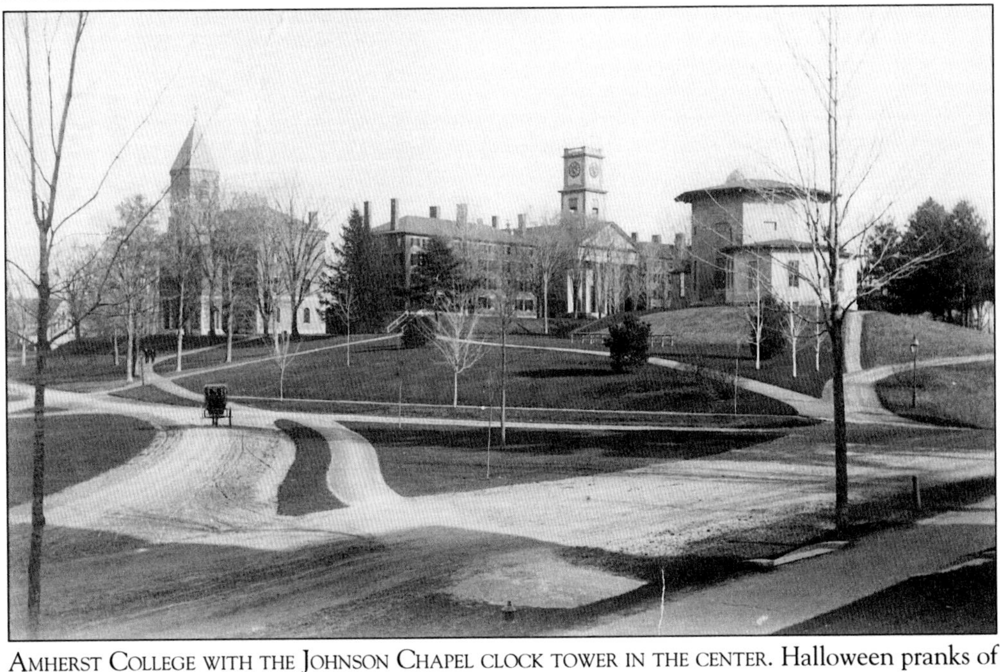

AMHERST COLLEGE WITH THE JOHNSON CHAPEL CLOCK TOWER IN THE CENTER. Halloween pranks of the 1870s at Amherst College included the stealing of the hands of the college clock. Students said the wind blew them off. When a cow was found on the second floor of South College, it was said, "no one put her there, she just went."

John and Irving Spear of Amherst in their World War I uniforms, 1917. WW I touched everyone in the valley, directly or indirectly. A single battle could kill or wound 120,000 Americans, as happened in the Argonne Forest. Twenty million people worldwide were killed by an influenza epidemic that broke out during the war. On November 7, 1918, Amherst and Hadley celebrated the end of the war with ringing bells, wild parades, and bonfires. But the war was not over.

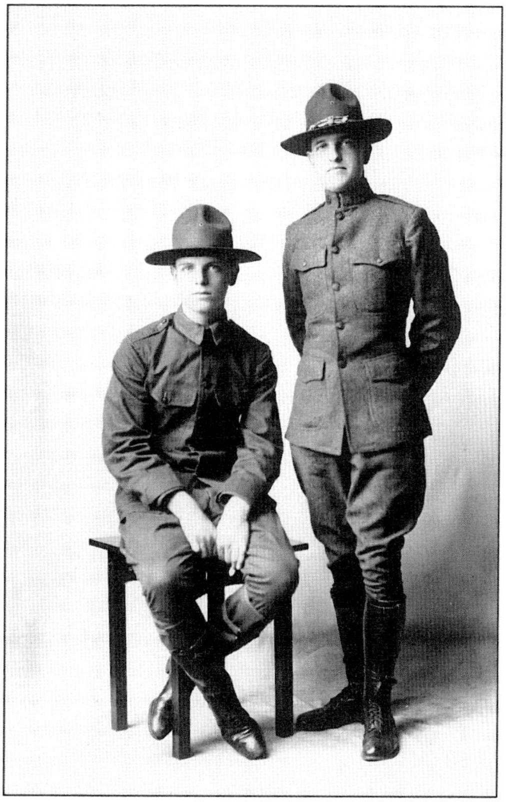

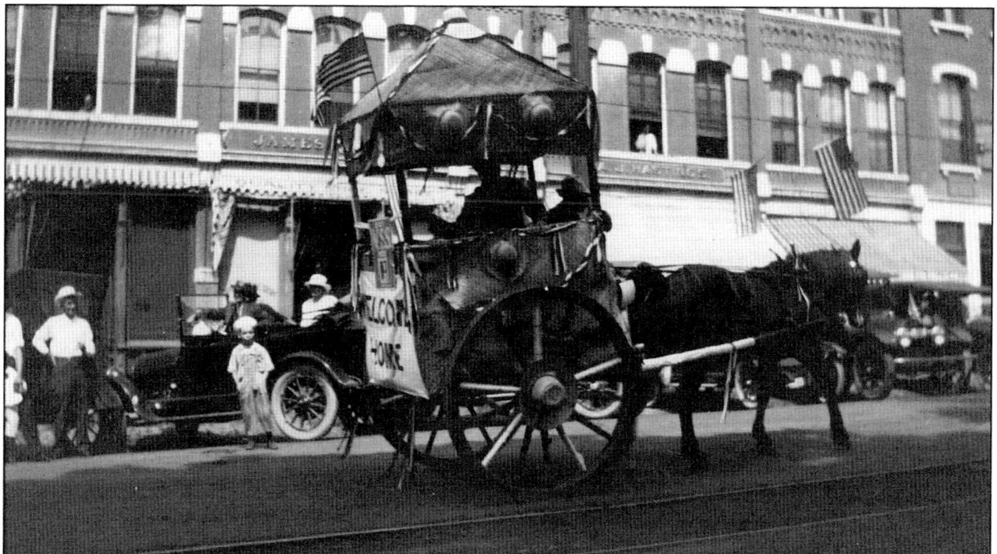

Celebrating the homecoming of WW I soldiers in Amherst, 1918. There were two false announcements of peace and two riotous celebrations before the Armistice was signed on November 11, 1918. The headline in *The Amherst Record* read, "Armistice Signed, Fighting Stops, Kaiser Takes a Sneak to Holland, Amherst Celebrates the Glorious Third Time."

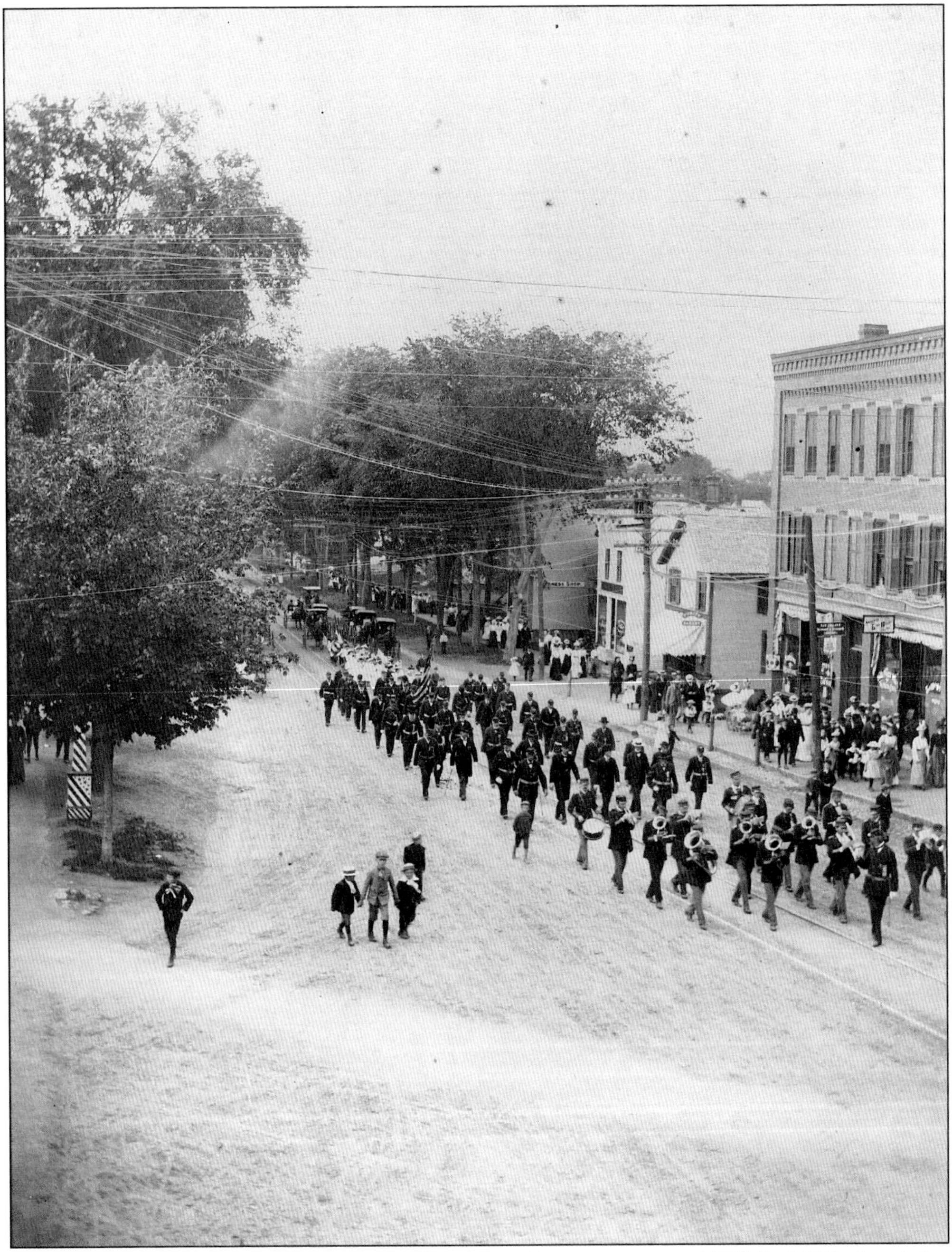

CIVIL WAR VETERANS PARADING ON SOUTH PLEASANT STREET IN ABOUT 1905. In 1919, Armistice Day became a legal holiday, though *The Amherst Record* thought it should be combined with Thanksgiving so businesses wouldn't lose two days of work. In 1954, after World War II and the Korean War, President Eisenhower changed the holiday's name to Veterans Day, to honor the dead of all American wars.

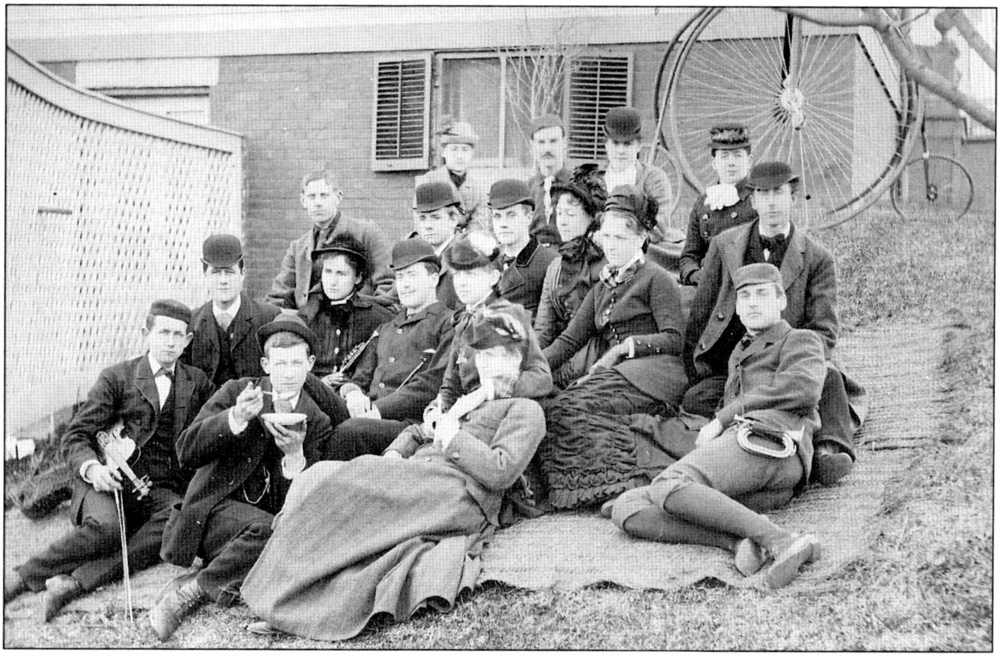

VICTORS' PORTRAIT. The first football team at the Massachusetts Agricultural College had no uniforms and played no games in their first season in 1878. It wasn't until 1881 that they played against another team. Impressed by their wins over both Williston and Wesleyan, team members had their picture taken with friends, horns, a piccolo, a violin, a bowl of soup, and two high-wheeler bicycles.

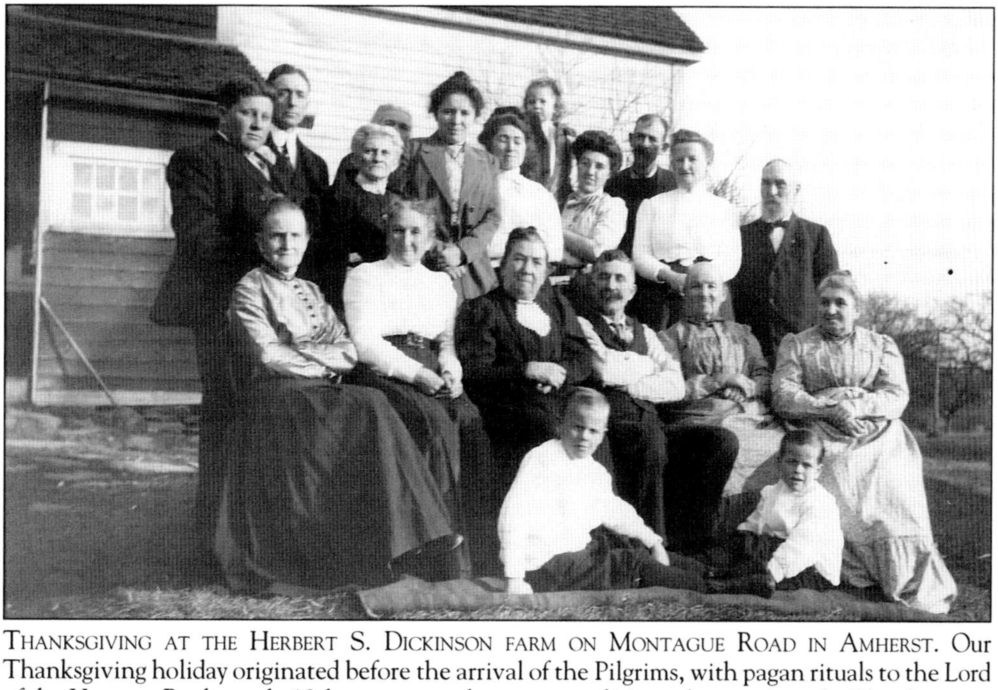

THANKSGIVING AT THE HERBERT S. DICKINSON FARM ON MONTAGUE ROAD IN AMHERST. Our Thanksgiving holiday originated before the arrival of the Pilgrims, with pagan rituals to the Lord of the Harvest. By the early 19th century each governor of Massachusetts issued a Thanksgiving Proclamation sometime during the fall, after the harvest was brought in.

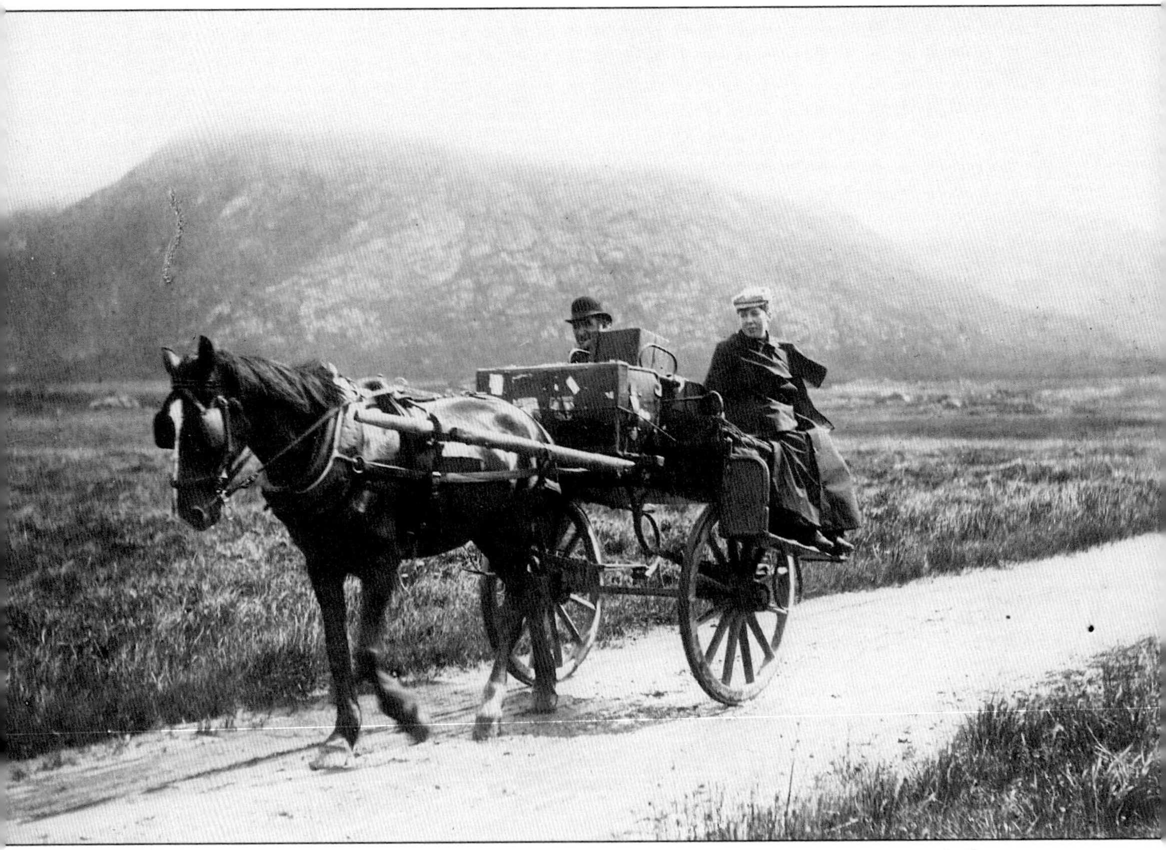

A CLIFTON JOHNSON PHOTOGRAPH OF AN IRISH COUPLE LEAVING THEIR HOMELAND. In 1847, Governor Briggs reminded everyone of the terrible famine in Ireland: "During the last winter, a cry for bread was heard throughout this land from a distant and famishing people. It was a voice of agony, such as was never before heard by the living generations of this continent." People in Amherst and Hadley gave thanks for what they had that year and gave generously to the Irish.

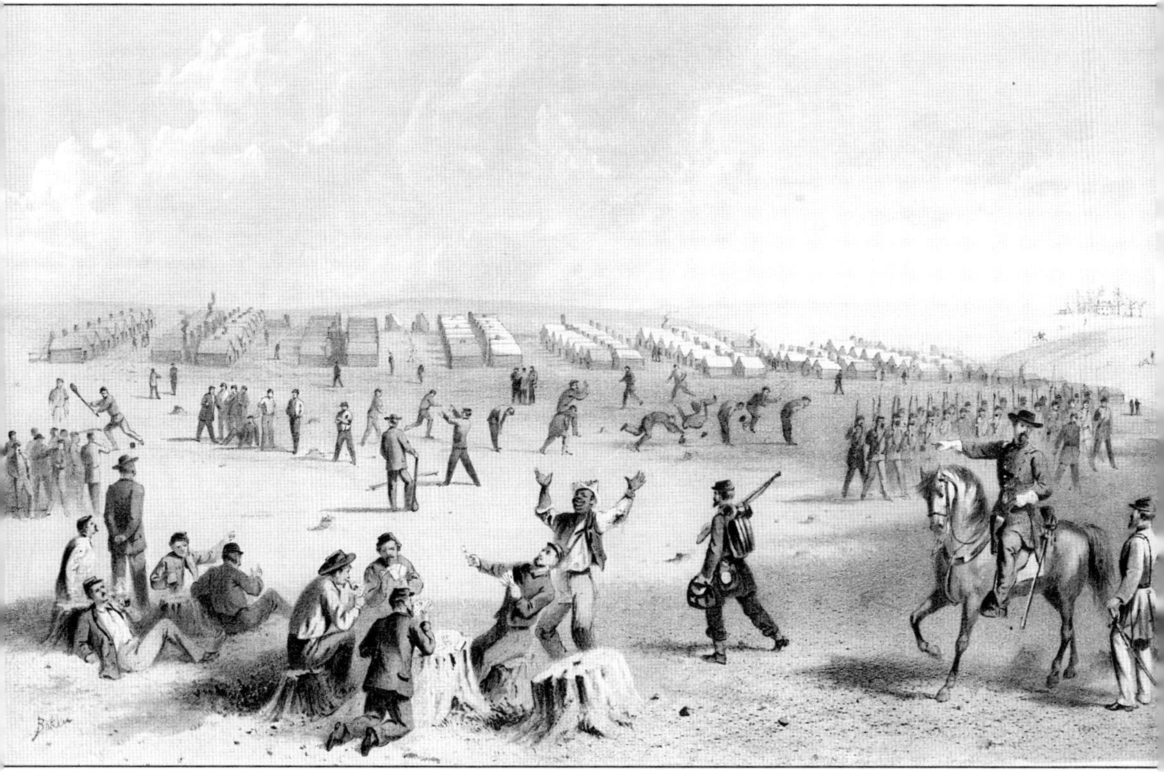

A LITHOGRAPH OF THE 37TH MASSACHUSETTS VOLUNTEERS IN THE CIVIL WAR BY J.H. BUFFORD. In 1862, the Amherst and Hadley boys of the 27th Civil War Regiment thought they would be eating salted horse for Thanksgiving. But folks from home sent a feast to the boys in the field. One soldier wrote, "There was a gleam of flashing ivories down the line, and individuals were wrestling with huge pieces of poultry, pie, cake, cheese, etc., in a most vigorous manner, till all cried enough."

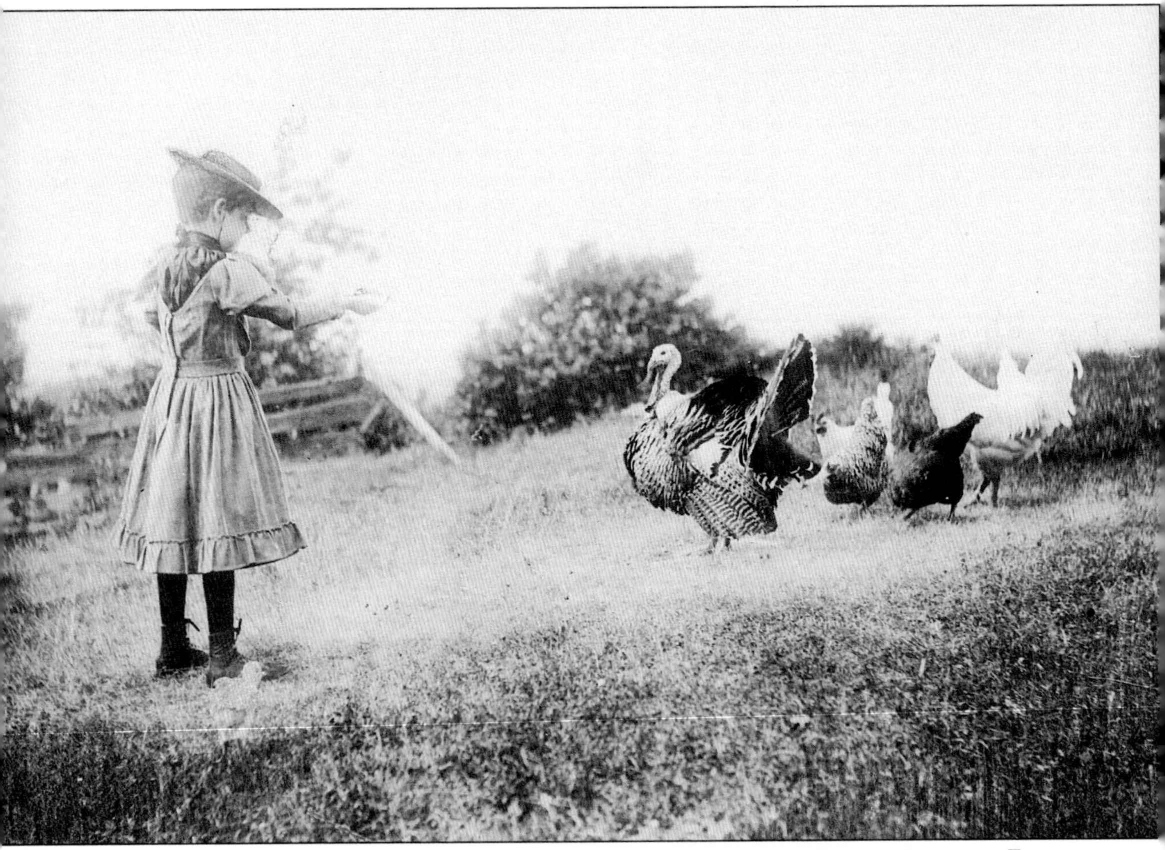

A HADLEY GIRL HOLDING OUT CORN FOR THE THANKSGIVING TURKEY, BY CLIFTON JOHNSON. Even during the Civil War the needy at home weren't forgotten: "We are gratified to learn that the materials of a good dinner on Thanksgiving day . . . were sent to many a poor family, as the aged and feeble ones in our midst . . . probably could not have enjoyed this luxury; thus carrying out the spirit and original intent of this festival in the good olden time." (*Hampshire and Franklin Express*, November 1862.)

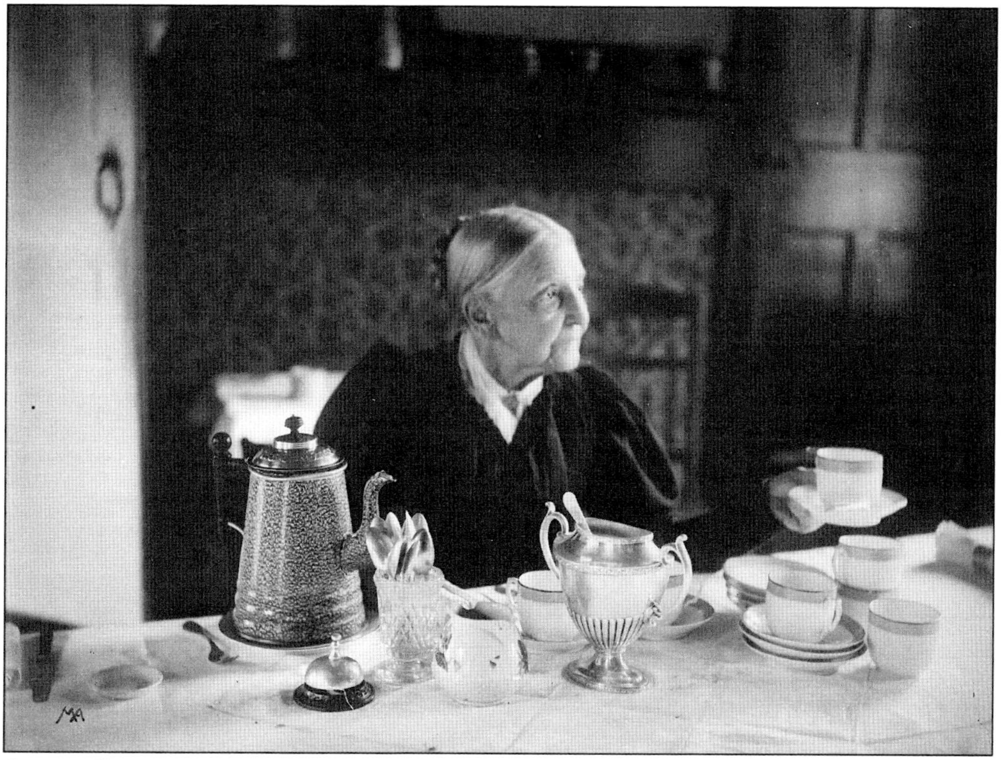

AURELIA DAVIS SERVING COFFEE AFTER THANKSGIVING DINNER IN HER SOUTH PLEASANT STREET HOME. Aurelia attended Mount Holyoke College in South Hadley in 1854 and lived by the Amherst Common until her death in about 1908.

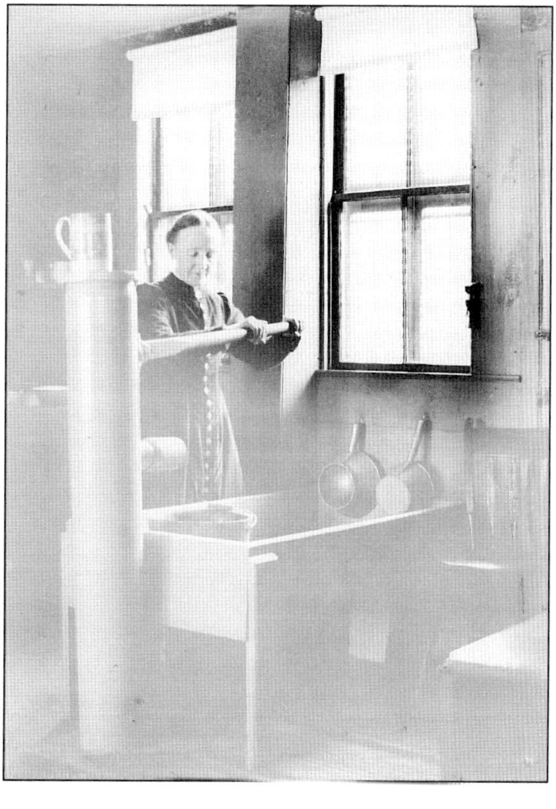

THE KITCHEN PUMP. The pump and the pumper got a workout at Thanksgiving time, as illustrated by this Clifton Johnson image taken in a Hadley home.

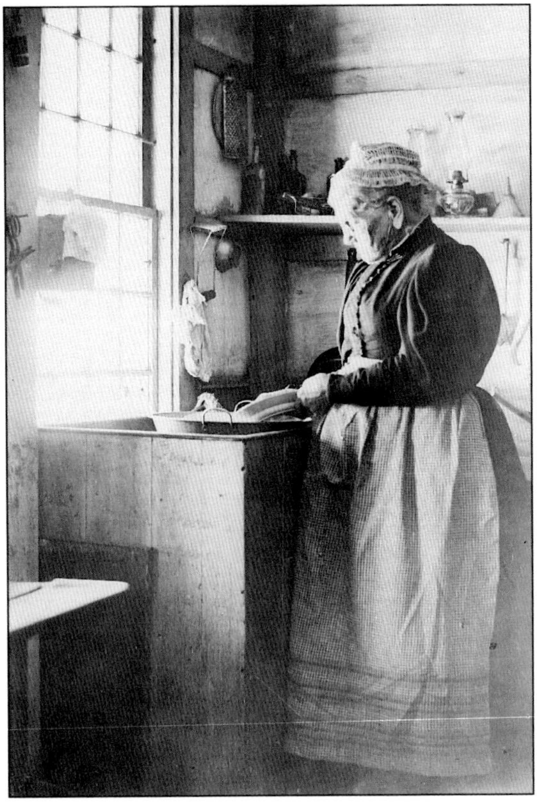

Washing dishes after Thanksgiving dinner in Hadley, by Clifton Johnson. In 1863 Lincoln made the last Thursday in November a national Thanksgiving holiday. In 1939, Roosevelt moved it to the third Thursday to give merchants an extra week of shopping days before Christmas. In that year, some refused to change, and some celebrated Thanksgiving twice.

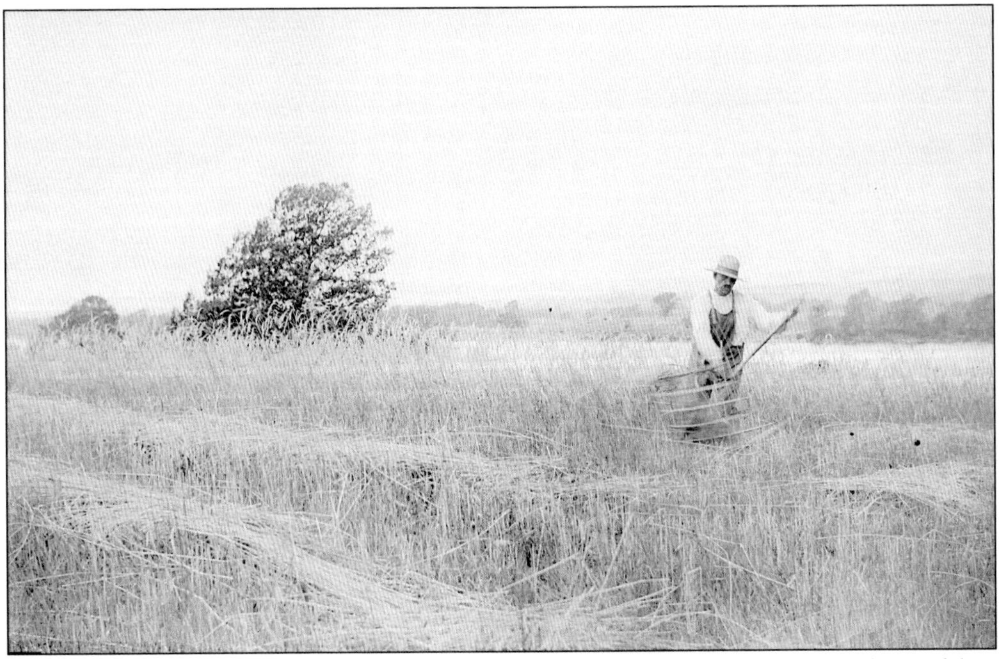

Cradling rye on the plains of Hadley, by Clifton Johnson. Harvest time was bountiful in Amherst, but especially in the fertile alluvial plains of Hadley. The towns produced milk, vegetables, fruit, meat, tobacco, and broom corn (for the manufacture of brooms).

WEAVING WORK. Horsehair sieves were woven for the bolting of the flour in the fall. Clifton Johnson photographed one of the Marsh sisters of Hadley at her loom.

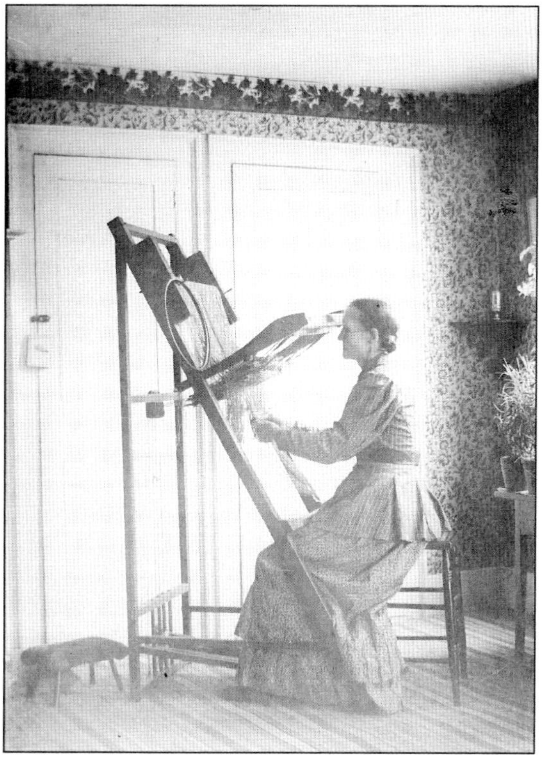

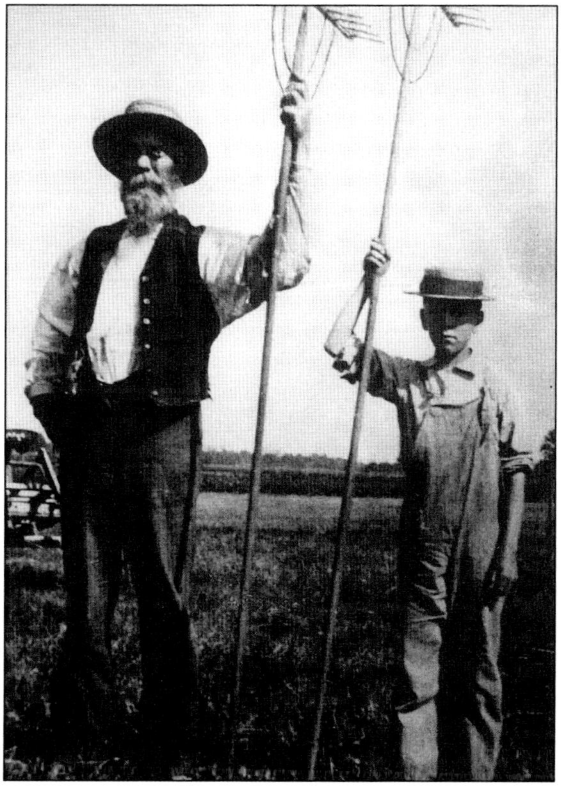

A STRIKING POSE. Stephen P. Puffer (1822–1913) and Stephen P. Puffer Jr. posed in classic American Gothic style with their hay rakes on their North Amherst farm.

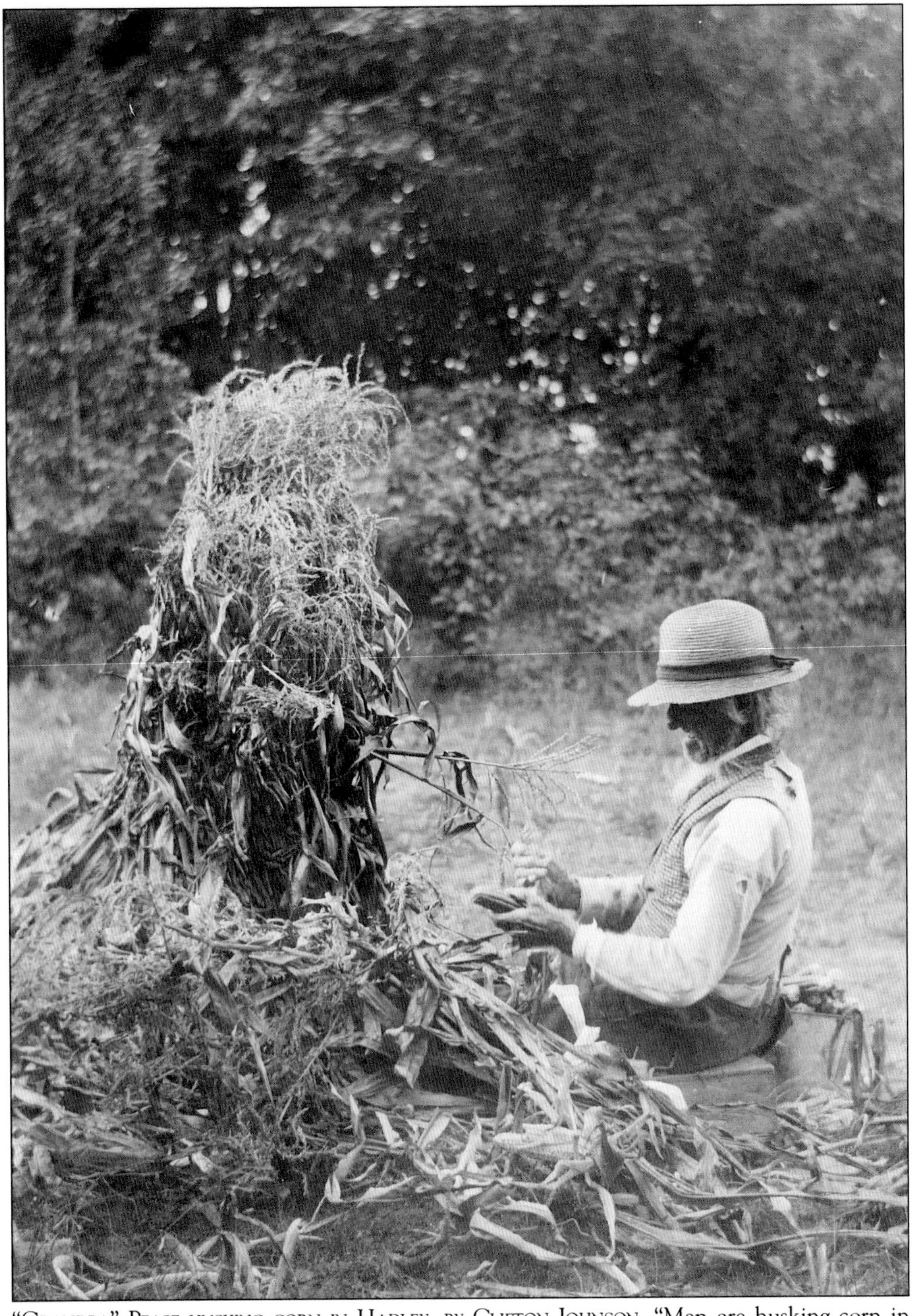

"GRANDPA" PEASE HUSKING CORN IN HADLEY, BY CLIFTON JOHNSON. "Men are husking corn in my neighbor's field: a good sight to see. Come now to my hillside and be still. It is only a little way to understanding if you will be still, only a little way to peace." (David Grayson, *The Countryman's Year*, October 9.)

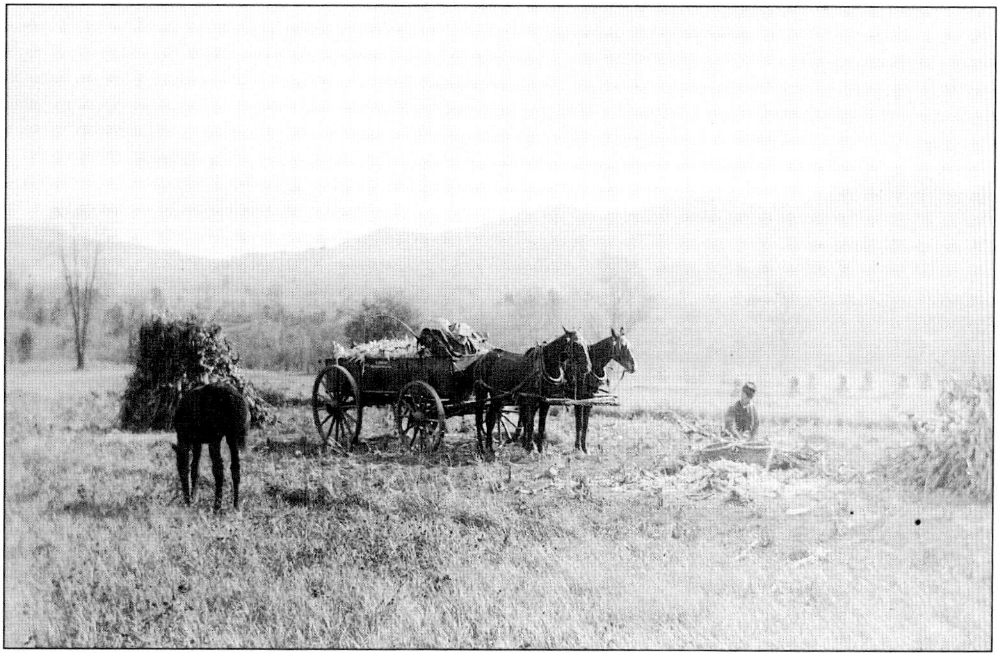

HUSKING CORN IN THE FORT MEADOW OF HADLEY, BY CLIFTON JOHNSON.

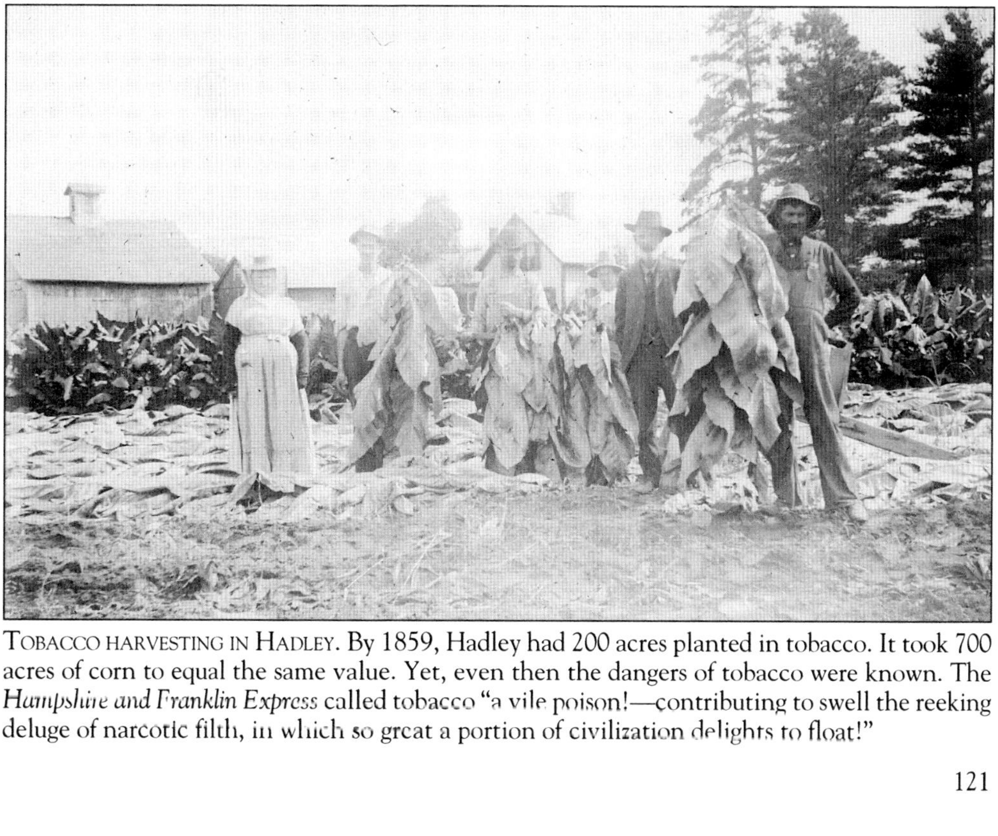

TOBACCO HARVESTING IN HADLEY. By 1859, Hadley had 200 acres planted in tobacco. It took 700 acres of corn to equal the same value. Yet, even then the dangers of tobacco were known. The *Hampshire and Franklin Express* called tobacco "a vile poison!—contributing to swell the reeking deluge of narcotic filth, in which so great a portion of civilization delights to float!"

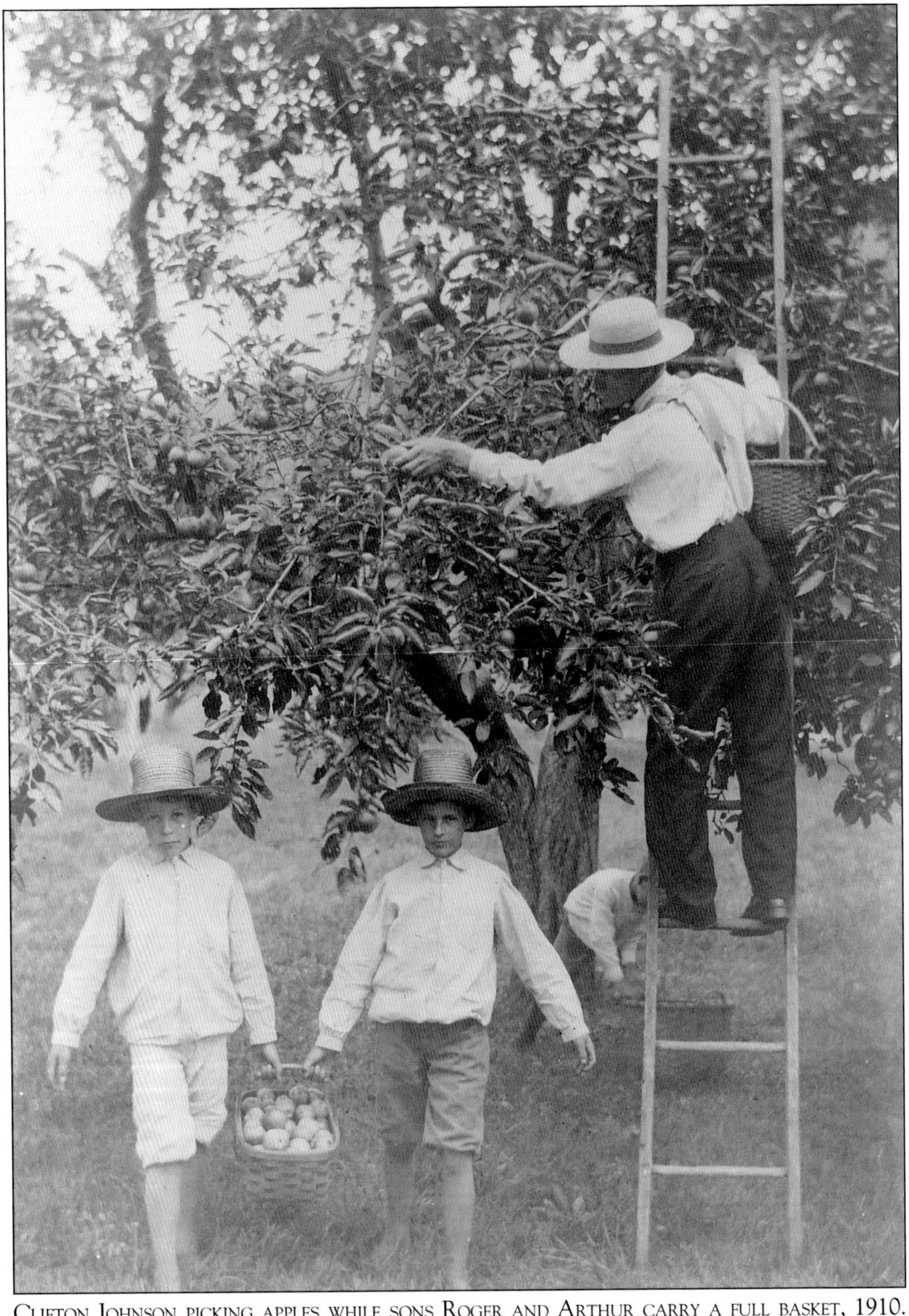

CLIFTON JOHNSON PICKING APPLES WHILE SONS ROGER AND ARTHUR CARRY A FULL BASKET, 1910. "Cool sharp mornings, inconceivably beautiful. I began picking my Baldwin apples. High up in one of the trees I felt vainglorious enough, remembering how . . . I set out that very tree, a frail sapling, with my own hands." (David Grayson, *The Countryman's Year*, October 8.)

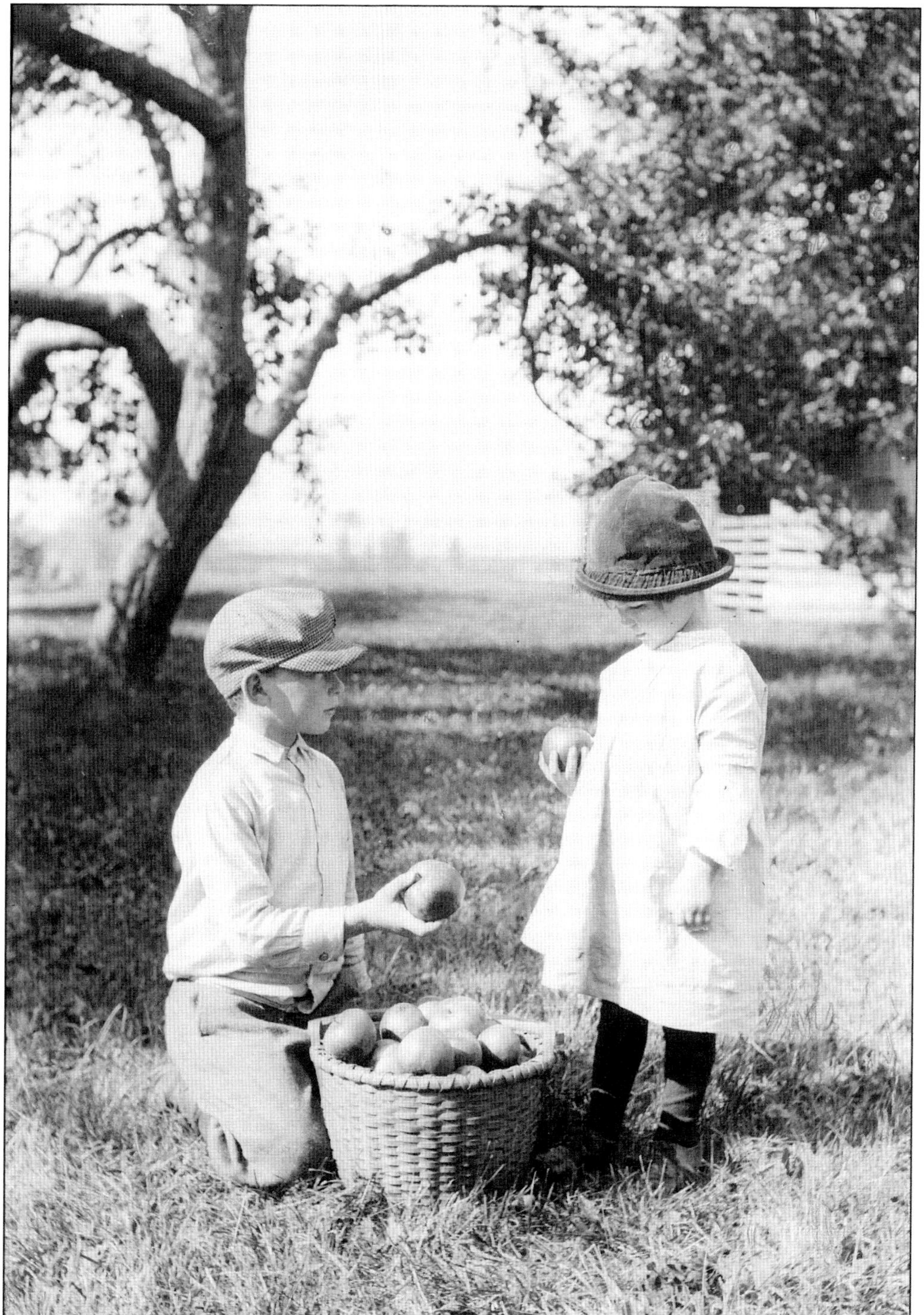

IRVING AND KATHERINE JOHNSON DURING THE APPLE HARVEST, BY CLIFTON JOHNSON ABOUT 1914. "I have seen it grow, pruned it, sprayed it, and am now reaping the rich fruit of it. This gives a kind of satisfaction that one can get, I think, in no other way." (David Grayson, *The Countryman's Year*, October 8.)

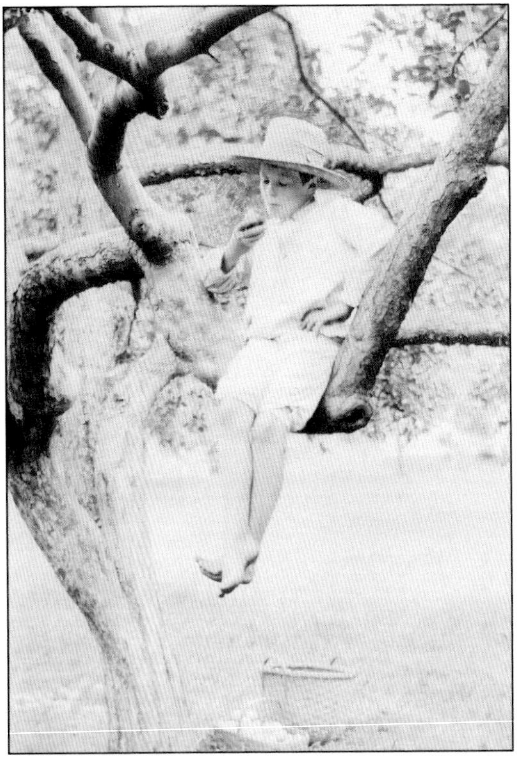

ROGER JOHNSON ENJOYING ONE OF AUTUMN'S EXQUISITE PLEASURES ABOUT 1909, IN A PHOTOGRAPH BY CLIFTON JOHNSON. "A perfect autumn day: New England at its best. I wish I could look long enough at the coloring on Mount Warner to keep it permanently in my inner eye. Such a tapestry of beauty: such sunlight: such crystal air!" (David Grayson, *The Countryman's Year*, October 10.)

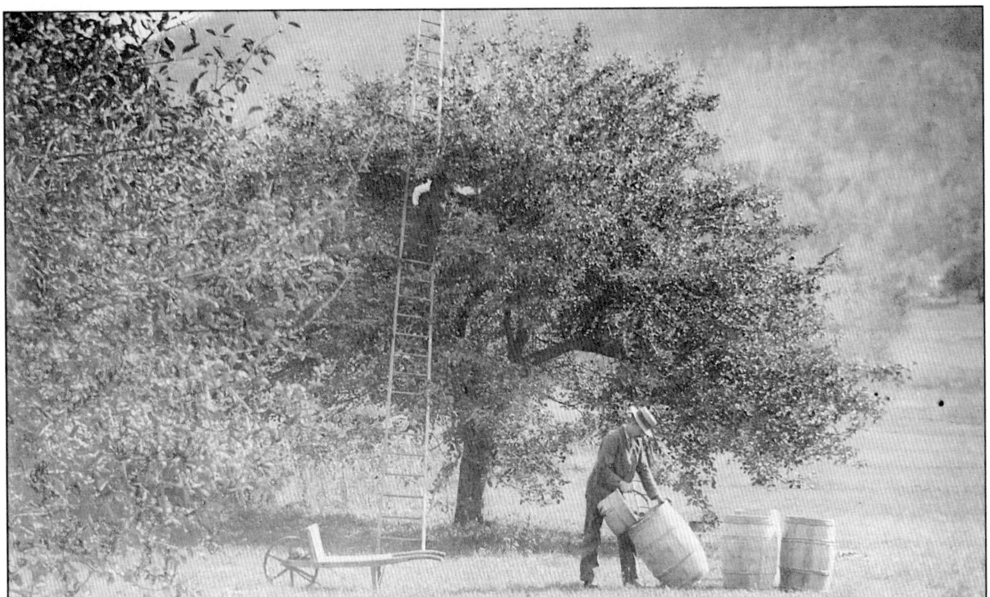

THE OCTOBER APPLE HARVEST IN HADLEY, BY CLIFTON JOHNSON. The harvest of 1878 was so great that the chaplain of the Massachusetts Agricultural College announced in the *New York Tribune* that the valley was being crushed by an apple glacier. The immense weight of apples crushed the lower layers of fruit until juice began to flow from windows. The Hadley meadows were said to have overflowed with cider and the swollen Connecticut River was 3% alcohol as far as Middletown, Connecticut.

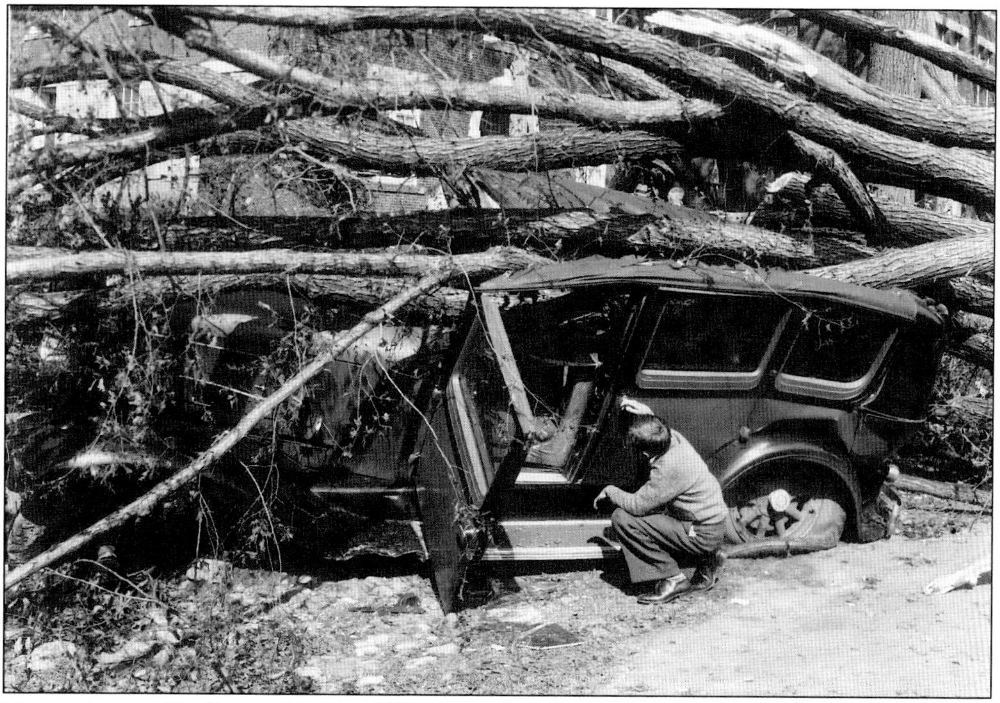

NATURE'S FURY. On September 20, 1938, a hurricane roared up the Connecticut River Valley. In New England, 431 people died. As the rivers rose, hundreds in the Hadley area were evacuated to the armory in Northampton and the state college in Amherst. This image depicts one of the many cars crushed by one of thousands of elm trees that came down.

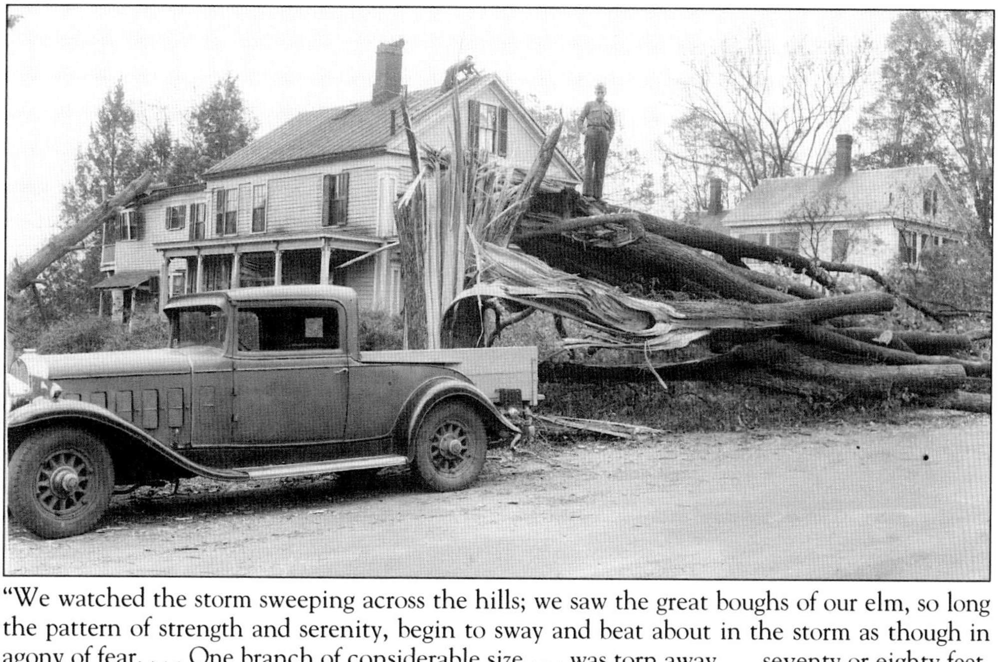

"We watched the storm sweeping across the hills; we saw the great boughs of our elm, so long the pattern of strength and serenity, begin to sway and beat about in the storm as though in agony of fear. . . . One branch of considerable size . . . was torn away . . . seventy or eighty feet, to tear through one of the windows of our home." (David Grayson, *Under My Elm*. Frederick, CO: Renaissance House, 1986, p. 142.)

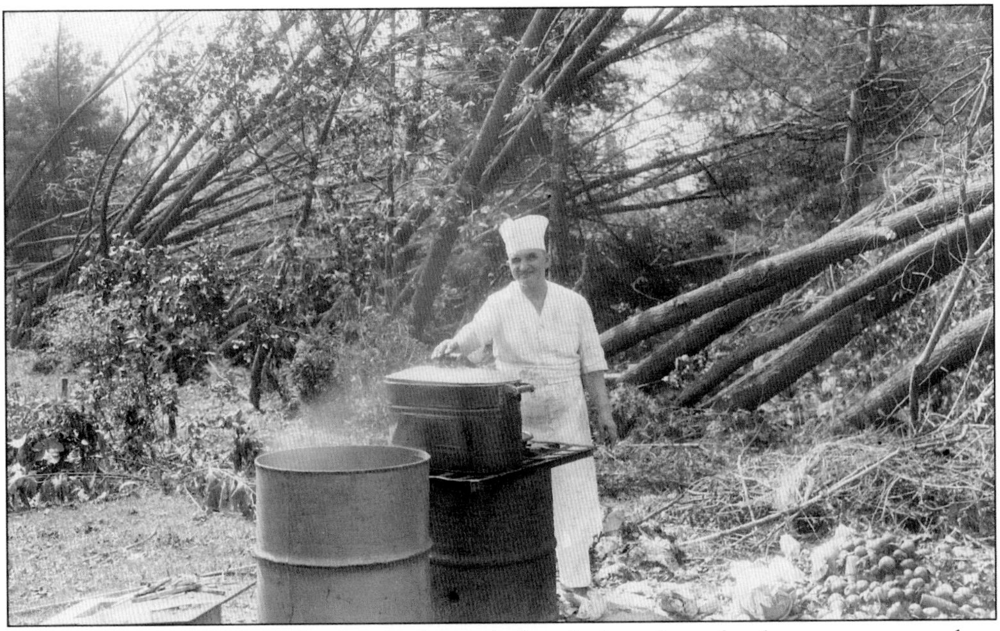

AN ACT OF KINDNESS. An unknown Amherst chef cooked outdoors for the emergency workers after the Hurricane of 1938. Because the area was cut off from the outside world, rumors were rampant that New London was on fire and under siege by four hundred looters, and that another hurricane was on its way.

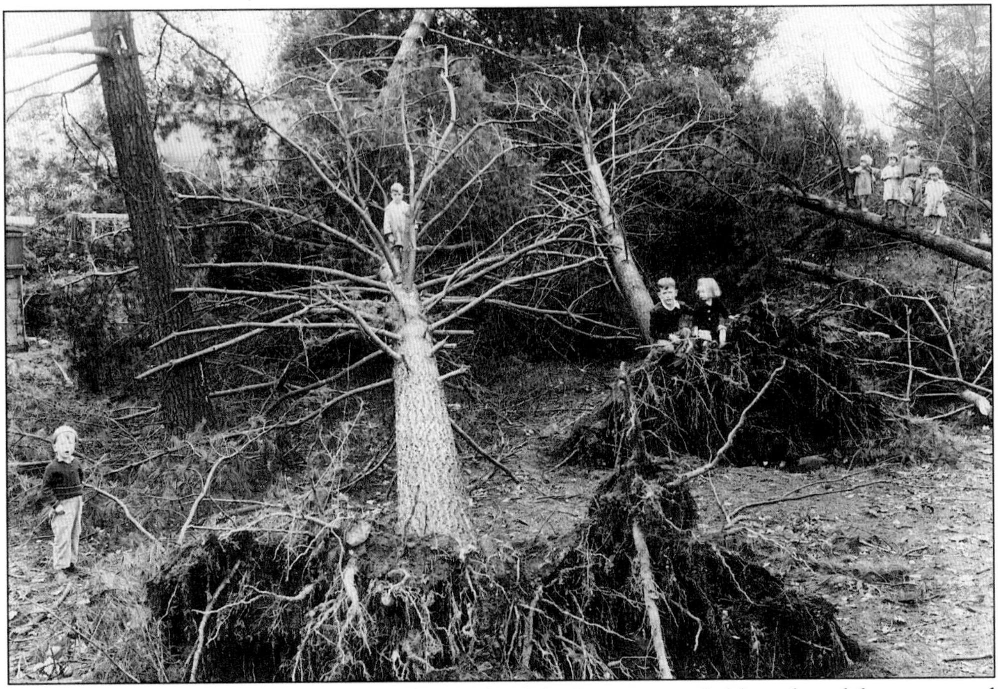

PLAYING AMONGST THE RUBBLE. In the aftermath of the hurricane, children found fortresses and castles among the fallen trees. Amherst had long been known as "the village among the trees" for its streets lined with elms. The town lost 1,500 ancient trees, the majority of them elms, which, because of disease, could not be replaced.

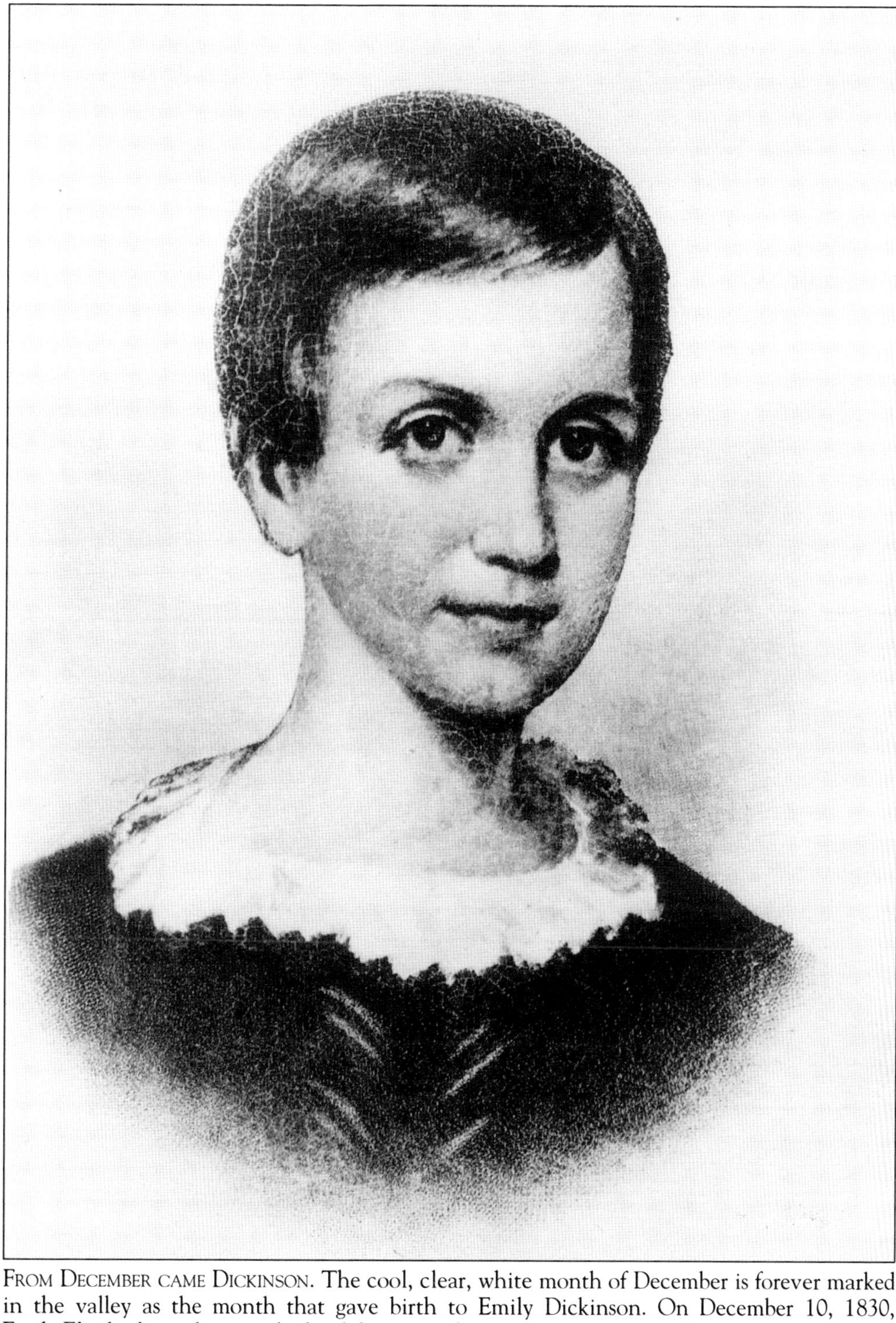

FROM DECEMBER CAME DICKINSON. The cool, clear, white month of December is forever marked in the valley as the month that gave birth to Emily Dickinson. On December 10, 1830, Emily Elizabeth was born in the brick homestead on Main Street. From there she would witness the cycle of seasons and the cycle of life, and fashion them into poetry like none the world had ever seen.

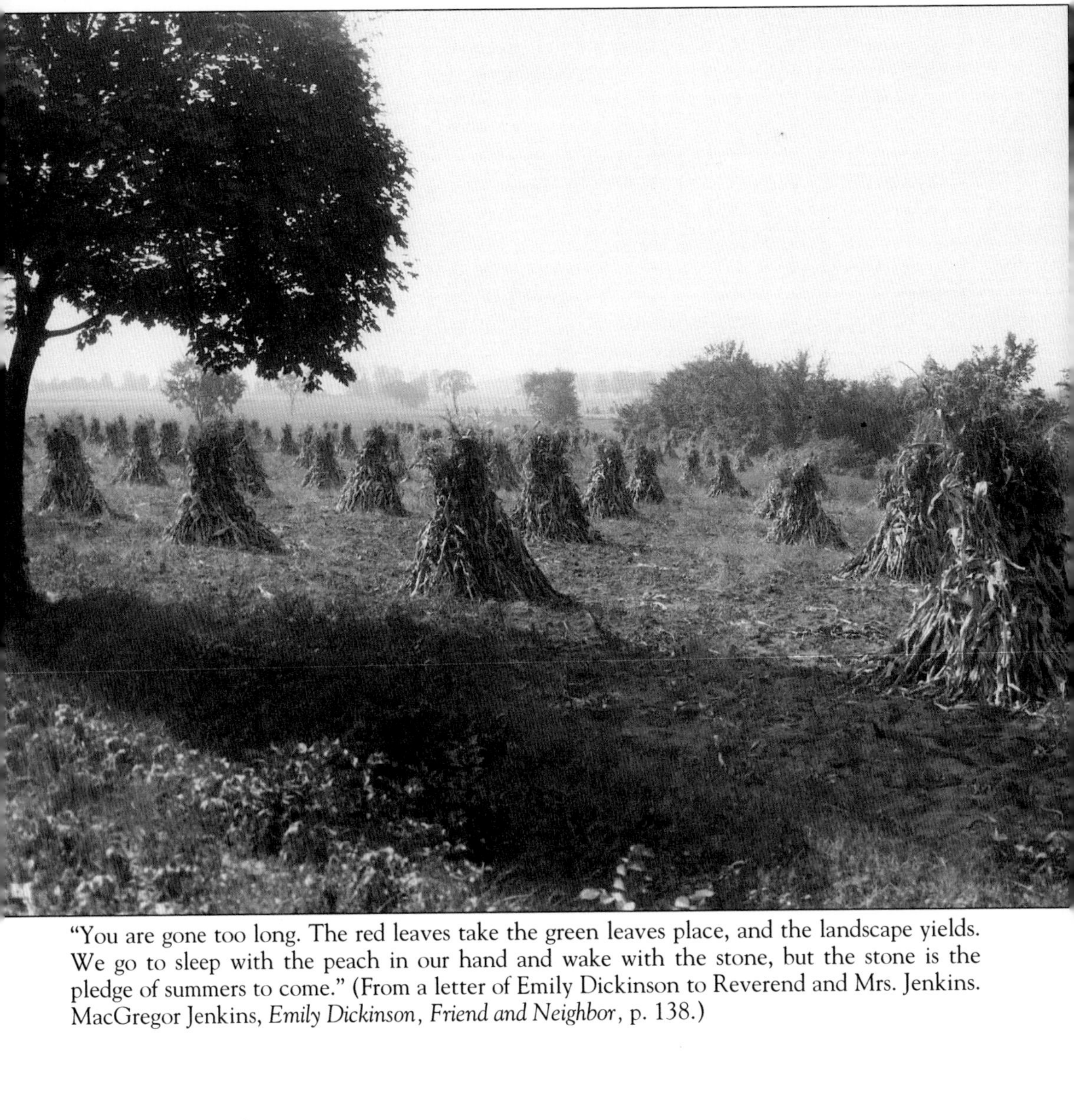

"You are gone too long. The red leaves take the green leaves place, and the landscape yields. We go to sleep with the peach in our hand and wake with the stone, but the stone is the pledge of summers to come." (From a letter of Emily Dickinson to Reverend and Mrs. Jenkins. MacGregor Jenkins, *Emily Dickinson, Friend and Neighbor*, p. 138.)